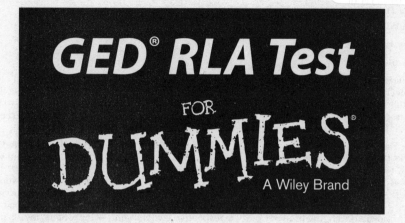

GED® RLA Test

FOR

DUMMIES®

A Wiley Brand

by Murray Shukyn, BA, and
Achim K. Krull, BA, MAT

FOR

DUMMIES®

A Wiley Brand

GED® RLA Test For Dummies®

Published by: **John Wiley & Sons, Inc.,** 111 River Street, Hoboken, NJ 07030-5774, www.wiley.com

Copyright © 2015 by John Wiley & Sons, Inc., Hoboken, New Jersey

Published simultaneously in Canada

For general information on our other products and services, please contact our Customer Care Department within the U.S. at 877-762-2974, outside the U.S. at 317-572-3993, or fax 317-572-4002. For technical support, please visit www.wiley.com/techsupport.

Wiley publishes in a variety of print and electronic formats and by print-on-demand. Some material included with standard print versions of this book may not be included in e-books or in print-on-demand. If this book refers to media such as a CD or DVD that is not included in the version you purchased, you may download this material at http://booksupport.wiley.com. For more information about Wiley products, visit www.wiley.com.

Library of Congress Control Number: 2015946516

ISBN 978-1-119-03005-8 (pbk); ISBN 978-1-119-03007-2 (ebk); ISBN 978-1-119-03006-5 (ebk)

Manufactured in the United States of America

10 9 8 7 6 5 4 3 2 1

Contents at a Glance

Introduction 1

Part I: Getting Started with the GED RLA Test 5
Chapter 1: Taking a Quick Glance at the GED RLA Test 7
Chapter 2: Prepping for the RLA Test 15
Chapter 3: Uncovering Your Strengths and Weaknesses with a Diagnostic Test 27
Chapter 4: Succeeding on the GED RLA Test 51

Part II: Enhancing Your RLA Skills 61
Chapter 5: Understanding the Written Word 63
Chapter 6: Analyzing Arguments and Weighing Evidence 93
Chapter 7: Mastering Language Conventions and Usage 119
Chapter 8: Penning Powerful Prose for the Extended Response 151

Part III: Putting Your RLA Knowledge and Skills to the Test 171
Chapter 9: Taking an RLA Practice Test 173
Chapter 10: Answers and Explanations for the RLA Practice Test 193

Part IV: The Part of Tens 201
Chapter 11: Ten Tips for Faster Reading and Improved Comprehension 203
Chapter 12: Avoiding Ten Tricky Writing Errors 211

Index 217

Table of Contents

Introduction 1
    About This Book 1
    Foolish Assumptions 2
    Icons Used in This Book 2
    Beyond the Book 2
    Where to Go from Here 3

Part I: Getting Started with the GED RLA Test 5

Chapter 1: Taking a Quick Glance at the GED RLA Test 7
    Knowing What to Expect: The GED Test Format 7
    Reviewing the GED RLA Test 8
    It's a Date: Scheduling the Test 9
        Determining whether you're eligible 10
        Recognizing when you can take the test 10
        Signing up 12
        Working with unusual circumstances 12
    Taking the GED Test When English Isn't Your First Language 12
    Taking Aim at Your Target Score 13
        Identifying how scores are determined 14
        Knowing what to do if you score poorly on one or more tests 14

Chapter 2: Prepping for the RLA Test 15
    Grasping What's on the Grammar and Writing Component 15
        Looking at the skills the grammar and writing component covers 16
        Understanding the format of the grammar and writing component 17
    Rocking the Reading Comprehension Component 17
        Checking out the skills required for the reading component 18
        Breaking down the format of the reading component 18
        Identifying the types of passages and how to prepare for them 19
            Literary passages 19
            Nonfiction passages 19
    Examining the Extended Response Item 20
        Eyeing the skills covered in the Extended Response 21
        Understanding the Extended Response format 21
        Planning to succeed on the Extended Response 22
    Preparing for the RLA Test with Tactics That Work 23
        Sharpening your reading and writing skills 23
        Navigating text to comprehend 25

Chapter 3: Uncovering Your Strengths and Weaknesses with a Diagnostic Test 27
    Taking the Diagnostic Test 27
    Answer Sheet for RLA Diagnostic Test 28
    Reasoning Through Language Arts Diagnostic Test 29
    The Extended Response 40
    Reviewing Answers and Explanations 44
    Sample Extended Response 49
    Scoring Your Extended Response 50

Chapter 4: Succeeding on the GED RLA Test **51**

Gearing Up for Test Time 51
Using the Diagnostic and Practice Tests to Your Advantage 52
Packing for Test Day 53
Getting Comfortable before the Test Begins 54
Brushing Up on Test-Taking Strategies 54
Watching the clock: Using your time wisely 55
Evaluating the different questions...56
Analysis 56
Application 57
Comprehension 57
Synthesis 57
Evaluation 57
Cognitive skills 58
Addressing and answering questions 58
Guess for success: Using intelligent guessing..................................58
Leaving time for review...59
Sharpening Your Mental Focus..59

Part II: Enhancing Your RLA Skills **61**

Chapter 5: Understanding the Written Word **63**

Recognizing and Ordering the Sequence of Events 63
Drawing Inferences..65
Plot...65
Setting...66
Characters 66
Ideas 68
Analyzing Relationships among Ideas 69
Sequence...69
Connection..69
Cause and effect...70
Conclusion..70
Deriving Meaning from Context..71
Figuring Out the Function of Details 72
Comparing Points of View 74
Determining the author's point of view 75
Analyzing the author's response to opposing viewpoints 76
Appreciating the Importance of Word Choice...78
Tuning in to variations in meaning and tone 78
Word choice for overall effect...78
Meaning and tone..79
Interpreting figurative language...80
Extracting Meaning from Flow 81
Taking a big picture look at meaning and flow 82
Recognizing the parts of the whole..83
Analyzing the transitions that tie it all together...............................83
Comparing Two Passages...85
Analyzing differences in perspective, tone, style, structure,
purpose, and impact 86
Perspective 86
Tone 87
Style 87
Purpose 87
Structure 88
Impact..88

Analyzing passages that present related ideas or themes 89
    Scope 90
    Purpose 90
    Emphasis 91
    Audience...91
    Impact 92

Chapter 6: Analyzing Arguments and Weighing Evidence **93**
  Identifying and Summarizing the Main Idea 93
    Inferring the main idea from details 96
    Drawing generalizations and hypotheses from the evidence 96
  Digging into the Details 99
    Summarizing details 99
    Following the train of thought 99
    Distinguishing between supported and unsupported claims 100
    Spotting valid and invalid reasoning 102
    Analyzing the evidence 104
      Is the evidence relevant? 104
      Is the evidence sufficient? 106
      What evidence was ignored? 106
    Analyze data, graphs, and pictures used as evidence 107
  Rooting Out Premises and Assumptions 110
    Finding the premise on which the argument is based 110
    Identifying assumptions 111
  Comparing Two Arguments 112
    Analyzing differences in interpretation and use of evidence................113
    Synthesizing two arguments 115
    Drawing new conclusions 115
    Applying information to other situations 116

Chapter 7: Mastering Language Conventions and Usage **119**
  Correcting Errors in Agreement 119
    Addressing subject-verb agreement..119
    Practicing subject-verb agreement..122
    Making pronouns agree with their antecedents 122
      Choosing the right verb when you have multiple pronouns.............123
      Giving yourself a refresher in reflexive pronouns 124
      Welcoming relative pronouns into the family 124
      Considering collective and proper pronouns 125
      Practicing your pronoun-antecedent agreement skills 125
  Choosing the Right Words...126
    Tuning your ear to homonyms..126
    Correcting errors with frequently confused words 129
    Eliminating informal language...131
  Fixing Broken Sentences 134
    Taking care of misplaced modifiers 134
    Achieving parallelism, coordination, and subordination 135
      Spotting and correcting faulty parallelism 136
      Identifying and fixing faulty coordination.........................136
      Pinpointing and correcting faulty subordination 137
      Testing your skills: Parallelism, coordination, and subordination..........137
    Tightening wordy sentences 138
      Using precise language..138
      Opting for active over passive voice 138
      Cutting out redundancy 139
      Avoiding overuse of be verbs..139
      Saying no to nominalizations..140

Watching out for prepositions 140
Purging phrasal verbs 140
Replacing negatives with positive statements 140
Practicing your word-slashing skills..141
Smoothing out awkward sentences...141
Using transitional words and phrases effectively 142
Eliminating sentence fragments and run-on or fused sentences............143
Detecting and fixing run-on or fused sentences................................144
Finding a home for sentence fragments 145
Practicing your sentence repair skills 145
Tweaking the Text: Capitalization, Contractions, Possession, and Punctuation 146
Brushing up on capitalization rules 146
Telling the difference between contractions and possessives 147
Fine-tuning your punctuation skills...147
Practicing with capitalization, contractions, possessives, and punctuation.......148

Chapter 8: Penning Powerful Prose for the Extended Response **151**
Wrapping Your Brain around the Extended Response Guidelines 151
Choosing a Side..153
Identifying the different positions 153
Examining the strengths and weaknesses of each argument...............155
Identifying premises and assumptions 155
Weighing the evidence 157
Testing for logical errors...159
Rooting out bias and emotional appeals.....................................160
Picking a position you can support 160
Writing a Clear, Direct Thesis Statement 161
Structuring Your Argument...161
Putting your main points in logical order..163
Building your arguments 163
Considering Your Purpose, Audience, and Message 165
Purpose 165
Audience 165
Message 166
Writing and Revising Your Essay..166
Choosing your words carefully...166
Varying your sentence patterns..167
Smoothing transitions..167
Detecting and eliminating errors in spelling, grammar, usage,
and punctuation 168
Rereading and revising your response 168

Part III: Putting Your RLA Knowledge and Skills to the Test **171**

Chapter 9: Taking an RLA Practice Test..**173**
Answer Sheet for Reasoning Through Language Arts Practice Test 174
Reasoning Through Language Arts Test 175
The Extended Response 189

Chapter 10: Answers and Explanations for the RLA Practice Test..........**193**
Answers and Explanations 193
Sample Extended Response 197
Answer Key...199

Part IV: The Part of Tens 201

Chapter 11: Ten Tips for Faster Reading and Improved Comprehension 203
Understanding Words from Context 203
Balancing Speed and Comprehension 204
Skimming on a Computer Screen..205
Remembering the Essay Models..206
Detecting Bias and Faulty Logic...206
Reading for Details (Picking Out Key Words)................................206
Tracking Tone in Longer Passages...207
Paraphrasing 207
Practicing Under Pressure 208
Maintaining Focus 209

Chapter 12: Avoiding Ten Tricky Writing Errors 211
Misusing Words 211
Overlooking Subject-Verb Disagreement 212
Mixing Verb Tenses...212
Using the First or Second Person in Analysis 213
Missing and Misplacing Commas 213
Being Inconsistent 214
Writing in Non-Standard English 214
Creating a Choppy Progression..214
Building Your Essay on Sloppy Thinking 215
Ignoring Proofreading Errors...215

Index 217

Introduction

Y ou've decided to take the General Education Development (GED) test to earn the equivalent of a high school diploma. Congratulations! You're about to clear a major hurdle standing between you and your educational and professional goals. But now you realize that you need extra guidance in reading and writing to tackle the GED Reasoning Through Language Arts test. Perhaps you took the test once or even twice and didn't do so well. Perhaps you've done an honest self-assessment and now realize that English was never your favorite or best subject. Whatever the reason, you need to quickly review the essentials and practice answering questions like those you'll encounter on the test. You want to know what to expect so you're not blindsided on test day.

Welcome to *GED RLA Test For Dummies* — your key to excelling on the GED Reasoning Through Language Arts test. Here, you find everything you need to do well on the test, from guidance on how to improve reading speed and comprehension to how to analyze arguments. We also bring you up to speed on proper English conventions and usage and explain how to write a top-notch essay for the Extended Response portion of the test. Along the way, you find plenty of practice questions to reinforce your newly acquired knowledge and skills.

About This Book

As we were writing *GED Test For Dummies,* 3rd edition (Wiley), we didn't have the space to cover all four sections of the GED test in great detail. In that book, we provided a general overview of the GED test and two full-length practice tests that covered all four sections — Reasoning Through Language Arts (RLA), Mathematical Reasoning, Science, and Social Studies.

Knowing that each section of the GED test can be taken separately and that test-takers probably need more guidance in some subject areas than in others, we decided to develop a separate workbook for each section — four workbooks, each with a balance of instruction and practice. In this book, we focus exclusively on the GED Reasoning Through Language Arts test. Our goal is twofold: to prepare you to answer correctly any RLA question you're likely to encounter on the test so that you receive a high score and to help you do well on your Extended Response essay.

We begin by giving you a sneak peek at the test format and an overview of what's on the GED RLA test. We then provide a diagnostic test that presents you with RLA questions, which challenge your reading and reasoning knowledge and skills and identify your unique strengths and weaknesses. The diagnostic test and the self-assessment form following the test guide you to specific chapters for instruction and practice. When you feel ready, you can then tackle the full-length Reasoning Through Language Arts practice test in Chapter 9 and turn to Chapter 10 for answers and explanations. Check the answers even for questions you answered correctly because the answers do provide additional learning materials.

We wrap up with two Part of Tens chapters — one that presents ten tips to improve your reading speed and comprehension and another that helps you steer clear of ten common writing errors.

Foolish Assumptions

When we wrote this book, we made a few assumptions about you, dear reader. Here's who we think you are:

- ✔ You're serious about earning a high-school diploma or GED endorsement for existing qualifications as quickly as you can.

- ✔ You're looking for additional instruction and guidance specifically to improve your score on the GED Reasoning Through Language Arts test, not the Math, Science, or Social Studies test.

- ✔ You've made earning a high-school diploma and an endorsement a priority in your life because you want to advance in the workplace or move on to college.

- ✔ You're willing to give up some activities so you have the time to prepare, always keeping in mind your other responsibilities, too.

- ✔ You meet your state's requirements regarding age, residency, and the length of time since leaving school that make you eligible to take the GED test. (See Chapter 1 for details.)

- ✔ You have sufficient English language skills to handle the test.

- ✔ You want a fun and friendly guide that helps you achieve your goal.

If any of these descriptions sounds like you, welcome aboard. We've prepared an enjoyable tour of the GED test.

Icons Used in This Book

Icons – little pictures you see in the margins of this book — highlight bits of text that you want to pay special attention to. Here's what each one means:

Whenever we want to tell you a special trick or technique that can help you succeed on the GED RLA test, we mark it with this icon. Keep an eye out for this guy.

This icon points out information you want to burn into your brain. Think of the text with this icon as the sort of stuff you'd tear out and put on a bulletin board or your refrigerator.

Take this icon seriously! Although the world won't end if you don't heed the advice next to this icon, the warnings are important to your success in preparing to take the GED RLA test.

We use this icon to flag example questions that are much like what you can expect on the actual GED Reasoning Through Language Arts test. So if you just want to get familiar with the types of questions on the test, this icon is your guide.

Beyond the Book

In addition to the book content, you can find valuable free material online. We provide you with a Cheat Sheet that addresses things you need to know and consider when getting ready for the GED Reasoning Through Language Arts test. You can access this material at www.dummies.com/cheatsheet/gedrlatest.

We also include additional articles at www.dummies.com/extras/gedrlatest that provide even more helpful tips and advice to help you score your best on the GED Reasoning Through Language Arts test.

Where to Go from Here

Some people like to read books from beginning to end. Others prefer to read only the specific information they need to know now. Here we provide a road map so you can find your way around.

Chapter 1 starts off with an overview of the GED test and how to register for the exam. Chapter 2 brings you up to speed on what the Reasoning Through Language Arts test covers. Chapter 3 is a must-read — a diagnostic test followed by a self-assessment to target areas where you need the most guidance and practice. Based on your self-assessment, you'll know which chapters to focus on in Part II of this book.

The chapters in Part II are the meat and potatoes — instruction and practice that covers reading comprehension, argument analysis, Standard English language conventions, and writing:

- ✔ **Reading comprehension:** The RLA test is essentially an open-book test in that it provides the content on which questions are based. That said, you have to be a very good and careful reader to identify the main ideas and pick out details from the reading passages on the test. In Chapter 5, we help you develop your reading comprehension skills.

- ✔ **Argument analysis:** The RLA test challenges your ability not only to read and understand the written word but also to evaluate arguments in terms of logic and supporting evidence. In Chapter 6, we explain how to pick apart arguments and separate fact from opinion.

- ✔ **English language conventions:** A significant portion of the GED RLA test presents you with writing errors in grammar, spelling, usage, punctuation, and other conventions and challenges you to choose the correction. In Chapter 7, we address the most common errors and explain how to correct them.

- ✔ **Extended Response:** Chapter 8 turns your attention to writing. Here, you find out what the Extended Response portion of the test is all about, how to compare two passages and determine which is most effective, and how to write an essay that clearly states your point of view and supports it with plenty of evidence in a well-reasoned persuasive essay.

When you're ready to dive into a full-length practice test that mimics the real GED Reasoning Through Language Arts test, check out Part III. After the test, you can check your answers with the detailed answer explanations we provide. (But be sure to wait until *after* you take the practice test to look at the answers!).

If you need a break, turn to the chapters in Part IV, where you can find ten tips to improve your reading speed and comprehension and descriptions of ten writing errors to avoid.

Part I
Getting Started with the GED RLA Test

In this part. . .

- ✔ Get oriented to the test format, question types, test scheduling, and scoring and find out what steps to take if English isn't your first language.

- ✔ Find out what's on the GED Reading Through Language Arts test and the knowledge and skills it requires you to demonstrate.

- ✔ Take a diagnostic test to identify your strengths and weaknesses and highlight the areas where you may need additional practice.

- ✔ Prepare for the actual test day and find out what you should or shouldn't do on the day(s) before and the day of the test, including during the exam.

Chapter 1

Taking a Quick Glance at the GED RLA Test

In This Chapter

▶ Warming up to the GED test format

▶ Checking out what's on the GED RLA test

▶ Registering for the test and choosing a test date

▶ Completing the GED test when English is your second language

▶ Understanding what your score means and how it's determined

The GED test offers high-school dropouts, people who leave school early, and people who were educated outside the United States an opportunity to earn the equivalent of a United States (U.S.) high-school diploma without the need for full-time attendance in either day or night school. The GED test is a recognized standard that makes securing a job or college placement easier.

The GED test complies with current Grade 12 standards in the U.S. and meets the College and Career Readiness Standards for Adult Education. The GED test also covers the Common Core Standards, used in most states in the United States. These standards are based on the actual expectations stated by employers and postsecondary institutions.

The GED test measures whether you understand what high-school seniors across the country have studied before they graduate. Employers need better-educated employees. In addition, some colleges may be uncertain of the quality of foreign credentials. The GED provides those assurances. When you pass the GED test, you earn a high-school equivalency diploma. That can open many doors for you — perhaps doors that you don't even know exist at this point.

You're permitted to take the GED in sections, so you can take the Reasoning Through Language Arts (RLA), Math, Science, and Social Studies tests in separate testing sessions. This flexibility enables you to focus your studies and practice on one section of the test at a time, and this book supports your efforts to do just that.

Ready to get started? This chapter gives you the basics of the GED RLA test: how the test is administered, what the RLA test section looks like, how to schedule the test (including whether you're eligible), and how your score is calculated (so you know what you need to focus on to pass).

Knowing What to Expect: The GED Test Format

A computer administers the GED test. That means that all the questions appear on a computer screen, and you enter all your answers into a computer. You read, evaluate, analyze, and write everything on the computer. Even when drafting an essay, you don't use paper. Instead, the test centers provide you with an erasable tablet. If you know how to use a computer and are comfortable with a keyboard and a mouse, you're ahead of the game. If not, practice your keyboarding. Also, practice reading from a computer screen, because reading from a screen is very different from reading printed materials. At the very least, you need to get more comfortable with computers, even if that means taking a short course at a local learning center. In the case of the GED test, the more familiar you are with computers, the more comfortable you'll feel taking the computerized test.

Under certain circumstances, as a special accommodation, the sections are available in booklet format. Check with the GED Testing Service to see what exceptions are acceptable.

The computer-based GED test allows for speedy detailed feedback on your performance. When you pass (yes, we said *when* and not *if,* because we believe in you), the GED Testing Service provides both a diploma and a detailed transcript of your scores, similar to what high-school graduates receive. They're now available online at `www.gedtestingservice.com` within a day of completing the test. You can then send your transcript and diploma to an employer or college. Doing so allows employers and colleges access to a detailed outline of your scores, achievement, and demonstrated skills and abilities. This outline is also a useful tool for you to review your progress. It highlights those areas where you did well and areas where you need further work. If you want to (or have to) retake the test, these results will provide a detailed guide to what you should work on to improve your scores. Requests for additional copies of transcripts are handled online and also are available within a day.

Reviewing the GED RLA Test

The Reasoning Through Language Arts (RLA) test is one long test that covers all the literacy components of the GED test. The 150-minute test is divided into three sections. First, you have 35 minutes on all content in question-and-answer format, then 45 minutes for the Extended Response (essay), followed by a 10-minute break, and then another 60 minutes for more general test items.

Time for the Extended Response can't be used to work on the other questions in the test, nor can you use leftover time from the other sections to work on the Extended Response.

Here's what you can expect on the RLA test:

- ✔ The literacy component asks you to correct text, respond to writings, and generally demonstrate a critical understanding of various passages. This task includes demonstrating a command of proper grammar, punctuation, and spelling.

- ✔ The Extended Response item, also known as "the essay," examines your skills in organizing your thoughts and writing clearly. Your response will be based on one or two source text selections, drawing key elements from that material to prepare your essay.

  The essay is evaluated both on your interpretation of the source texts and the quality of your writing. You type on the computer, using a tool that resembles a word processor. It has neither a spell-checker nor a grammar-checker. How well you use spelling and grammar as you write is also part of your evaluation. You'll have an erasable tablet on which to prepare a draft before writing the final document.

- ✔ The scores from both components will be combined into one single score for the RLA test.

The question-answer part of this test consists mainly of various types of multiple-choice questions (also called items) and the occasional fill-in-the-blank question. Most items will be in the traditional multiple-choice format with four answer choices, but you'll also see drag-and-drop and drop-down menu items. For details on the different question types, see Chapters 2 and 3.

These items are based on source texts, which are materials presented to you for your response. Some of this source material is nonfiction from science and social studies content as well as from the workplace. About 25 percent is based on literature. Here's a breakdown of the materials:

- **Workplace materials:** These documents include work-related letters, memos, and instructions that you may see on the job.

- **U.S. founding documents and documents that present part of the Great American Conversation:** These bits may include extracts from the Bill of Rights, the Constitution, and other historical documents. They also may include opinion pieces on relevant issues in American history and civics.

- **Informational works:** These texts include documents that present information (often dry and boring information), such as the instructional manual that tells you how to set up an Internet connection on your tablet. They also include materials that you may find in history, social studies, or science books.

- **Literature:** These sources include extracts from novels, plays, and similar materials.

You find a variety of problems in the RLA test, including the following:

- **Correction:** In these items, you're asked to correct sentences presented to you.

- **Revision:** In these items, you're presented with a sentence that has a word or phrase underlined. If the sentence needs a correction, one of the answer choices will be better than the words or phrase underlined. If no correction is needed, either one of the answer choices will be the same as the underlined portion or one of the choices will be something like "no correction needed."

- **Construction shift:** In these types of problems, you have to correct a sentence by altering the sentence structure. The original sentence may not be completely wrong, but it can be improved with a little editing. In these cases, the question presents you with optional rewording or allows you to change the sentence order in a paragraph.

- **Text analysis:** These problems require you to read a passage and respond in some manner. It may be an analysis of the content, a critique of the style, review for biases or other influences, or responses to something in the content.

Because the computerized GED test is new and still evolving as we write this book, be sure to check out the latest and greatest about the GED test at www.gedtestingservice.com.

If you can't wait to get started practicing for the RLA test, you may skip to Chapter 3 to take a diagnostic version of the test or check out the chapters in Part 5 that cover the skills and knowledge required in greater detail.

It's a Date: Scheduling the Test

To take the GED test, you schedule it based on the available testing dates. Each state or local testing center sets its own schedule for the GED test, which means that your state decides how and when you can take each section of the test. It also determines how often you can retake a failed section and how much such a retake will cost. Because a computer administers the test, many testing centers schedule an individual appointment. Your test starts when you start and ends when your allotted time is completed. The test centers are small computer labs, often containing no more than 15 seats, and actual testing facilities are located in many communities in your state.

You book your appointment through the GED Testing Service (www.gedtestingservice. com). Your local GED test administrator can give you all the information you need about scheduling the test. In addition, local school districts and community colleges can provide information about local test centers in your area.

Sending a specific question or request to the website may come with a charge for the service. To save money, you're better off asking a person at your local testing center. That way, you don't have to pay for the privilege of asking a question, and your answer will be based on rules and conditions specific to your area.

The following sections answer some questions you may have before you schedule your test date, including whether you're even eligible to take the test, when you can take the test, and how to sign up to take the test.

Determining whether you're eligible

Before you schedule your test, make sure you meet the requirements to take the GED test. You're eligible to apply to take the GED test only if

- **You're not currently enrolled in a high school.** If you're currently enrolled in a high school, you're expected to complete your diploma there. The purpose of the GED test is to give people who aren't in high school a chance to get an equivalent high-school diploma.

- **You're not a high-school graduate.** If you're a high-school graduate, you should have a diploma, which means you don't need to take the GED test. However, you can use the GED to upgrade or update your skills and to prove that you're ready for further education and training.

- **You meet state requirements regarding age, residency, and the length of time since leaving high school.** Check with your local GED test administrator to determine your state's requirements concerning these criteria. Residency requirements are an issue, because you may have to take the test in a different jurisdiction, depending on how long you've lived at your present address.

Recognizing when you can take the test

If you're eligible, you can take the GED test whenever you're prepared. You can apply to take the GED test as soon as you want. Just contact your local testing center or www. gedtestingservice.com for a test schedule. Pick a day that works for you.

You can take all four sections of the GED test together. That takes about seven hours. However, the test is designed so that you can take each section separately, whenever you're ready. In most areas, you can take the test sections one at a time, in the evening or on weekends, depending on the individual testing center. If you pass one test section, that section of the GED test is considered done, no matter how you do on the other sections. If you fail one section, you can retake that section of the test. The scheduling and administration of the test vary from state to state, so check with the GED Testing Service site or your local high-school guidance office.

Because the test starts when you're ready and finishes when you've used up the allocated time, you should be able take it alone and not depend on other people. For you, that means you may be able to find locations that offer the testing in evenings or on weekends as well as during regular business hours. Even better, because you don't have to take the test with a group, you may be able to set an individual starting time that suits you.

If circumstances dictate that you must take the paper version of the test, you'll probably have to forgo the flexibility afforded by the computer. Check well in advance to see what the rules are for you.

You can also apply to take the test if you're not prepared, but if you do that, you don't stand a very good chance of passing. If you do need to retake any section of the test, use your time before your next test date to get ready. You can retake the test three times in a year without waiting, but after the third failed attempt you must wait 60 days. In most jurisdictions, taking the test costs money (check with your local testing center to find out specifics for your area). The GED Testing Service does offer a discounted retake up to twice a year, but these promotions change. Some states include free retakes in the price of the test. Check with the GED Testing Service or your state when ready about what special discounts may be available. To save time and money, prepare well before you schedule the test. Refer to the later section "Knowing what to do if you score poorly on one or more tests" for details.

Are special accommodations available?

If you need to complete the test on paper or have a disability that makes it impossible for you to use the computer, your needs can be accommodated. However, other specifics apply: Your choice of times and testing locations may be much more restricted, but times to complete a test may be extended. Remember also that the GED testing centers will ask for documentation of the nature of the accommodation required.

The GED testing centers make every effort to ensure that all qualified people have access to the tests. If you have a disability, you may not be able to register for the tests and take them the same week, but, with some advanced planning, you can probably take the tests when you're ready. Here's what you need to do:

- Check with your local testing center or check out www.gedtestingservice.com/testers/accommodations-for-disability.

- Contact the GED Testing Service or your local GED test center and explain your disability.

- Request any forms that you have to fill out for your special circumstances.

- Ensure that you have a recent diagnosis by a physician or other qualified professional.

- Complete all the proper forms and submit them with medical or professional diagnosis.

- Start planning early so that you're able to take the tests when you're ready.

Note that, regardless of your disability, you still have to be able to handle the mental and emotional demands of the test.

The GED Testing Service in Washington, D.C., defines specific disabilities, such as the following, for which it may make special accommodations, provided the disability severely limits your ability to perform essential skills required to pass the GED test:

- Medical disabilities, such as cerebral palsy, epilepsy, or blindness

- Psychological disabilities, such as schizophrenia, major depression, attention deficit disorder, or Tourette's syndrome

- Specific learning disabilities, including perceptual handicaps, brain injury, minimal brain dysfunction, dyslexia, and developmental aphasia

Signing up

When you're actually ready to sign up for the test, follow these steps:

1. **Contact your local GED test administrator to make sure you're eligible.**

   Refer to the earlier section "Determining whether you're eligible" for some help.

2. **Ask the office for an application (if needed) or an appointment.**

3. **Complete the application (if needed).**

4. **Return the application to the proper office, with payment, if necessary.**

   The fees vary state by state, so contact your local administrator or testing site to find out what you have to pay to take the tests. In some states, low-income individuals may be eligible for financial assistance.

Note: You can also do all of this online, including submitting the payment, with your computer, tablet, or smartphone. Go to www.gedtestingservice.com to start the process.

Never send cash by mail to pay for the GED test. Most local administrators have payment rules and don't accept cash.

Working with unusual circumstances

If you feel that you may have a special circumstance that prevents you from taking the GED test on a given day, contact the GED test administrator in your area. If, for example, the test is going to be held on your Sabbath, the testing center may make special arrangements for you.

When applying for special circumstances, keep the following guidelines in mind:

- Document everything in your appeal for special consideration.

- Contact the GED test administrator in your area as early as you can.

- Be patient. Special arrangements can't be made overnight. The administrator often has to wait for a group with similar issues to gather so he can make arrangements for the entire group.

- Ask questions. Accommodations can be made if you ask. For example, special allowances include extended time for various disabilities, large print and Braille for visual impairments, and age (for individuals older than 60 who feel they may have a learning disability).

Taking the GED Test When English Isn't Your First Language

English doesn't have to be your first language for you to take the GED test. The GED test is offered in English, Spanish, and French. If you want to take the test in Spanish or French, contact your local GED test administrator to apply. Individuals who speak other languages as their first language, however, must take the test in English. If that is you, you should take a test of your English skills before taking the GED test.

Websites that can help you plan to take the GED test

The Internet is a helpful and sometimes scary place. Some websites are there to help you in your GED test preparation, while others just want to sell you something. You have to know how to separate the good from the bad. Here are a couple of essential ones (most are accessible through www.gedtestingservice.com):

✔ adulted.about.com/od/getting yourged/a/stateged.htm is a website that links to the GED test eligibility requirements and testing locations in your state.

✔ usaeducation.info/Tests/GED/ International-students.aspx is a site that explains GED test eligibility for foreign students.

If you're curious and want to see what's out there, type "GED test" into any search engine and relax while you try to read about 22 million results, ranging from the helpful to the helpless. We suggest leaving this last activity until after you've passed the tests. As useful as the Internet can be, it still provides the opportunity to waste vast amounts of time. And right now, you need to spend your time preparing for the test — and leave the rest for after you get your diploma.

If English, Spanish, or French isn't your first language, you must decide whether you can read and write English as well as or better than 40 percent of high-school graduates, because you may be required to pass an English as a Second Language (ESL) placement test. If you write and read English well, prepare for and take the test (either in English or in Spanish or French). If you don't read or write English well, take additional classes to improve your language skills until you think you're ready. An English Language Proficiency Test (ELPT) is also available for people who completed their education in other countries. For more information about the language component of the GED test, check out www.gedtestingservice.com/testers/special-test-editions.

In many ways, the GED test is like the Test of English as a Foreign Language (TOEFL) comprehension test. If you've completed the TOEFL test with good grades, you're likely ready to take the GED test. If you haven't taken the TOEFL test, enroll in a GED test-preparation course to see whether you have difficulty understanding the subjects and skills assessed on the test. GED test courses provide you with some insight into your comprehension ability with a teacher to discuss your skills and struggles.

Taking Aim at Your Target Score

To pass, you need to score a minimum of 150 on each section of the test, and you must pass each section of the test to earn your GED diploma. If you achieve a passing score, congratulate yourself: You've scored better than at least 40 percent of today's high-school graduates, and you're now a graduate of the largest virtual school in the country. And if your marks are in the honors range (any score over 170), you're ready for college or career training.

Be aware that some colleges require scores higher than the minimum passing score. If you plan to apply to postsecondary schools or some other form of continuing education, check with their admissions office for the minimum admission score requirements.

The following sections address a few more points you may want to know about how the GED test is scored and what you can do if you score poorly on one or more of the test sections.

Identifying how scores are determined

Correct answers may be worth one, two, or more points, depending on the item and the level of difficulty. The Extended Response, the essay, is scored separately. However, the Extended Response is only part of the RLA and Social Studies sections. On each test section, you must accumulate a minimum of 150 points.

Because you don't lose points for incorrect answers, make sure you answer all the items on each test. After all, a correct guess can get you a point. Leaving an answer blank, on the other hand, guarantees you a zero. The information and practice in this book provide you with the knowledge and skills you need to answer most questions on the RLA section with confidence and to narrow your choices when you're not quite sure which answer choice is correct.

Knowing what to do if you score poorly on one or more tests

If you discover that your score is less than 150 on any test section, start planning to retake the test(s) — and make sure you leave plenty of time for additional study and preparation.

As soon as possible after obtaining your results, contact your local GED test administrator to find out the rules for retaking the failed section of the test. Some states may ask that you wait a certain amount of time and/or limit the number of attempts each year. Some may ask that you attend a preparation course and show that you've completed it before you can retake the GED. Some may charge you an additional fee. However, you need to retake only those sections of the test that you failed. Any sections you pass are completed and count toward your diploma. Furthermore, the detailed evaluation of your results will help you discover areas of weakness that need more work before repeating any section of the test.

One advantage of taking the GED test on a computer is that you can receive, within a day, detailed feedback on how you did, which includes some specific recommendations of what you need to do to improve your scores.

No matter what score you receive on your first round of the section, don't be afraid to retake any section that you didn't pass. After you've taken it once, you know what you need to work on, and you know exactly what to expect on test day.

Chapter 2

Prepping for the RLA Test

The Reasoning Through Language Arts (RLA) test evaluates your skills in comprehending and applying concepts in grammar and writing. (*Grammar* is the basic structure of language — you know: subjects, verbs, sentences, fragments, punctuation, and all that.) Most of what you're tested on (both in writing and grammar) is stuff you've picked up over the years, either in school or just by speaking, reading, and observing, but, to help you prepare better for this test, we give you some more skill-building tips in this chapter.

The RLA test is divided into three sections. You start off with a 35-minute question-and-answer section that focuses on writing and reading comprehension, and then you spend 45 minutes writing an Extended Response (the essay). After a 10-minute break, you finish with a 60-minute question-and-answer section that presents more questions on reading and writing. The length of the two question-and-answer sections may vary slightly, but the overall time is always 150 minutes, including the 10-minute break.

In this chapter, we provide all you need to know to prepare for the RLA test and its different components. From reading everything you can to practicing your writing, grammar, and spelling to improving your reading comprehension and speed, this chapter, along with those in Part II, equip you with what you need to nail the test.

Grasping What's on the Grammar and Writing Component

Although the GED test doesn't label question sets with the words *writing* or *grammar*, the concepts are worked into almost everything on the test. To pass this component of the RLA test, you need to demonstrate that you have a command of the conventions of Standard English. You need to know the appropriate vocabulary to use and avoid slang. Texting short-cuts may save you time while communicating with your friends, but they're not acceptable in formal writing. You need to be able to spell, identify incorrect grammar, and eliminate basic errors, including such common errors as run-on sentences or sentence fragments.

To help you succeed, we provide insightful information in the following sections about what skills this part of the test covers, what you can do to brush up on those skills, and how the questions are presented. With this information in hand, you can be confident in your ability to tackle any type of grammar or writing question on test day.

Looking at the skills the grammar and writing component covers

The grammar and writing component of the RLA test evaluates you on the following types of skills related to grammar. Note that unlike the other GED test sections, this component of the RLA test expects that you know or at least are familiar with the rules of grammar. Just looking at the passages provided won't do you much good if you don't understand the basics of these rules already.

- **Mechanics:** You don't have to become a professional grammarian to pass this test, but you need to know or review basic grammar. Check out Chapter 7 to review what you should know or may have forgotten. The mechanics of writing include the following:

  - **Capitalization:** You have to recognize which words should start with a capital letter and which words shouldn't. All sentences start with a capital letter, but so do titles, like *Miss, President,* and *Senator,* when they're followed by a person's name. Names of cities, states, and countries are also capitalized.

  - **Punctuation:** This area of writing mechanics includes everyone's personal favorite: commas. (Actually, most people hate commas because they aren't sure how to use them, but the basic rules are simple.) The more you read, the better you get at punctuation. If you're reading and don't understand why punctuation is or isn't used, check with your grammar guidebook or the Internet.

    A general rule: Don't use a comma unless the next group of words is a complete sentence. For example: "As agonizing as it was to leave her friends, college was what she wanted." *College was what she wanted* is a complete sentence and can stand alone, so using a comma here is correct.

  - **Spelling:** You don't have to spot a lot of misspelled words, but you do have to know how to spell contractions and possessives and understand the different spellings of *homonyms* — words that sound the same but have different spellings and meanings, like *their* and *there.*

  - **Contractions:** This area of writing mechanics has nothing to do with those painful moments before childbirth! Instead, *contractions* are formed when the English language shortens a word by leaving out a letter or a sound. For example, when you say or write *can't,* you're using a shortened form of *cannot.* In this example, *can't* is the contraction.

    The important thing to remember about contractions is that the *apostrophe* (that's a single quotation mark) takes the place of the letter or letters that are left out.

  - **Possessives:** Do you know people who are possessive? They're all about ownership, right? So is the grammar form of possessives. *Possessives* are words that show ownership or possession, usually by adding an apostrophe to a person's or object's name. If Marcia owns a car, that car is *Marcia's* car. The word *Marcia's* is a possessive. Make sure you know the difference between singular and plural possessives. For example: "The girl's coat is torn." (*Girl* and *coat* are singular, so the apostrophe goes before the *s.*) "The girls' coats are torn." (*Girls* and coats are plural, so the apostrophe goes after the *s.*) When working with plural possessives, form the plural first and then add the apostrophe.

- **Organization:** On the test, you're asked to correct passages by changing the order of sentences or leaving out certain sentences when they don't fit. You have to work with passages to turn them into logical, organized paragraphs. You may be asked to work with paragraphs to form a better composition by changing them around, editing them by improving or adding topic sentences, or making sure that all the sentences are about the same topic. The important thing to remember is that the questions all offer you a choice of answers. That means you have only a limited number of options for making the passages better. Read the questions carefully, and you should have no problems.

✔ **Sentence structure:** Every language has rules about the order in which words should appear in a sentence. You get a chance to improve sentences through your understanding of what makes a good sentence. Extensive reading before the test can give you a good idea of how good sentences are structured and put together. The advice here is read, read, and read some more.

✔ **Usage:** This broad category covers a lot of topics. Grammar has a wide variety of rules, and these questions test your knowledge and understanding. Subjects and verbs must agree. Verbs have tenses (for example, present and future) that must be consistent. Pronouns must refer to nouns properly. If the last three sentences sound like Greek to you, make sure you review grammatical usage rules. Usage also covers vocabulary and acceptable Standard English usage. People have become very comfortable with short forms used in texting, but "LOL" and "C U L8R" aren't acceptable in formal writing.

Having a firm grasp of these writing mechanics can help you get a more accurate picture of the types of questions you'll encounter on this part of the test. The chapters in Part II of this book help you master the basics.

Understanding the format of the grammar and writing component

The grammar and writing component consist of a set of questions, mainly multiple-choice but also drag-and-drop or other technologically enhanced question formats and the occasional fill-in-the-blank question. One type of question asks you to read, revise, and edit documents that may include how-to info, informational texts, and workplace materials. Don't worry; almost all of the questions are some form of multiple-choice, which means you don't have to come up with the answers all on your own. And the best part: Practicing for this component helps you understand the grammar and other language skills needed for the Extended Response. It even carries over to the other GED test sections.

To answer the questions in this part of the RLA test, read the information presented to you carefully. Reading the questions before reading the entire text is often helpful because then you know what to look for. And because you're dealing with grammar, as you read each passage, you can ask yourself, "Can I correct this passage? If so, how?"

Rocking the Reading Comprehension Component

You may not understand why the GED test examines your knowledge of literature comprehension. However, in today's society, being able to comprehend, analyze, and apply something you've read is the strongest predictor of career and college readiness and an important skill set to have. In the following sections, we explore the four aspects of good reading skills: comprehension, application, analysis, and synthesis.

Checking out the skills required for the reading component

The questions on the RLA reading portion of the test focus on the following skills, which you're expected to be able to use as you read both fiction and nonfiction passages:

- **Comprehension:** Questions that test your *comprehension* skills assess your ability to read a source of information, understand what you've read, and restate the information in your own words. If you understand the passage, you can rephrase what you read while retaining the meaning of the passage. You can also create a summary of the main ideas presented in the passage and explain the ideas and implications of the passage.

- **Application:** Questions that test your *application* skills assess your ability to use the information you read in the passage in a new situation, such as when you're answering questions. Application-focused questions are most like real life because they often ask you to apply what you read in the passage to a real-life situation. Being able to read and understand a users' manual in order to use the product it came with is a perfect example of using your application skills in real life.

- **Analysis:** Questions that test your *analysis* skills assess your ability to draw conclusions, understand consequences, and make inferences after reading the passage. To answer these questions successfully, you have to make sure your conclusions are based solely on the written text in the passage and not on outside knowledge or the book you read last week. Questions that focus on your ability to analyze what you read try to find out whether you appreciate the way the passage was written and see the cause-and-effect relationships within it. They also expect you to know when a conclusion is being stated and analyze what it means in the context of the passage.

- **Synthesis:** Questions that test your *synthesis* skills assess your ability to take information in one form and in one location and put it together in another context. Here, you get a chance to make connections between different parts of the passage and compare and contrast them. You may be asked to talk about the tone, point of view, style, or purpose of a passage — and saying that the purpose of a passage is to confuse and confound test-takers isn't the answer.

Some reading-comprehension questions on the test may ask you to use information in the source text passages combined with information from the text in the questions to answer them. So make sure you read everything that appears on-screen — you never know where an answer may come from.

Breaking down the format of the reading component

The RLA reading comprehension section measures your ability to understand and interpret fiction and nonfiction passages. It's plain and simple — no tricks involved. You don't have to do any math to figure out the answers to the questions. You just have to read, understand, and use the material presented to you to answer the corresponding questions.

The passages in this test are similar to the works a high-school student would come across in English class. To help you feel more comfortable with the RLA reading comprehension, we're here to give you a better idea of what this test looks like on paper.

Most source texts (the reading passages) are presented on the left side of a split screen, with the question on the right. A source text or passage will be between 450 and 900 words. The passages in this test may come from workplace (on-the-job) materials or from academic reading materials. Seventy-five percent of the source text will be from informational texts — nonfiction documents. The remaining 25 percent is based on literary texts, including plays, poetry, short stories, and novels. With each source text, you have to answer four to eight questions.

Text passages are text passages. Although the next section describes what types of passages appear on the RLA test to help you prepare, don't worry so much about what type of passage you're reading. Instead, spend your time understanding what information the passage presents to you.

Identifying the types of passages and how to prepare for them

To help you get comfortable with answering the questions on the reading comprehension portion of the RLA test, you want to have a good idea of what these types of questions look like. The good news is that in this section, we focus on the two main types of passages you'll see: literary and nonfiction. We also give you some practical advice you can use as you prepare for this portion of the test.

Literary passages

The RLA reading component may include passages from the following literary texts (and plenty of questions to go with them):

- **Drama:** *Drama* (that is, a play) tells a story, using the words and actions of the characters. The description of the place and costumes are in the stage directions or in the head of the director. As you read passages from drama, try to imagine the dramatic scene and see the characters and their actions in your head. Doing so makes drama easier to understand.

  Stage directions are usually printed in italics, *like this.* Even though you're not acting in the play, pay attention to the stage directions. They may provide valuable information you need to answer the questions that follow the passage.

- **Prose fiction:** *Prose fiction* refers to novels and short stories. As you may already know, *fiction* is writing that comes straight from the mind of the author (in other words, it's made up; it's not about something that really happened). The only way to become familiar with prose fiction is to read as much fiction as you can. After you read a book, try to talk about it with other people who have read the book.

Nonfiction passages

Nonfiction passages may come from many different sources. Here's a list of some of the kinds of passages you may see, and of course, answer questions about:

- **Critical reviews of visual and performing arts:** These prose passages are reviews written by people who have enough knowledge of the visual or performing arts to be critical of them. You can find examples of good critical reviews in the library, in some daily papers, and on the Internet. Type in "critical review" into your favorite search engine, and you'll get more critical reviews than you have time to read.

  To prepare for this part of the test, try to read critical reviews of books, movies, restaurants, and the like as often as you can. The next time you go to a movie, watch television, or attend a play, write your own critical review (what you thought of the piece of work). Put some factual material into your review and make suggestions for improvement. Compare what the real critics have to say with your own feelings about the movie, television show, or play. Do you agree with their opinions?

✔ **Nonfiction prose:** *Nonfiction prose* is prose that covers a lot of ground — and all the ground is real. Nonfiction prose is material that the author doesn't create in his or her own mind; it's based on fact or reality. In fact, this book is classified as nonfiction prose, and so are the newspaper articles you read every day. The next time you read the newspaper or a magazine, tell yourself, "I'm reading nonfiction prose." Just don't say it out loud in a coffee shop or in your break room at work, or people may start to look at you in strange ways.

✔ **Workplace and community documents:** You run across these types of passages in the job- and community-related areas of life. The following are some examples:

• **Corporate statements:** Companies and organizations issue policies for employee behavior, rules for hiring and firing, goals for the corporation, even statements on environmental stewardship. These assertions tell the world what the company intends to accomplish and what the basic rules of behavior within the company are. The goal statement for your study group may be as follows: "We're all going to pass the GED test on our first attempt."

• **Historic documents, founding documents, legal documents:** These texts may include extracts from the Constitution or other founding documents, extracts from treaties, or legal documents. The founding and historical documents are obviously older materials, with a somewhat different writing style from what you may see in a modern legal document. Other documents may include leases, purchase contracts, and bank statements. If you aren't familiar with these kinds of documents, collect some examples from banks or libraries and review them. Have a look at the terms in your lease, mortgage, or credit card statement. If you can explain these types of documents to a friend, you understand them.

• **Letters:** You certainly know what a *letter* is: a written communication between two people. It's not very often that you get to read other people's letters without getting into trouble — here's your chance.

• **Manuals:** Every time you purchase a major appliance, an electronic gadget, or a power tool, you get a user's manual that tells you how to operate the device. Some manuals are short and straightforward; others are so long and complicated that the manufacturers put them on CD-ROMs to save printing costs.

Regardless of what type of passage the questions in the reading component are based on, you have two challenges. The first is grammar. Grammar doesn't change with the type of passage, so although you should be familiar with the various types of passages, you need to be most familiar with the rules of grammar so you can use them to improve the passages. The second is reading skills. You need to answer questions, using the four skills outlined in the earlier section "Checking out the skills required for the reading component": comprehension, application, analysis, and synthesis.

Examining the Extended Response Item

In spite of its name, the Extended Response doesn't consist of a real research essay so much as a series of related paragraphs. You aren't expected to produce a book-length opus complete with documented research. Rather, you're expected to write a coherent series of interrelated paragraphs on a given topic and use the rules of grammar and correct spelling. Part of that essay will be an analysis of materials presented to you, and part will be preparation of logical argument. Examiners look for an essay that's well organized and sticks to the topic given.

In the following sections, we explain what you need to know about the Extended Response and give you some tools for writing a successful essay.

Eyeing the skills covered in the Extended Response

The evaluation of your essay focuses on three major criteria or skills. By having a clear understanding of the main skills covered in this part of the test, you can ensure that you address all of them when writing your essay that will translate into success in terms of your essay score. The GED Testing Service defines the three essay criteria you need to address as follows:

- **Creation of argument and use of evidence:** This criterion refers to how well you answer the topic, including whether the focus of the response shifts as you write. Stay on topic.

- **Development and organizational structure:** This criterion refers to whether you show the reader through your essay that you have a clear idea about what you're writing and that you're able to establish a definable plan for writing the essay. The evaluation expects that you'll present your arguments in a logical sequence and back those arguments with specific supporting evidence from the source text. Remember, you must use specific detail from the source texts; you can elaborate, but your answer must be based on the source text.

- **Clarity and command of Standard English conventions:** This criterion refers to your ability to appropriately use what the GED Testing Service calls "on-demand, draft writing." That includes the application of the basic rules of grammar, such as sentence structure, mechanics, usage, and so forth. It's also looking for stylistic features, such as transitional phrases, varied sentence structure, and appropriate word choices.

The evaluation grades your essay on a three-point scale. You receive 2, 1, or 0 points, depending on your success in each of these three categories. You can check out a guide for teachers on the RLA Extended Response at www.gedtestingservice.com/uploads/files/949aa6a0418791c4f3b962a4cd0c92f4.pdf. Here, you can see a sample essay prompt and breakdown of how it's evaluated. It includes a very detailed look at the criteria and what the evaluators look for in an essay that receives a passing score.

Read the sections on what constitutes a passing score very carefully. If you don't pass the essay, you probably won't accumulate a high enough score on the other sections to pass the RLA test, and that means you'll have to retake the entire test.

Understanding the Extended Response format

This 45-minute part of the Reasoning Through Language Arts (RLA) test has only one item: a prompt on which you have to write a short essay (usually 600 to 800 words).

For this part of the test, you're given one topic and a few instructions. Your task is to write an essay of three or more paragraphs on that topic. Remember that you can't write about another topic or a similar topic; if you do, you'll receive zero points for your essay, and you'll have to retake the entire RLA test.

The focus for the evaluation of this part of the GED test is on your reading comprehension, analysis and organization, and writing skills.

The test presents you with one or two passages of argumentation. The writer of each passage takes a position on an issue and defends that position with evidence and the power of reason. You must examine the positions, determine which is the stronger and best defended, and write an essay explaining why you made that choice. You have to do that regardless of how you feel about the issue. The point is to analyze and show that you understand the strategies used to defend positions.

As part of that process, you must analyze the arguments for logical consistency, illogical conclusions, and false reasoning. This area is where your critical analysis skills come into play. Does Point A from the author really make sense? Is it valid and backed by facts?

Finally, you must write your answer in a clear, concise, and well-organized response. The evaluation examines how well you write, including the following aspects:

- Your style
- Varied sentence structure and vocabulary
- Use of transitional sentences
- Appropriate vocabulary
- Correct spelling and grammar, including word usage and punctuation

You have an erasable tablet for rough notes, points, and draft organization. Use it. The computer screen has a window that offers a mini-word processor with some basic functions, such as cut and paste and undo and redo. However, it doesn't offer a spell-checker or grammar-checker.

Planning to succeed on the Extended Response

The Extended Response essay requires some very specific skills, ranging from grammar and proper language usage to comprehension and analysis skills. If you've ever had an argument about who has the best team or which employer is better, you already know how to assess arguments and respond. Now you need to hone those skills. As you prepare for the RLA Extended Response, do the following:

- **Read, read, and read some more.** Just like for the other parts of the RLA test (and most other subtests on the GED test), reading is important. Reading exposes you to well-crafted sentences, which can help you improve your own writing. Reading also expands your horizons and provides you with little bits of information you can work into your essay.

  As you read, make an outline of the paragraphs or chapters you read to see how the material ties together. Try rewriting some of the paragraphs from your outline, and compare what you write to the original. Yours may not be ready for prime time, but this little exercise gives you practice in writing organized, cohesive sentences and paragraphs, which can go a long way in this part of the test.

- **Practice editing your own work.** After the test starts, the only person able to edit your essay is you. If that thought scares you, practice editing your own work now. Take a writing workshop, or get help from someone who knows how to edit. Practice writing a lot of essays, and don't forget to review and edit them as soon as you're done writing.

- **Review how to plan an essay.** Few people can sit down, write a final draft of an essay the first time around, and receive a satisfactory grade. Instead, you have to plan what you're going to write. The best way to start is to jot down everything you know about a topic without worrying about the order. From there, you can organize your thoughts into groups. Check out Chapter 8 for more help on planning your essay.

- **Practice writing on a topic (and not going off topic!).** Your essay must relate to the given topic as closely as possible. If the test asks you to write about your personal goals, and you write about a hockey game you once played in, you can kiss your good score on this part of the test goodbye.

TIP

To help you practice staying on topic, read the newspaper and write a letter to the editor or a response to a columnist. Because you're responding to a very narrow topic that appeared in a particular newspaper article, you have to do so clearly and concisely — if you ever want to see it in print. (You can also practice staying on topic by picking a newspaper article's title and writing a short essay about it. Then read the actual story and see how yours compares.)

✔ **Think about, and use, appropriate examples.** You're dealing with information presented in the source text. You'll find information in the source text for and against the position you are to argue. When you take a position, you need to use materials from the source text to support your position. Use that information. Look for flaws in the logic. You can find good examples of such arguments in the editorial section of a newspaper or in blogs. Look at how the writers develop their arguments, use logic to support their positions, and perhaps use false logic or flawed reasoning to persuade the readers.

✔ **Practice general writing.** If writing connected paragraphs isn't one of your fortes, practice doing so! Write long emails. Write long letters. Write to your member of Congress. Write to your friends. Write articles for community newspapers. Write short stories. Write anything you want — whatever you do, just keep writing.

✔ **Write practice essays.** Check out the diagnostic test in Chapter 3 and the practice test in Chapter 9. The test includes an RLA-style extended response essay with prompts in actual test format. Write an essay based on the topic given. You can also practice essays by taking newspaper or blog editorials and writing rebuttals. Then ask a knowledgeable friend or former teacher to grade them for you. You may also consider taking a preparation class in which you're assigned practice topics to write about. When you think you're finished practicing, practice some more.

Preparing for the RLA Test with Tactics That Work

The RLA test requires a number of skills, from knowing proper spelling, usage, and punctuation to reading quickly and accurately. You can master all of these skills with practice. The following sections give some advice on how to do that.

Sharpening your reading and writing skills

To succeed on the RLA test, you can prepare in advance by reviewing rules of grammar, punctuation, and spelling and by familiarizing yourself with the format and subject matter of the test. Here are some of the best ways you can prepare:

✔ **Read as often as you can.** This strategy is the best one and is by far the simplest, because reading exposes you to correct grammar. What you read makes a difference. Reading catalogs may increase your product knowledge and improve your research skills, but reading literature is preferable because it introduces you to so many rules of grammar. Reading fiction exposes you to interesting words and sentences. It shows you how paragraphs tie into one another and how each paragraph has a topic and generally sticks to it.

You should also read nonfiction — from instructions to business letters, from press releases to history books and historical documents. Nonfiction is generally written at a higher reading level than fiction and uses a very formal style, the kind expected of you when you write an essay for the Extended Response item. Older documents can be a special problem because the writing style is very different from what's common today. Getting familiar with such documents will help you to better results and even help with your Social Studies test.

Read everything you can get your hands on — even cereal boxes — and identify what kind of reading you're doing. Ask yourself questions about your reading and see how much of it you can remember.

✔ **Develop your reading speed.** Reading is wonderful, but reading quickly is even better; it gets you through the test with time to spare. Check out *Speed Reading For Dummies* by Richard Sutz and Peter Weverka (Wiley), or do a quick Internet search to find plenty of material that can help you read faster. Whatever method you use, try to improve your reading rate without hurting your overall reading comprehension.

✔ **Master the rules of basic grammar.** On this test, you don't have to define a gerund and give an example of one, but you do have to know about verb tenses, subject-verb agreement, pronoun-antecedent agreement, possessives, and other basic grammar. As your knowledge of grammar and punctuation improves, have a bit of fun by correcting what you read in small-town newspapers and low-budget novels — both sometimes have poor editing.

✔ **Practice grammar and proper English in everyday speaking.** As you review the rules of grammar, practice them every day as you talk to your friends, family, and coworkers. Although correct grammar usually "sounds" right to your ears, sometimes it doesn't because you and the people you talk to have become used to using incorrect grammar. If you see a rule that seems different from the way you talk, put it on a flashcard and practice it as you go through your day. Before long, you'll train your ears so that correct grammar sounds right.

Correcting other people's grammar out loud doesn't make you popular, but correcting it in your head can help you succeed on this test. Also, listen for and avoid slang or regional expressions. *Y'all* may be a great favorite in the South but wouldn't work well on a college application.

✔ **Understand punctuation.** Know how to use commas, semicolons, colons, and other forms of punctuation. To find out more about punctuation and when and why to use its different forms, head to Chapter 7.

✔ **Practice writing.** Write as much and as often as you can, and then review it for errors. Look for and correct mistakes in punctuation, grammar, and spelling. If you can't find any, ask someone who knows grammar and punctuation for help.

✔ **Keep a journal or blog.** Journals and blogs are just notebooks (physical or virtual) in which you write a bit about your life every day. They both provide good practice for personal writing. Blogging or responding to blogs gives you practice in public writing because others see what you write. Whether you use a personal journal or a public blog, though, keep in mind that the writing is the important part. If public writing encourages you to write more and more often, do it. If not, consider the private writing of a journal or diary.

✔ **Improve your spelling.** As you practice writing, keep a good dictionary at hand. If you're not sure of the spelling of any word, look it up. We hear you. How do you look up the spelling of a word if you can't spell it? Try sounding out the word phonetically and look in an online dictionary. Type in the word and select the word that looks familiar and correct. If that doesn't work, ask someone for help. Add the word to a spelling list and practice spelling those words. In addition, get a list of common homonyms — words that sound the same but are spelled differently and have different definitions — and review them every day. (You need to know, for example, the difference between *their, there,* and *they're* and *to, two,* and *too.*) Many dictionaries contain a list of homonyms.

✔ **Keep in mind that these questions are some form of multiple-choice.** Among the various answer choices, the test questions give you the correct answer. Of course, they also tell you three other answers that are incorrect, but all you have to do is find the correct one! The answers offered may not always be complete, so remember to pick the *most correct* answer from among those offered. As you practice speaking and writing, you tune your ears so the correct answer sounds right, which, believe it or not, makes finding the correct answer easier on the test.

✔ **Take practice tests.** Take as many practice tests as you can. Be strict about time limitations, and check your answers after you're finished. Don't move on until you know and understand the correct answer. (Check out Chapter 3 for diagnostic questions and Chapter 9 for a full-length sample test.) The time you spend taking and reviewing these tests is well worth it.

Navigating text to comprehend

After you know what to read to prepare for this test, you need to focus on how to read. You can't easily skim the type of prose that appears on the test. You need to read each question and passage completely to find the right answer. Here are some tactics that will help you do just that:

✔ **Read carefully.** When you read, read carefully. If reading novels, plays, or historical documents is unfamiliar to you, read these items even more carefully. The more carefully you read any material, the easier it'll be for you to get the right answers on the test.

✔ **Ask questions.** Ask yourself questions about what you just read. Could you take a newspaper column and reduce the content to four bulleted points and still summarize the column accurately? Do you understand the main ideas well enough to explain them to a stranger? (Note that we don't advise going up to strangers to explain things to them in person. Pretend you're going to explain it to a stranger and do all the talking in your head. If you want to explain what you read to someone in person, ask your friends and family to lend you an ear — or two.)

Ask for help if you don't understand something you read. You may want to form a study group and work with other people. If you're taking a test-preparation course, ask the instructor for help when you need it. If you have family, friends, or coworkers who can help, ask them.

✔ **Use a dictionary.** Not many people understand every word they read, so use a dictionary. Looking up unfamiliar words increases your vocabulary, which in turn makes passages on the Reasoning Through Language Arts test easier to understand. If you have a thesaurus, use it, too. Often, knowing a synonym for the word you don't know is helpful. Plus, it improves your Scrabble game. You can find a dictionary online at dictionary.com and a thesaurus at thesaurus.com. You can also search for dictionaries by well-known publishers such as Webster's and Oxford.

✔ **Use new words.** A new word doesn't usually become part of your vocabulary until you put it to use in your everyday language. When you come across a new word, make sure you know its meaning and try to use it in a sentence. Then try to work it into conversation for a day or two. After a while, this challenge can make each day more exciting. If you don't know what you don't know, you can find lists of important words online. To find such lists, search the web for "the 100 most commonly misspelled or misunderstood words," "words important to pass the SAT," "homonyms," and "common phrases that you're using wrong." These lists can be a good start to increasing your vocabulary.

✔ **Practice.** Take the Reasoning Through Language Arts diagnostic test in Chapter 3 and the full-length practice test in Chapter 9. Do the questions and check your answers. Checking your answers and reading the detailed answer explanations are important because they help you find out *why* each answer choice is correct or incorrect. Don't move on to the next answer until you understand the preceding one. If you want more practice tests, look for additional test-prep books at your local bookstore or library. Our *GED Test For Dummies* (Wiley) includes additional practice tests for all four sections of the GED test, including the RLA, Math, Science, and Social Studies sections. You can also find some abbreviated tests on the Internet. Type in "GED test questions" or "GED test questions + free" into your favorite search engine and check out some of the results. The GED Testing Service also offers free sample tests; check it out at www. gedtestingservice.com/educators/freepracticetest.

Take as many practice tests as you can. Stick to the time limits, and keep the testing situation as realistic as possible. When you go to the test center for the official test, you'll feel more at ease because you practiced.

All the information you need to answer the reading questions is given in the passages or in the text of the questions that accompany the passages. You're not expected to recognize the passage or know the answers to questions about what comes before it or what comes after it in context of the entire work. You do not need to rely of previous knowledge to answer the questions. The passages are complete in themselves, so just focus on what you read.

Many people get hung up on the drama passages. Don't stress. Keep in mind that these literary genres are just different ways of telling a story and conveying feelings. If you're not familiar with them, read plays before taking the test. Discuss what you've read with others; you may even want to consider joining (or starting) a book club that discusses novels and plays.

Chapter 3

Uncovering Your Strengths and Weaknesses with a Diagnostic Test

- -

In This Chapter

▶ Taking a sample RLA test to diagnose areas of strength and weakness

▶ Checking your answers and reading explanations to gain additional insight

▶ Noting areas you need to work on

- -

*B*efore committing to any serious training regimen for the GED Reasoning Through Language Arts (RLA) test, take the diagnostic test in this chapter and check the answers and explanations in order to identify the skills you need to work on most. This approach enables you to focus your efforts on your weakest areas so you don't waste a lot of time on what you already know.

Taking the Diagnostic Test

The GED RLA test is comprised of about 50 questions and an Extended Response essay prompt and takes nearly two and a half hours to complete. The good news is that the diagnostic test isn't quite that long and requires less of a time commitment. Simply follow the instructions to mark your answer choices and write a sample essay.

Unless you require accommodations, you'll be taking the GED test on a computer. Instead of marking your answers on a separate answer sheet, like you do for the practice tests in this book, you'll see clickable ovals and fill-in-the-blank text boxes, and you'll be able to click with your mouse and drag and drop items where indicated. We formatted the questions and answer choices in this book to make them appear as similar as possible to the real GED test, but we had to retain some A, B, C, D choices for marking your answers, and we provide a separate answer sheet for you to do so.

Answer Sheet for RLA Diagnostic Test

1. Ⓐ Ⓑ Ⓒ Ⓓ	21. Ⓐ Ⓑ Ⓒ Ⓓ	
2. Ⓐ Ⓑ Ⓒ Ⓓ	22. Ⓐ Ⓑ Ⓒ Ⓓ	
3. Ⓐ Ⓑ Ⓒ Ⓓ	23. Ⓐ Ⓑ Ⓒ Ⓓ	
4. Ⓐ Ⓑ Ⓒ Ⓓ	24. Ⓐ Ⓑ Ⓒ Ⓓ	
5. Ⓐ Ⓑ Ⓒ Ⓓ	25. [ ]	
6. Ⓐ Ⓑ Ⓒ Ⓓ	26. Ⓐ Ⓑ Ⓒ Ⓓ	
7. Ⓐ Ⓑ Ⓒ Ⓓ	27. Ⓐ Ⓑ Ⓒ Ⓓ	
8. Ⓐ Ⓑ Ⓒ Ⓓ	28. [ ]	
9. Ⓐ Ⓑ Ⓒ Ⓓ	29. Ⓐ Ⓑ Ⓒ Ⓓ	
10. Ⓐ Ⓑ Ⓒ Ⓓ	30. Ⓐ Ⓑ Ⓒ Ⓓ	
11. Ⓐ Ⓑ Ⓒ Ⓓ	31. Ⓐ Ⓑ Ⓒ Ⓓ	
12. Ⓐ Ⓑ Ⓒ Ⓓ	32. Ⓐ Ⓑ Ⓒ Ⓓ	
13. Ⓐ Ⓑ Ⓒ Ⓓ	33. Ⓐ Ⓑ Ⓒ Ⓓ	
14. Ⓐ Ⓑ Ⓒ Ⓓ	34. Ⓐ Ⓑ Ⓒ Ⓓ	
15. Ⓐ Ⓑ Ⓒ Ⓓ	35. Ⓐ Ⓑ Ⓒ Ⓓ	
16. Ⓐ Ⓑ Ⓒ Ⓓ	36. Ⓐ Ⓑ Ⓒ Ⓓ	
17. Ⓐ Ⓑ Ⓒ Ⓓ	37. Ⓐ Ⓑ Ⓒ Ⓓ	
18. Ⓐ Ⓑ Ⓒ Ⓓ	38. Ⓐ Ⓑ Ⓒ Ⓓ	
19. Ⓐ Ⓑ Ⓒ Ⓓ	39. Ⓐ Ⓑ Ⓒ Ⓓ	
20. Ⓐ Ⓑ Ⓒ Ⓓ	40. Ⓐ Ⓑ Ⓒ Ⓓ	

Reasoning Through Language Arts Diagnostic Test

Time: 65 minutes for 40 questions

Directions: You may answer the questions in this section in any order. Mark your answers on the answer sheet provided.

Questions 1–4 refer to the following excerpt written by Dale Shuttleworth (originally printed in the Toronto Star, *January 2008).*

What Is the History of the Social Enterprise Movement?

The Center for Social Innovation, a renovated warehouse in the Spadina Ave. area of Toronto, houses 85 "social enterprises," including organizations concerned with the environment, the arts, social justice, education, health, technology, and design. Tribute has been paid to the "social enterprise movement" in Quebec and Vancouver for providing the impetus for this very successful venture.

Toronto, Ontario, also has provided leadership in the areas of community education and community economic development — essential components in the creation of social enterprises. In 1974, the Toronto Board of Education assisted in the establishment of the Learnxs Foundation Inc. as part of its Learning Exchange System.

The foundation represented an additional source of support for the burgeoning "alternatives in education" movement. In 1973, the Ontario government had imposed ceilings on educational spending and, together with reduced revenue due to declining enrollment, the Toronto board had limited means to fund innovative and experimental programs. The Learnxs Foundation was an independent "arms-length" nonprofit charitable enterprise, which could solicit funds from public and private sources and generate revenue through the sale of goods and services to support innovative programs within the Toronto system.

What followed during the 1970s was a series of Learnxs-sponsored demonstration projects as a source of research and development in such areas as: school and community programs to improve inner-city education; a series of small enterprises to employ 14- to 15-year-old school leavers; Youth Ventures — a paper recycling enterprise employing at-risk youth; Artsjunction — discarded material from business and industry were recycled for use as craft materials for visual arts classes; Toronto Urban Studies Centre — a facility to encourage the use of the city as a learning environment; and Learnxs Press — a publishing house for the production and sale of innovative learning materials.

The York Board of Education and its school and community organizations jointly incorporated the Learning Enrichment Foundation (LEF), modeled on Learnxs. Originally devoted to multicultural arts enrichment, LEF during the 1980s joined with parental groups and the school board to establish 13 school-based childcare centers for infants, pre-school and school-age children.

In 1984, LEF was asked by Employment and Immigrant Canada to convene a local committee of adjustment in response to York's high rate of unemployment and plant closures. Outcomes of the work of the Committee included:

York Business Opportunities Centre: In 1985, with support from the Ontario Ministry of Industry, Trade & Technology, LEF opened the first small business incubator operated by a nonprofit charitable organization.

Microtron Centre: This training facility was devoted to micro-computer skills, word and numerical processing, computer-assisted design, graphics and styling, and electronic assembly and repair.

Microtron Bus: This refurbished school bus incorporated eight workstations from the Microtron Centre. It visited small business, industry and service organizations on a scheduled basis to provide training in word and numerical processing for their employees and clients.

In 1996, the Training Renewal Foundation was incorporated as a nonprofit charity to serve disadvantaged youth and other displaced workers seeking skills, qualifications and employment opportunities. Over the years, TRF has partnered with governments, employers and community organizations to provide a variety of services including job-creation programs for: immigrants and refugees, GED high school equivalency, café equipment technicians, coffee and vending service workers, industrial warehousing and lift truck operators, fully expelled students, youth parenting, construction craft workers and garment manufacturing.

1. The Learnxs Foundation supported

   (A) homeless people

   (B) scholarships for computer studies students

   (C) innovative programs

   (D) art programming

2. The Center for Social Innovation is

   (A) a social housing enterprise

   (B) a center housing social enterprises

   (C) a renovated warehouse

   (D) a small enterprise to employ school leavers

3. The Microtron bus helped

   (A) provide transportation for the Microtron Center

   (B) provide training in word and numerical processing to employees and clients

   (C) train auto mechanics in computerized controls in new cars

   (D) the center establish social enterprises

4. The Training Renewal Foundation serves

   (A) as a social innovator for youth

   (B) as a patron of the center

   (C) a training center for the homeless

   (D) as a business incubator

Questions 5–7 refer to the following excerpt.

How Must Employees Behave?

It is expected that employees behave in a respectful, responsible, professional manner. Therefore, each employee must do the following:

- Wear appropriate clothing and use safety equipment where needed.

- Refrain from the use and possession of alcohol and/or illicit drugs and associated paraphernalia throughout the duration of the workday.

- Refrain from associating with those who pass, use, and are under the influence of illicit drugs and/or alcohol.

- Address all other employees and supervisors with courtesy and respect, using nonoffensive language.

- Accept the authority of supervisors without argument. If an employee considers an action unfair, he or she should inform the Human Resources department.

- Respect the work environment of this company and conduct oneself in a manner conducive to the growth and the enhancement of this business.

- To keep the premises secure, refrain from inviting visitors to the workplace.

- Promote the dignity of all persons, regardless of gender, creed, or culture and conduct oneself with dignity.

If the employee chooses *not* to comply, the following will occur:

- On the first offense, the employee meets with his or her supervisor. A representative from Human Resources may choose to attend.

- On the second offense, the employee meets with the Vice President of Human Resources before returning to work.

- On the third offense, the employee is dismissed.

5. Which requirement relates to employee appearance?

   (A) The employee must refrain from using alcohol.

   (B) The employee must not use associated paraphernalia.

   (C) The employee must wear appropriate clothing.

   (D) The employee must use courtesy and respect.

6. Which requirement is concerned with the growth and enhancement of the business?

   (A) conducive to growth

   (B) enhancement of self

   (C) dressing unprofessionally

   (D) personal conduct

7. What are the penalties for continued noncompliance?

   (A) The employee meets with the president of the company.

   (B) The employee must avoid his or her supervisor.

   (C) The employee has to take behavior classes.

   (D) The employee is fired.

Questions 8–15 refer to the following business letter.

CanLearn Study Tours, Inc., 2500 Big Beaver Road, Troy, MI 70523

Dr. Dale Worth, PhD Registrar BEST Institute of Technology, 75 Ingram Drive Concord, MA 51234

Dear Dr. Worth:

Our rapidly changing economic climate has meant both challenges never before known. It has been said that only those organizations who can maintain loyalty and commitment among their employees, members, and customers will continue to survive and prosper in this age of continuous learning and globalization.

Since 1974, CanLearn Study Tours, Inc., have been working with universities, colleges, school districts, voluntary organizations, and businesses to address the unique learning needs of their staff and clientele. These have included educational travel programs that explore the following, artistic and cultural interests, historic and archeological themes, environmental and wellness experiences, and new service patterns. Professional development strategies have been organized to enhance international understanding and boost creativity. Some organizations' have used study tours to build and maintain their membership or consumer base. Other organizations discover a new soarce of revenue in these difficult economic times.

The formats have varied from a series of local seminars to incentive conferences or sales promotion meetings. Our professional services, including the best possible transportation and accommodation at the most reasonable rates, have insured the success of these programs.

We would appreciate the opportunity to share our experiences in educational travel and discuss the ways we may be of service to your organization.

Yours sincerely, Todd Croft, MA, President, CanLearn Study Tours, Inc.

8. Sentence 1: **Our rapidly changing economic climate has meant both challenges never before known.**

    Which improvement should be made to Sentence 1?

    (A) insert *and opportunities* between *challenges* and *never*

    (B) change *has meant* to *have meant*

    (C) change *known* to *none*

    (D) insert comma after *climate*

9. Sentence 2: **It has been said that only those organizations who can maintain loyalty and commitment among their employees, members, and customers will continue to survive and prosper in this age of continuous learning and globalization.**

    Which change should be made to Sentence 2?

    (A) insert a comma after *commitment*

    (B) change *has been* to *had been*

    (C) change *who* to *that*

    (D) change *those* to *these*

10. Sentence 3: **Since 1974, CanLearn Study Tours, Inc. <u>have been working</u> with universities, colleges, school districts, voluntary organizations, and businesses to address the unique learning needs of their staff and clientele.**

    Which is the best way to write the underlined portion of Sentence 3?

    (A) had been working

    (B) has been working

    (C) will be working

    (D) shall be working

11. Sentence 4: **These have included educational travel programs that explore the following, artistic and cultural interests, historic and archeological themes, environmental and wellness experiences, and new service patterns.**

    Which correction should be made to Sentence 4?

    (A) insert a comma after *have included*

    (B) change the comma after *following* to a colon

    (C) change the comma after *interests* to a semicolon

    (D) no changes required

12. Sentence 6: **Some organization's have used study tours to build and maintain their membership and consumer base.**

    Which correction should be made to Sentence 6?

    (A) change *organization's* to *organizations*

    (B) change *Some* to *All*

    (C) change *their* to *there*

    (D) change *have used* to *has used*

13. Sentence 7: **Other organizations <u>discover a new soarce of revenue in these</u> difficult economic times.**

    Which change should be made to the underlined portion in Sentence 7?

    (A) discovering a new soarce of revenue in these

    (B) discover a new source of revenue in these

    (C) discover a new soarce, of revenue, in these

    (D) recover a new soarce of revenue in these

14. Sentence 8: **The formats has varied from a series of local seminars to incentive conferences or sales promotion meetings.**

    Which revision should be made to Sentence 8?

    (A) add a comma after *seminars*

    (B) add an apostrophe after *sales*

    (C) change *formats* to *format*

    (D) add a period after *seminars*

15. Sentence 9: **Our professional services, including the best possible transportation and accommodation at the most reasonable rates, have insured the success of these programs.**

    Which correction should be made to Sentence 9?

    (A) change *services* to *service*

    (B) replace *insured* with *ensured*

    (C) remove the comma after *services*

    (D) replace the comma after *rates* with a semicolon

Questions 16–18 refer to the following excerpt from Washington Irving's "Rip Van Winkle" (1819).

Whoever has made a voyage up the Hudson must remember the Kaatskill Mountains. They are a dismembered branch of the great Appalachian family, and are seen away to the west of the river, swelling up to a noble height, and lording it over the surrounding country. Every change of season, every change of weather, indeed, every hour of the day, produces some change in the magical hues and shapes of these mountains, and they are regarded by all the good wives, far and near, as perfect barometers. When the weather is fair and settled, they are clothed in blue and purple, and print their bold outlines on the clear evening sky; but, sometimes, when the rest of the landscape is cloudless, they will gather a hood of gray vapors about their summits, which, in the last rays of the setting sun, will glow and light up like a crown of glory.

At the foot of these fairy mountains, the voyager may have described the light smoke curling up from a village, whose shingle-roofs gleam among the trees, just where the blue tints of the upland melt away into the fresh green of the nearer landscape. It is a little village of great antiquity, having been founded by some of the Dutch colonists, in the early times of the province, just about the beginning of the government of the good Peter Stuyvesant (may he rest in peace!), and there were some of the houses of the original settlers standing within a few years, built of small yellow bricks brought from Holland, having latticed windows and gablefronts, surmounted with weather-cocks.

16. How would you set out to find the Kaatskill Mountains?

    (A) Ask directions.

    (B) Journey up the Hudson.

    (C) Look for a dismembered branch.

    (D) Notice fresh green.

17. According to the passage, wives tell the weather

    (A) with perfect barometers

    (B) by the clear evening sky

    (C) through gray vapors

    (D) with magical hues and shapes

18. What clues might you look for as a sign that you are close to the village?

    (A) fairy mountains

    (B) shingle-roofs

    (C) light smoke curling

    (D) blue tints

Questions 19–22 refer to the following excerpt from Richard Wright's "The Man Who Was Almost a Man," from Eight Men *(1961).*

Dave struck out across the fields, looking homeward through paling light. . .One of these days he was going to get a gun and practice shooting, then they couldn't talk to him as though he were a little boy. He slowed, looking at the ground. Shucks, Ah ain scareda them. . .even ef they are biggern me! Aw, Ah know whut Ahma do. Ahm going by ol Joe's sto n git that Sears-Roebuck catlog n look at them guns. Mebbe Ma will lemme buy one when she gits mah pay from ol man Hawkins. Ahma beg her t gimme some money. Ahm ol ernough to hava gun. Ahm seventeen. Almost a man. He strode, feeling his long loose-jointed limbs. Shucks, a man oughta hava little gun aftah he done worked hard all day.

He came in sight of Joe's store. A yellow lantern glowed on the front porch. He mounted steps and went through the screen door, hearing it bang behind him. There was a strong smell of coal oil and mackerel fish. He felt very confident until he saw fat Joe walk in through the rear door, then his courage began to ooze.

"Howdy, Dave! Whutcha want?"

"How yuh, Mistah Joe? Aw, Ah don wanna buy nothing. Ah jus wanted t see ef yuhd lemme look at tha catlog erwhile."

"Sure! You wanna see it here?"

"Nawsuh. Ah wants t take it home wid me. Ah'll bring it back termorrow when Ah come in from the fiels."

"You plannin on buying something?"

"Yessuh."

"Your ma lettin you have your own money now?"

"Shucks. Mistah Joe, Ahm gittin t be a man like anybody else!"

19. Dave wanted "to get a gun" to

    (A) show he wasn't "scareda" the others

    (B) prove he wasn't unemployed

    (C) make his Ma proud

    (D) impress Joe

20. From where did Dave hope to get a gun?

    (A) from "Joe's sto"

    (B) from "ol man Hawkins"

    (C) from Ma

    (D) from the Sears-Roebuck "catlog"

21. How would you find Joe's store at night?

    (A) by the smell of mackerel

    (B) by a yellow lantern glow

    (C) by the banging screen door

    (D) by the smell of coal oil

22. Why do you think Dave asked to take the catalog home?

    (A) He lost his nerve.

    (B) It was too dark to read.

    (C) He needed it to convince Ma to give him the money to buy a gun.

    (D) He makes his own money.

Questions 23–29 refer to the following excerpt, which is adapted from Customer Service For Dummies *by Karen Leland and Keith Bailey (Wiley).*

---

(1) This step requires you to listen to each customers assessment of the problem. (2) Your job when she explains the situation from her perspective is to fully absorb what she is saying about her unique set of circumstances. (3) After you identify the customer's problem, the next step, obviously, is to fix it. (4) Sometimes, you can easily remedy the situation by changing an invoice, redoing an order, waving or refunding charges, or replacing a defective product. (5) At other times fixing the problem is more complex because the damage or mistake cannot be repaired simply. (6) In these instances, mutually exceptable compromises need to be reached.

(7) Whatever the problem, this step begins to remedy the situation and gives the customer what she needs to resolve the source of the conflict. (8) Don't waste time and effort by putting the horse before the cart and trying to fix the wrong problem. (9) Its easy to jump the gun and think that you know what the customer is about to say because you've heard it all a hundred times before. (10) Doing so loses you ground on the recovery front and farther annoys the customer. (11) More often than not, what you think the problem is at first glance, is different from what it becomes upon closer examination.

23. Sentence 1: **This step requires <u>you to listen to each customers assessment</u> of the problem.**

    Which correction should be made to the underlined portion in Sentence 1?

    (A) you to listen each customers assessment

    (B) you to listen to each customers' assessment

    (C) you to listen to each customers asessment

    (D) you to listen to each customer's assessment

24. Sentence 4: **Sometimes, you can easily remedy the situation by changing an invoice, redoing an order, waving or refunding charges, or replacing a defective product.**

    Which correction should be made to Sentence 4?

    (A) change *redoing* to *re-doing*

    (B) change *invoice* to *invoise*

    (C) change *waving* to *waiving*

    (D) change *defective* to *defected*

25. Sentence 6: **In these instances, mutually exceptable compromises need to be reached.**

    What one word is misspelled or misused in Sentence 6? [____]

26. Sentence 7: **Whatever the problem, this step begins to remedy the situation and gives the customer what she needs to resolve the source of the conflict.**

    Which is the best way to begin Sentence 7? If the original is the best way, choose Choice (A).

    (A) Whatever the problem,

    (B) This step begins to remedy,

    (C) What she needs to resolve,

    (D) To remedy the situation,

27. Sentence 8: **Don't waste time and effort by putting the horse before the cart and trying to fix the wrong problem.**

    Which change should be made to Sentence 8?

    (A) change *waste* to *waist*

    (B) revise to read *the cart before the horse*

    (C) change *trying* to *try*

    (D) change *Don't* to *Doesn't*

28. Sentence 9: **Its easy to jump the gun and think that you know what the customer is about to say because you've heard it all a hundred times before.**

    What word(s) is/are used incorrectly in Sentence 9? [____]

29. Sentence 10: **Doing so loses you ground on the recovery front and farther annoys the customer.**

    Which change should be made to the underlined portion in Sentence 10?

    (A) with the recovery front and farther

    (B) on the recover front and farther

    (C) on the recovery front and further

    (D) on the recovery, and farther

Questions 30–34 refer to the following business letter.

GED Enterprises LLC, 1655 Elizabeth Drive, Ajax, England 51221

To Whom It May Concern:

(1) We are delighted to provide a refference for Michael Jaxon. (2) He was employed by the training division of our company for six years, he provided excellent services, both recruiting and training clients to participate in our coffee vending machine repair division for the period of June 2010 to October 2014.

(3) As part of that programme, he

- prepared PowerPoint presentations for new recruits
- reviewed, revised, and upgraded training procedures
- prepared a repair manual for the graduating technicians
- organizes communications with other companies in the industry

(4) Mr. Jaxon has always been an excellent representative for our company, which has trained some 45 new repair personnel in the past year. (5) Mr. Jaxon's concerted efforts to network with others in the coffee industry contributed greatly to his success. (6) He has showed a high level of commitment to his job; and he will pursue his work with both competence and efficiency.

(7) I have developed a great respect for Mr. Jaxons' personal communication skills and dedication to his work and our program. (8) I wish him all the best for the future.

Jules Klaus, PhD

President

30. Sentence 2: **He was employed by the training division of our company for six years, he provided excellent services, both recruiting and training clients to participate in our coffee vending machine repair division for the period of June 2010 to October 2014.**

What revisions should be made to Sentence 2?

(A) break the sentence into two sentences after the word *services* by replacing the comma with a period and capitalizing *both*

(B) replace *was employed* with *had been employed*

(C) break the sentence into two sentences after the word *years,* replacing the comma with a period and capitalizing the word *he*

(D) capitalize *Coffee Vending Machine Repair Division*

31. Sentence 3: **As part of that programme, he**

- **prepared PowerPoint presentations for new recruits**
- **reviewed, revised, and upgraded training procedures**
- **prepared a repair manual for the graduating technicians**
- **organizes communications with other companies in the industry**

What change should be made to Sentence 3?

(A) change *programme* to *program*

(B) change *organizes* to *organized*

(C) remove the comma after *revised*

(D) change *procedures* to *proceedures*

32. Sentence 4: **Mr. Jaxon has always been an excellent representative** for our company, which has trained some 45 new repair personnel in the past year.

What is the best rewording for the underlined portion of this sentence?

(A) had always been

(B) always had been

(C) always was

(D) no change required

33. Sentence 6: **He has shown a high level of commitment to his job; and he will pursue his work with both competence and efficiency.**

What change should be made to this sentence?

(A) change *shown* to *showed*

(B) change *commitment* to *comitment*

(C) change *has* to *had*

(D) remove the semicolon before *and*

34. Sentence 7: **I have developed a great respect for Mr. Jaxons' personal communication skills and dedication to his work and our program.**

What correction does this sentence require?

(A) move the apostrophe from *Jaxons'* to *Jaxon's*

(B) change *personal* to *personnel*

(C) insert a comma after *dedication*

(D) No change required

> *Questions 35–38 refer to the following excerpt from Saul Bellow's "Something to Remember Me By" (1990).*

It began like any other winter school day in Chicago — grimly ordinary. The temperature a few degrees above zero, botanical frost shapes on the windowpane, the snow swept up in heaps, the ice gritty and the streets, block after block, bound together by the iron of the sky. A breakfast of porridge, toast, and tea. Late as usual, I stopped for a moment to look into my mother's sickroom. I bent near and said, "It's Louie, going to school." She seemed to nod. Her eyelids were brown, her face was much lighter. I hurried off with my books on a strap over my shoulder.

When I came to the boulevard on the edge of the park, two small men rushed out of a doorway with rifles, wheeled around aiming upward, and fired at pigeons near the rooftop. Several birds fell straight down, and the men scooped up the soft bodies and ran indoors, dark little guys in fluttering white shirts. Depression hunters and their city game. Moments before, the police car had loafed by at ten miles an hour. The men had waited it out.

This had nothing to do with me. I mention it merely because it happened. I stepped around the blood spots and crossed into the park.

35. What do you find out about the state of Louie's home life?

   (A) He ate porridge, toast, and tea.

   (B) He carried books on a strap.

   (C) His face was much lighter.

   (D) His mother was sick.

36. What were the men doing in the doorway?

   (A) hunting for game

   (B) having target practice

   (C) staying out of the weather

   (D) hiding from police

37. What is the importance of the term *depression hunters* in this passage?

   (A) It tells you the state of mind of the men.

   (B) A lot of people hunted in the Depression.

   (C) They were reacting to the grim weather.

   (D) The fact that people had to hunt pigeons for food in the cities reinforces the image of great hardship.

38. Why didn't Louie tell the police about what he saw?

   (A) He was in a hurry to get to school.

   (B) His mother was sick.

   (C) It had nothing to do with him.

   (D) The guys were his friends.

Questions 39 and 40 refer to the following excerpt from Russell Hart's Photography For Dummies, *2nd Edition (Wiley).*

If you've ever had to figure out where to stick batteries in your child's latest electronic acquisition, then loading batteries in your point-and-shoot shouldn't be a challenge. Turn off your camera when you install them; the camera may go crazy opening and closing its lens. (Some cameras turn themselves off after you install new batteries, so you have to turn them back on to shoot.)

With big point-and-shoot models, you typically open a latched cover on the bottom to install batteries. More compact models have a battery compartment under a door or flap that is incorporated into the side or grip of the camera. You may have to pry open such doors with a coin.

More annoying are covers on the bottom that you open by loosening a screw. (You need a coin for this type, too.) And most annoying are battery covers that aren't hinged and come off completely when you unscrew them. If you have one of these, don't change batteries while standing over a sewer grate, in a field of tall grass, or on a pier.

Whether loading four AAs or a single lithium, make sure that the batteries are correctly oriented as you insert them. You'll find a diagram and/or plus and minus markings, usually within the compartment or on the inside of the door.

If your camera doesn't turn on and the batteries are correctly installed, the batteries may have lost their punch from sitting on a shelf too long. Which is where the battery icon comes in.

If your camera has an LCD panel, an icon tells you when battery power is low.

39. What is the easiest model in which to replace the batteries?

(A) compact models

(B) big point-and-shoots

(C) screw bottoms

(D) covers not hinged

40. Why should you avoid locations such as sewer grates and tall grass when changing batteries?

(A) Water can get in the camera.

(B) Your lens may get dirty.

(C) Your card may be ruined.

(D) The battery cover may be lost.

The Extended Response

> **Time:** 45 minutes for 1 essay
>
> **Directions:** The following articles present arguments both for and against making cyberbullying a criminal offense. In your response, analyze the positions presented in each article and explain which you think is best supported. You must use specific and appropriate evidence to support your arguments. Use the following sheets of lined paper for your response. You should expect to spend up to 45 minutes in planning, drafting, and editing your response.

Pro

Some youth deliberately set out to harm others; this act is called bullying. However, when it happens by using social media, texting, and other technologies, it is called cyberbullying. That, too, should be a crime, especially because the intent to hurt and harm is there. Worse, considering how pervasive media technology is today, the bullying never stops; it follows the victims wherever and whenever they try to escape. The resulting evidence of the harm is also clear. The number of young people who have in desperation committed suicide after months and years of horrific abuse shows that.

Cyberbullying is a form of abuse, just like cyberstalking. It relentlessly hounds a designated target, even following the victim when he or she moves or changes schools. In a recent case, a teen was raped, and photographs of the rape were distributed to classmates in her school. Comments that followed taunted her as a slut — it was her fault; she was asking for it — to the point that she transferred schools. The teen reported the rape to the police who took little action, and the perpetrators remained free. She received an endless stream of abusive emails and texts. Meetings with the principal of both high schools and parents of the bullies solved nothing. Even after transferring, the bullies found her again and the harassment started again. Only after being faced with community outrage did the police take action, and then only after the teen had committed suicide.

This was not an isolated case. Nearly half of all teens report they have been victims of cyber-bullying. There have been multiple suicides in many countries. The police are often unwill-ing or unable to take action, claiming that cyberbullying itself does not constitute a crime.

Education programs don't work, either. Virtually all schools these days have antibullying programs. Even grade-school children are taught about bullying and to show respect for others. They are also educated on how to be safe online. Yet cyberbullying continues.

The threat of a criminal record is a deterrent and, at the very least, will give the police a tool with which to fight cyberbullying. Arresting bullies will certainly stop them in their tracks. It might also give the victims a tool for seeking redress. All the other initiatives have failed, so what choice is left?

Against

There are several considerations in the debate on criminalizing cyberbullying. There are already laws against cyberbullying if it crosses the line into criminal harassment. That is a chargeable offense. Second, how can one keep a clear line between cyberbullying and an abrogation of the freedom of speech guaranteed by the Constitution? Further, does the threat of a criminal record really deter people from such activities?

The whole issue is unclear: How do you define cyberbullying? Mostly, it consists of wild accusations and name-calling. It may be crude and rude, but it is not a crime unless it crosses the line and becomes slanderous or libelous. If there is no physical harm done and no intent to drive someone to self-harm, why treat verbal abuse as a crime? If it continues and crosses into destruction of reputation, then it does become criminal harassment. Existing laws can deal with this issue. Although this may be interpreted differently in different jurisdictions, it is a criminal offense under existing laws.

There are other tools. A young teen texted nude photos of her boyfriend's ex-girlfriend to friends. She also posted a copy on the former girlfriend's Facebook page. All were minors at the time. She was recently convicted of distributing child pornography, even though she, too, was a minor at the time. Existing laws punished the crime.

The other issue often raised is that cyberbullying has driven victims to suicide or attempts at self-harm. This is certainly true, but what is not proven is that the cyberbullying was the sole cause. Were the victims already suffering from depression? Were there other issues in their lives that made them unstable and prone to self-harm?

Proponents also argue that the fear of a criminal charge will be a deterrent. But if that is the case, why do so many people still drive drunk or continue to indulge in recreational drugs? There are clear consequences for these acts if caught, but they certainly do not stop these incidents. Teens are not the most rational beings, and the idea that their actions might result in criminal charges is not really foremost in their minds.

We must also remember that the Constitution guarantees the right to free speech. When the law tries to tell people they cannot say something, at what point does that infringe on that right? Some social media have taken a solid first step. They no longer permit people to have accounts in false names. Just a limitation of anonymity will reduce cyberbullying and do so without limiting free speech.

Education is a better approach. Let's get the schools and parents, community groups, and churches all involved in teaching our teens to have respect for others. Teach teens that words can hurt and that hurting others is never an appropriate thing to do.

Reviewing Answers and Explanations

After you take the diagnostic test, you're ready to check your answers to see how well or how poorly you did. We strongly encourage you to read the answer explanations. Doing so will help you understand why some answers were correct and others not, especially when the choices were really close. In addition, the answer explanations shed light on which skills you need to work on most. Your wrong answers can pinpoint areas where you need further study. One wrong answer may indicate you need to review common spelling mistakes, while a different error may mean you need to look up punctuation rules. You can discover just as much from your errors as from the correct answers.

1. **(C) innovative programs.** The column states that the Learnxs Foundation supports innovative programs, which you can deduce from the second paragraph. All the other answers except for Choice (A) are mentioned or implied in the column; however, they aren't correct answers to the question. You have to read carefully and double-check the facts. Just because something is mentioned or is familiar doesn't mean it's the right answer to the question. See Chapter 5 for more about improving reading and comprehension skills.

2. **(B) a center housing social enterprises.** The column specifically states that the center houses 85 social enterprises. Choice (A) is totally wrong and can be instantly eliminated on first reading. The other answers have a ring of correctness because the column is about social enterprises, charities, and school leavers. For example, the column states that the center is located in a renovated warehouse, and houses various kinds of enterprises, but these answers have nothing to do with the question or what the center is and thus are wrong. This question is an example of one requiring careful reading. For more about improving reading and comprehension skills, turn to Chapter 5.

3. **(B) provide training in word and numerical processing to employees and clients.** The column is very specific about the purpose of the Microtron bus. It provided services to employees and clients of small businesses in word and numerical processing. The other answers sound as though they may be right, but after rereading the column, you can see that they aren't.

When you're trying to answer these questions under time constraints, try to remember exactly what was stated in the passage. If you only *think* you remember, go back as quickly as you can and skim the piece for key words. In this case, the key word is *Microtron*. Sometimes, reading the question first before reading the passage is a more effective approach. See Chapter 5 for suggestions on how to improve reading and comprehensions skills.

4. **(D) as a business incubator.** The passage very precisely spells out the mandate of the Training Renewal Foundation: to serve disadvantaged youth and displaced workers seeking skills, qualifications and employment opportunities. Choices (A) and (B) may be worthy activities for any charity, but they aren't stated as part of the mandate and, thus, are wrong answers. Choice (C) is just wrong and is a play on another meaning of *serves*. You can immediately exclude this answer and have only three others to consider. Chapter 5 covers reading and comprehension.

5. **(C) The employee must wear appropriate clothing.** Employees must wear appropriate clothing to project a professional appearance and maintain safety standards. The other requirements, such as refraining from alcohol use, not associating with paraphernalia, being respectful, and using nonoffensive language, don't relate to appearance. As you read the source text, you have to remember the key wording of the question—in this case, *appearance*. See Chapter 5 for more about improving reading and comprehension skills.

6. **(D) personal conduct.** The key wording states that employees must conduct themselves professionally so that the business grows and improves. Choice (A) sounds good but is really a meaningless phrase in this context because it merely restates "leading to growth" without referring to the clear requirement to "conduct oneself in a manner conducive to

growth." Choices (B) and (C) may or may not help the business grow. The only answer that is specifically linked to the question is Choice (D). To improve your reading and comprehension skills, see Chapter 5.

7. **(D) The employee is fired.** Read the three stages of action for noncompliance. The question asks for penalties for continuing noncompliance. Only one option is correct: repeated instances of noncompliance lead to dismissal. The other options aren't backed up by the passage, nor do they answer the question. See Chapter 5 for more about improving reading and comprehension skills.

8. **(A) insert *and opportunities* between *challenges* and *never*.** Although the word *both* refers to two options, the text you're given here offers only one option — *challenges*. If you insert *and opportunities* between *challenges* and *never,* you include a second option and correct the sentence. Choice (B) introduces a new a subject-verb agreement error. Choice (C) changes words that sound alike (a homonym error) and adds the wrong word. Choice (D) introduces a punctuation error. This sentence doesn't require a comma. For guidance in detecting and eliminating grammar, punctuation, and usage errors, turn to Chapter 7.

9. **(C) change *who* to *that*.** An organization is never a *who;* only people can be referred to as *who.* An organization is a collective noun made up of people, but the collective noun itself is an impersonal entity and doesn't qualify as a *who.* Although the sentence may appear long and therefore may benefit from rewriting, the sentence is technically correct. Although commas do serve to make sentences clearer, as demonstrated in Choice (A), you don't want to insert them unless punctuation rules make them correct. Choice (B) introduces a tense error. The sentence refers to a statement made and completed in the past, so the present perfect tense (*has been*) is appropriate. The suggestion is to replace that with the past perfect (*had been*), but that wording requires that the action happened in the past before something else also in the past. That is incorrect in this case. Chapter 7 covers verb tenses.

10. **(B) has been working.** This is a subject-verb agreement error. CanLearn Study Tours is a single entity because it's one company. Therefore, it's a singular noun and needs the singular verb *has* rather than the plural *have.* A company is always an *it.* Even though a company is made up of a lot of people, or several different components, it's still a singular entity. Choices (A), (C), and (D) merely change the tense, which in this case is also wrong. Choice (A) suggests the past perfect, but that tense requires this statement to have taken place in the past before something else, which isn't the case. There is no time comparison here. Choices (C) and (D) are future tenses, which are also inappropriate because the sentence talks about what the company has done, not what it will do. To find out more about correcting errors in subject-verb agreement, turn to Chapter 7.

11. **(B) change the comma after *following* to a colon.** You need to insert a colon before the list to introduce it. Choice (A) asks for a comma in an incorrect location. Choice (C) asks you to change one comma to a semicolon. Semicolons are typically used to join two closely related sentences into one, but these sentences don't need that treatment. Choice (D) asks you to change spelling, but its revised spelling in fact introduces a spelling error; the existing word is correct. Chapter 7 covers common punctuation errors.

12. **(A) change *organizations'* to *organizations*.** A stray apostrophe has landed on this sentence. The one after *organizations'* is unnecessary because you're not trying to show possession here. Choice (B) is incorrect because the passage doesn't refer to *all* organizations. Choice (C) would introduce a homonym error, and Choice (D) inserts the wrong tense. Get comfortable with the uses of apostrophes — especially those used for possession — before taking the GED RLA test. For more about using apostrophes correctly, turn to Chapter 7.

13. **(B) discover a new source of revenue in these.** You need to correct the spelling error by changing *soarce* to *source.* Choice (A) changes the verb to a participle, an incorrect verb form in this case. Choice (C) inserts an unnecessary comma. Choice (D) suggests substituting a word, which is simply wrong for this sentence. Turn to Chapter 7 for guidance on correcting common errors.

14. **(C) change *formats* to *format*.** Formats is plural, but *has* is a singular verb. Verbs and their subjects must agree. You can either make *formats* singular or *has varied* plural. The only option offered is to change *formats* to the singular, so that is your answer. A comma isn't required after *seminar* or an apostrophe after *sales*. The apostrophe would indicate ownership, which isn't the case here. A period after *seminars* would create two sentence fragments. Study both subject-verb agreement and pronoun-antecedent agreement before taking the RLA test. To find out more about subject-verb agreement, turn to Chapter 7.

15. **(B) replace *insured* with *ensured*.** Choice (B) corrects the spelling error by changing *insured* to *ensured*. Using *insure* is a common error. Use *insure* only when you mean the service you buy to protect your car, house, health, life, and so on. This example has nothing to do with insurance, so use *ensure* instead. Choice (A) is wrong because the company offers more than one service. The comma after *services* is required to set apart the adjective phrase "including. . . ," so Choice (C) is wrong. Choice (D) misuses a semicolon; adding a semicolon here would create two sentence fragments, a major grammar error. For a list of commonly confused words, see Chapter 7.

16. **(B) Journey up the Hudson.** To get to the Kaatskill Mountains, you need to journey up the Hudson. A dismembered branch and fresh green aren't locations that can better help you locate the mountains. Although asking directions may work, this approach isn't mentioned in the passage. See Chapter 5 for more about improving reading and comprehension skills.

17. **(D) with magical hues and shapes.** The wives use the magical hues and shapes of the mountains to forecast the weather. Other factors, such as the evening sky or gray vapors, aren't good indicators. A barometer is an instrument to measure air pressure. Although barometers help predict the weather, that isn't what the wives use. For tips on improving your reading and comprehension skills, check out Chapter 5.

18. **(C) light smoke curling.** To help you locate the village, you first need to look for light smoke curling from chimneys. You can't see the other sign, shingle-roofs, until after you can see the smoke. Blue tints aren't signs for locating villages but rather refer to the distant uplands. Chapter 5 covers reading and comprehension.

19. **(A) show he wasn't "scareda" the others.** He wants to show the other field hands that he isn't scared of them. Dave mentions that he isn't afraid of them just before he first discusses buying the gun. Choice (B) may be true because the money to buy a gun implies he has a job, but this information isn't stated in the text. Similarly, Choices (C) and (D) refer to something not stated in the text and are therefore wrong. Answering this question correctly requires a close reading; see Chapter 5 for details.

20. **(D) from the Sears-Roebuck "catlog."** Dave had to purchase the gun through the Sears-Roebuck catalog. Joe didn't keep guns in his store. Neither Mr. Hawkins nor Ma is a source of guns. Before you choose an answer, check the passage to make sure it's right. For additional tips, see Chapter 5.

21. **(B) by a yellow lantern glow.** Joe kept a yellow lantern glowing on the porch. Other answer choices, such as *the smell of mackerel, the banging screen door,* or *the coal oil smell* may also help you find the store, but they aren't the best indicators. Again, you must read the text and rank the options for best choice based on the information given. See Chapter 5 for more about improving reading and comprehension skills.

22. **(A) He lost his nerve.** Dave lost his nerve and was afraid to ask Joe to see guns in the catalog. The text states "his courage began to ooze" when Joe walked in. The other possibilities — it was too dark, he needed to convince Ma to give him the money to buy a gun, and he made his own money — aren't the best answers. That he needed to convince Ma to let him have his own money was true, but it isn't the main point made in the text. The issue of convincing Ma that he be allowed to get a gun isn't mentioned. To find out more about improving reading and comprehension skills, turn to Chapter 5.

23. **(D) you to listen to each customer's assessment.** The *assessment* belongs to each customer and requires a possessive form of customer: *customer's*. The other answers aren't correct, nor do they improve the sentence. Choice (C) introduces a spelling error. Because

customer is singular, the apostrophe before the *s* in *customer's* is necessary. Choice (A) offers no possessive apostrophe, while Choice (B) uses it as if *customer* were plural. For more about forming the possessive, turn to Chapter 7.

24. **(C) change *waving* to *waiving*.** *Waving* means "to motion with the hand," while *waive* means "to dismiss." It may be interesting to wave at a charge, but the proper meaning of the sentence is to dismiss (or not collect) the charge. These two words are *homonyms* (words that sound the same but have different spellings and meanings). Choice (B) introduces a new spelling error, and Choice (D) changes the meaning of the word by replacing it with a close but misused variation. For a list of commonly confused words, turn to Chapter 7.

25. **exceptable.** *Exceptable* means "able to be made an exception," which isn't the sentiment you need here. The correct word to use is *acceptable.* The more reading you do as you prepare for the test, the better you get at recognizing misspellings. Chapter 7 helps you increase your sensitivity to such errors.

26. **(A) Whatever the problem,.** A gift for you: No correction is required. If you chose Choice (D), keep in mind that this sentence has one subject and two verbs. These types of sentences don't require a comma between the two verbs. Not sure about subjects and verbs? Here, the subject is *step,* and the two verbs are *begins* and *gives.* If the sentence had a second subject before the second verb, it would need a comma. For additional guidance in detecting and eliminating grammar, punctuation, and usage errors, turn to Chapter 7.

27. **(B) revise to read *the cart before the horse*.** If you live anywhere near Amish country, you know that the horse comes before the cart. Or you may have heard the idiomatic expression "Don't put the cart before the horse." In either case, the proper correction is to reverse the order of *horse* and *cart.* Choice (A) is a homonym error: *waste* and *waist.* The former refers to loss, while the latter is where your belt goes. Choice (C) introduces a parallelism error — *putting the cart* and *trying to fix* must be kept as parallel structures. Choice (D) is a subject-verb agreement error: *Don't* means "do not" and refers to the subject *you.* *Doesn't* means "does not" and refers to the implicit subject *he, she,* or *it.* Because this is a command, the implied subject is *you.* Therefore, *don't* is correct as is. See Chapter 7 for more about commonly confused words and expressions.

28. **Its.** *Its* is possessive (meaning that it shows that something belongs to *it*), whereas *it's* stands for "it is." Here, the sentence clearly means "it is." Confusing these two words is a common error that's usually tested in some way. Master the difference between *its* and *it's.* For more about forming the possessive, see Chapter 7.

29. **(C) on the recovery front and further.** *Farther* always refers to distance. *Further* is a matter of degree. Here, you want degree, not distance. Think of it this way: You'd run *far,* not *fur.* If you didn't know the answer, this question is a good example of one that you can answer by intelligent guessing. Choice (A) isn't correct because *with* isn't the proper word in this case. Choice (B) doesn't make sense in the context of the sentence. So now you just need to guess between Choices (C) and (D). Turn to Chapter 7 for a list of commonly confused words.

30. **(C) break the sentence into two after the word *years*, replacing the comma with a period and capitalizing *he*.** Choice (A) has the right idea but the wrong location; it would create a sentence fragment after the word *both.* Choice (B) introduces a new error by using the wrong tense under these circumstances. The past perfect is required only when comparing an action in the past to an action in the more distant past. The capitals suggested in Choice (D) aren't required. See Chapter 7 for additional guidance in correcting punctuation errors.

31. **(B) change *organizes* to *organized*.** This is a case of faulty parallelism. Every bullet is in the past tense except the last one. It should be in the same tense as the rest. The word *programme* is correctly spelled. This choice is a red herring, taking advantage of the differences between British and American English. In British English, *programme* is the preferred spelling, and the letter's return address indicates that the author is from England. Both spellings are still considered acceptable in American English. The comma in Choice (C) is required, and the suggested change to *proceedure* in Choice (D) introduces a misspelling, so it's wrong. We cover parallelism errors in greater depth in Chapter 7.

32. **(D) no change required.** The original wording splits the verb by inserting *always* between the auxiliary verb and the participle. This construction isn't always an error and, in this case, is fine. Choices (A) and (B) introduce the wrong tense into the sentence, and Choice (C) is no improvement; the original perfect tense is preferable because the action is completed in the past. For additional guidance in detecting and eliminating grammar, punctuation, and usage errors, turn to Chapter 7.

33. **(D) remove the semicolon before *and*.** You can join two complete sentences with either a semicolon or a conjunction. You don't use both a semicolon and a coordinate conjunction. Choice (A) creates a new error by using the wrong participle. Choice (B) adds a spelling error. Choice (C) introduces a new tense error. To find out more about correcting punctuation errors, turn to Chapter 7.

34. **(A) move the apostrophe from *Jaxons'* to *Jaxon's*.** The sentence refers to the skills Mr. Jaxon possesses. Because his name doesn't end in *s*, the apostrophe needs to come before the *s*. The change in Choice (B) introduces a new error, the misuse of the words *personal* and *personnel*. Because the letter discusses Mr. Jaxon's skills, they're *personal* skills. *Personnel* refers to staff. If the sentence were dealing only with his abilities with staff, such a use may be correct. Choice (C) is wrong because no comma is needed at this point. For more about forming the possessive, turn to Chapter 7.

35. **(D) His mother was sick.** Louie was living with his mother, who was very ill and confined to bed. Other answers describing Louie's breakfast, his books, and his complexion aren't good descriptions of the focus of his home life. See Chapter 5 for more about improving reading and comprehension skills.

36. **(A) hunting for game.** The men were hunting pigeons (game) for food. You can see that having target practice, staying out of the weather, and hiding from the police are inappropriate answers. They aren't the key points, and you'd know that if you'd read the passage thoroughly. We provide suggestions for improving reading and comprehension skills in Chapter 5.

37. **(D) The fact that people had to hunt pigeons for food in the cities reinforces the image of great hardship.** The term *depression hunters* and the other stark details help you realize the setting is the Great Depression. That timeframe then reinforces the grimness of the scene. Although the men may be depressed and the weather bad, those things have nothing to do with the question. And although Choice (B) may be true, it doesn't answer the question either. See Chapter 5 for more about improving reading and comprehension skills.

38. **(C) It had nothing to do with him.** What Louie saw had nothing to do with him, and he didn't want to get involved. Other possible answers — that he was hurrying to school, his mother was sick, or he was friends with the guys — don't relate directly to why Louie wouldn't tell the police. See Chapter 5 for more about improving reading and comprehension skills.

39. **(B) big point-and-shoots.** The easiest model in which to replace batteries is the point-and-shoot camera. The other answer choices — compact models, screw bottoms, and different types of covers — don't relate directly to the question. The only other type of camera, the more compact model, is only mentioned as an example of one you may have to pry the battery compartment open on — a more difficult process. For more about improving reading and comprehension skills, turn to Chapter 5.

40. **(D) The battery cover may be lost.** Avoid all the locations mentioned so you don't lose your battery cover if you drop it. Sewer grates and tall grass are places where the cover can easily be lost. The rest of the answer choices refer to issues other than losing battery covers. This type of question requires nothing more than basic careful reading skills. See Chapter 5 for more about improving reading and comprehension skills.

Sample Extended Response

The following sample essay would receive solid marks. It isn't perfect, but as the GED Testing Service tells you, you're not expected to write the perfect essay. You're expected to write a good, first-draft-quality response. When you prepare your essay, consider allocating your time like this: 10 minutes to read and analyze the source passages, 10 minutes to put together the quotes you intend to use to support your argument, 10 minutes to prepare your rough draft, and the remaining 15 minutes to write your actual essay, proofread it, and make any final adjustments.

Compare the following sample to the response you wrote and check out the scoring criteria in the following section to find out what evaluators look for in a response.

By its very nature, this issue is extremely emotional. And that makes it very difficult to prepare a rational argument. The first article describes the harm caused by cyberbullying and describe some unsuccessful efforts to intervene and later punish. The second article explains why criminalizing cyberbullying is unnecessary. Despite the harm cyberbullying causes, the second article is the better argued. It presents a rational case, backed by facts, without resorting to emotional prodding of one's conscience.

The first article very clearly makes the case that cyberbullying should be a crime. There's very little argument about the nature of the horrible crime the first article describes it, nor are the events in dispute. Nor would anyone argue that cyberbullying does no harm. The article further states that often intervention at the parent or school level has little effect. Again, this is not in dispute. However, the passage does use emotionally loaded terms, such as "hounding" and "community outrage." Further, while it presents one case in detail, it does not present little further evidence, neither examples nor statistics to back the case.

In contrast, the second article goes through the arguments against criminalizing cyberbullying in a logical manner. The first argument is the problem of defining what exactly cyberbullying is. It points out that mere name-calling is not a crime. It goes on to state that if and when such actions go too far, there's always recourse to existing laws. Harassments, libel, and slander are all covered under existing laws. Luring someone into self-harm is a criminal offense. Passing on nude or seminude photographs of someone can lead to child pornography charges. In most cases, existing laws will cover cyberbullying when it crosses a line.

The second article also examines the issue of self-harm as it arises from cyberbullying. Just because someone tragically commits suicide when bullied, either using electronic media or the old-fashioned bully in the school hallway, that does not automatically mean that the bullying was the cause. Most of us have endured bullying of some form in our lives and have dealt with it without suicide.

The final point that the second article raises, which the first passage ignores, is the right to free speech. While there are obviously reasonable limitations on free speech, we have to be very careful before considering restrictions of such a basic right.

While cyberbullying is an unfortunate reality of the life of today's teens, it is not necessary to expand criminal laws to cover such events. Existing laws will deal with extreme cases, an education, with parental and school involvement, will help limit such events. Finally, the removal of anonymity from social media should have an effect, again without limiting free speech or criminalizing such activities.

Scoring Your Extended Response

You can evaluate your Extended Response yourself, using the scoring criteria in Table 3-1. Most items have a potential score of 2 (completely accomplished), 1 (moderately accomplished), or 0 (poorly/not accomplished), while others have a score of 1 (done) or 0 (not done). A perfect score is 20 points. Remember, some spelling and grammar errors are tolerated. You're expected to produce a good, first-draft answer, not a polished final essay. Using this table to evaluate your essay can give you a good idea of your score on the GED Extended Response, but it's only an example of the scoring criteria used by the GED Testing Service. It can't predict how you'll do on the actual GED test.

Table 3-1	GED Extended Response Scoring Criteria	
Essay Answer Assessment	*Issue*	*Score*
Purpose	Your style and wording reflect an understanding of the audience for which you're writing and the purpose of your essay. You use a formal style.	Yes = 1 No = 0
Introduction	Your opening sentence/paragraph clearly identifies the topic.	Yes = 1 No = 0
Focus	Your details, arguments, and supporting evidence stay on topic, all referring to your thesis.	2 1 0
Content	Your points are factually correct.	2 1 0
	You show a clear understanding of subject-specific vocabulary.	2 1 0
	You correctly apply information from the source text.	2 1 0
	You correctly introduce your own knowledge to support ideas from the source text.	Yes = 1, No = 0
Quotations	You use quotes or content from the source test to support your thesis.	2 1 0
Grammar and style	You use varied sentence structure and appropriate vocabulary.	2 1 0
	You avoid colloquialisms and make no spelling mistakes.	2 1 0
	Your writing is grammatically correct.	2 1 0
Conclusion	Your conclusion restates your thesis and point of view and quickly and clearly summarizes your supporting evidence.	Yes = 1 No = 0

Score: 2 = completely accomplished, 1 = moderately accomplished, and 0 = poorly accomplished or not accomplished at all. Yes/No: Yes = 1; No = 0.

If you had trouble analyzing the two passages, turn to Chapters 5 and 6 for additional guidance on how to read, comprehend, and analyze arguments. If you had more trouble expressing your ideas in writing, see Chapter 8 for guidance on organizing and writing an Extended Response essay.

The GED Testing Service adjusts its marking schemes from time to time. Check out its website at www.gedtestingservice.com for up-to-date information on scoring criteria for essays and find some sample essay answers with detailed explanations of the reasons for the scores given.

Chapter 4

Succeeding on the GED RLA Test

● ●

In This Chapter

▶ Getting ready in the weeks and days leading up to the test

▶ Leveraging the power of the diagnostic and practice tests

▶ Knowing what to expect on test day

▶ Nailing down important test-taking strategies

▶ Staying calm and relaxed while you take the test

● ●

*Y*ou may never have taken a standardized test before. Or if you have, you may wake up sweating in the middle of the night from nightmares about your past experiences. Whether you've experienced the joys or sorrows of standardized tests, to succeed on the GED RLA test, you must know how to perform well on this type of test, which consists mostly of multiple-choice questions.

The good news is, you've come to the right spot to find out more about this type of test. This chapter explains some important pointers on how to prepare on the days and nights before the test, what to do on the morning of the test, and what to do during the test to be successful. You also discover some important test-taking strategies to build your confidence.

Gearing Up for Test Time

Doing well on the GED RLA test involves more than walking into the test site and answering the questions. You need to be prepared for the challenges in the test. To ensure that you're ready to tackle the test head-on, do the following leading up to the test:

✔ **Get enough sleep.** We're sorry if we sound like your parents, but it's true: You shouldn't take tests when you're approaching exhaustion. Plan your time so you can get a good night's sleep for several days before the test and avoid excess caffeine. If you prepare ahead of time, you'll be ready, and sleep will come easier.

✔ **Eat a good breakfast.** A healthy breakfast fuels your mind and body. You have to spend several hours taking the test, and you definitely don't want to falter during that time. Eat some protein, such as eggs, bacon, or sausage with toast for breakfast. Avoid sugars (such as doughnuts, jelly, and fruit) because they can cause you to tire easily. You don't want your empty stomach fighting with your full brain.

✔ **Take some deep breaths.** During your trip to the testing site, prepare yourself mentally for the test. Clear your head of all distractions, practice deep breathing, and imagine yourself acing the test. Don't panic.

✔ **Start at the beginning, not the end.** Remember that the day of the test is the end of a long journey of preparation and not the beginning. It takes time to build mental muscles.

✔ **Be on time.** Make sure you know what time the test begins and the exact location of your test site. Arrive early. If necessary, take a practice run to make sure you have enough time to get from your home or workplace to the testing center. You don't need the added pressure of worrying about whether you can make it to the test on time. In fact, this added pressure can create industrial-strength panic in the calmest of people.

Traffic congestion happens. No one can plan for it, but you can leave extra time to make sure it doesn't ruin your day. Plan your route and practice it. Then leave extra time in case a meteor crashes into the street and the crowd that gathers around it stalls your progress. Even though the GED test is now administered on a computer and not everyone has to start at the same time, test centers are open only for certain hours, and if they close before you finish, you won't get any sympathy. Check the times the test center is open. Examiners won't show you a lot of consideration if you show up too late to complete the test because you didn't check the times. They have even less sympathy if you show up on the wrong date.

Using the Diagnostic and Practice Tests to Your Advantage

Taking diagnostic and practice GED RLA tests is important for a few reasons, including the following:

✔ **They help you prepare for the test.** Practice tests, the diagnostic test in particular, shed light on knowledge and skills you need to focus on leading up to the actual test.

✔ **They give you an indication of how well you know the material.** One or two tests won't give you a definitive answer to how you'll do on the actual test, because you need to do four or five tests to cover all possible topics, but they do give you an indication of where you stand.

✔ **They confirm whether you know how to use the computer to answer the questions.** You don't get this information by taking the practice tests in the book, but you can go online at www.gedtestingservice.com/educators/freepracticetest to take a computer-based practice test.

✔ **They familiarize you with the test format.** You can read about test questions, but you can't actually understand them until you've worked through several.

✔ **They can ease your stress.** A successful run-through on a practice test allows you to feel more comfortable and confident in your own abilities to take the GED test successfully and alleviate your overall anxiety.

Turn to Chapter 3 to take the diagnostic test or to Chapter 9 to take the practice test. These tests are an important part of any preparation program. They're the feedback mechanism that you may normally get from a private tutor. To get the most out of any practice test, be sure to check your answers after each test and read the answer explanations. If possible, take the additional practice tests at the GED Testing Service site mentioned earlier and tackle a few more sample questions at www.gedtestingservice.com/testers/sample-questions. You can also access more online practice tests through the latest edition of our *GED Test For Dummies*. Use your favorite Internet search engine to find more practice tests online. The GED Testing Service also offers GED Ready tests that you can purchase through authorized outlets.

Packing for Test Day

The GED test may be the most important exam you ever take. Treat it seriously and come prepared. Make sure you bring the following items with you on test day:

- ✔ **You:** The most important thing to bring to the GED test is obviously you. If you enroll to take the test, you have to show up; otherwise, you'll receive a big fat zero and lose your testing fee. If something unfortunate happens after you enroll, contact the test center and explain your situation to the test administrators. They may reschedule the test with no additional charge.

- ✔ **Correct identification:** Before test officials let you into the room to take the test, they want to make sure you're you. Bring the approved photo ID; your state GED office can tell you what's an approved form of photo ID. Have your ID in a place where you can reach it easily. And when asked to identify yourself, don't pull out a mirror and say, "Yep, that's me."

- ✔ **Registration receipt and any fees you still owe:** The same people don't run all test centers. With some, you may have to pay in advance, when booking the test. If so, bring your receipt to avoid any misunderstandings. Others may allow you to pay at the door. If so, find out whether you can use cash, check, or debit or credit card. The amount of the GED test registration fee also varies from state to state. (Check with your local administrator to confirm when and where the fee has to be paid and how to pay it.) If you don't pay, you can't play or, in this case, take the test.

  If needed, you may be able to get financial assistance to help with the testing fees. Further, if you do the test one section at a time, which we recommend, you can probably pay for each test section separately. Check with your state or local education authorities.

- ✔ **Registration confirmation:** The registration confirmation is your proof that you did register. If you're taking the test in an area where everybody knows you and everything you do, you may not need the confirmation, but we suggest you take it anyway. It's light and doesn't take up much room in your pocket.

- ✔ **Other miscellaneous items:** In the instructions you receive after you register for the test, you get a list of what you need to bring with you. Besides yourself and the items we list previously, other items you want to bring or wear include the following:

  - **Comfortable clothes and shoes:** When you're taking the test, you want to be as relaxed as possible. Uncomfortable clothes and shoes may distract you from doing your best. You're taking the GED test, not modeling the most recent fashions. Consider dressing in layers; you don't want to be too hot or too cold.

  - **Reading glasses:** If you need glasses to read a computer monitor, don't forget to bring them to the test. Bring a spare pair, if you have them. You can't do the test if you can't read the screen. And before you go, make sure your reading glasses work with a computer screen. The focal distance for reading print materials and computer screens is different, depending on your prescription.

The rules about what enters the testing room are strict. Don't take any chances. If something isn't on the list of acceptable items and isn't normal clothing, leave it at home. Laptops, cellphones, and other electronic devices will most likely be banned from the testing area. Leave them at home or locked in your car. The last place on earth to discuss whether you can bring something into the test site is at the door on test day. If you have questions, contact the test center in advance. Check out www.gedtestingservice.com to start the registration process and find a list of sites close to your home with their addresses and phone numbers. You can also call 877-EXAM-GED (877-392-6433) to have real people answer your questions.

Whatever you do, be sure not to bring the following with you to the GED testing center:

- ✔ Books
- ✔ Notes or scratch paper
- ✔ MP3 players or tablets
- ✔ Cellphone (leave it at home or in your car)
- ✔ Anything valuable, like a laptop computer, that you don't feel comfortable leaving outside the room while you take the test

Getting Comfortable before the Test Begins

You usually take the GED RLA test in an examination room with at least one official (sometimes called a *proctor* or *examiner*) who's in charge of administering the test. (Some locations have smaller test centers that have space for no more than 15 test-takers at a time.) In either case, the test is the same.

As soon as you sit down to take the GED RLA test, spend a few moments to relax and get comfortable before the test actually starts. You're going to be in the chair for quite some time, so settle in. Keep these tips in mind before you begin:

- ✔ **Make sure that the screen is at a comfortable height and adjust your chair to a height that suits you.** Unlike a pencil-and-paper test, you'll be working with a monitor and keyboard. Although you can shift the keyboard around and maybe adjust the angle of the monitor, generally you're stuck in that position for the duration of the test. If you need to make any adjustments, make them before you start. You can even adjust the color scheme of the on-screen materials. You want to feel as physically comfortable as possible.

- ✔ **Go to the bathroom before you start.** This suggestion may sound silly, but it all contributes to being comfortable. You don't need distractions. You get a ten-minute break between some sections of the test, but otherwise, even if permitted during the test, bathroom breaks take time away from the test.

The proctor reads the test instructions to you and lets you log into the computer to start the test. Listen carefully to these instructions so you know how much time you have to take the test as well as any other important information.

Brushing Up on Test-Taking Strategies

You can increase your score by mastering a few smart test-taking strategies. To help you do so, we give you some tips in these sections on how to

- ✔ Plan your time
- ✔ Determine the question type
- ✔ Figure out how to answer the different types of questions
- ✔ Guess intelligently
- ✔ Review your work

Watching the clock: Using your time wisely

When you start the computerized version of the GED RLA test, you may feel pressed for time and have the urge to rush through the questions. We strongly advise that you don't. You have sufficient time to do the test at a reasonable pace. You have only a certain amount of time for each section in the GED exam, so time management is an important part of succeeding on the test. You need to plan ahead and use your time wisely.

Although you're required to complete each of the other three GRE tests in single sittings, with the RLA test, you get a ten-minute break after the Extended Response (also known as the essay).

During the test, the computer keeps you constantly aware of the time with a clock in the upper right-hand corner. Pay attention to the clock. When the test begins, check that time, and be sure to monitor how much time you have left as you work your way through the test. The GED RLA test is 150 minutes long and is broken down into three sections with a ten-minute break before the last section:

Section 1	35 minutes	Tests all content
Section 2	45 minutes	Extended Response (essay)
Break	10 minutes	
Section 3	60 minutes	Tests all content

The time you're given for Sections 1 and 3 may vary a little, but the total test time is always 150 minutes.

As you start, quickly scroll through the test and find out how many questions you have to answer. (Not all RLA tests have the same number of questions.) Quickly divide the time by the number of questions. Doing so can give you a rough idea of how much time to spend on each question. For example, on Section 3 of the RLA test, suppose that you see you have 40 questions to answer. You have 60 minutes to complete the section. Divide the time by the number of questions to find out how much time you have for each item: $60/40 = 3/2 = 1\frac{1}{2}$ minutes or 1 minute and 30 seconds per item. As you progress, repeat the calculation to see how you're doing. Remember, too, that you can do questions in any order, except for the Extended Response item. Do the easiest questions first. If you get stuck on a question, leave it and come back to it later if you have time. Keeping to that schedule and answering as many questions as possible are essential.

If you don't monitor the time for each question, you won't have time to answer all the questions on the test. Keep in mind the following general time-management tips to help you complete each exam on time:

- ✔ **Tackle questions in groups.** For example, calculate how much time you have for each item on each test. Multiply the answer by 5 to give you a time slot for any five test items. Then try to answer each group of five items within the time you calculated. Doing so helps you complete all the questions and leaves you several minutes for review.

- ✔ **Keep calm and don't panic.** The time you spend panicking could be better spent answering questions.

- ✔ **Practice using the diagnostic and practice tests in this book.** The more you practice timed sample test questions, the easier managing a timed test becomes. You can get used to doing something in a limited amount of time if you practice. Refer to the earlier section "Using the Diagnostic and Practice Tests to Your Advantage" for more information.

When time is up, immediately stop and breathe a sigh of relief. When the test ends, the examiner will give you a log-off procedure. Listen for instructions on what to do or where to go next.

Evaluating the different questions

Although you don't have to know much about how the test questions, or items, were developed to answer them correctly, you do need some understanding of how they're constructed. Knowing the types of items you're dealing with can make answering them easier — and present fewer surprises.

To evaluate the types of questions that you have to answer, keep these tips in mind:

- **As soon as the computer signals that the test is running, start by skimming the questions.** Don't spend a lot of time doing so — just enough to spot the questions you absolutely know and the ones you know you'll need more time to answer.

- **Rely on the Previous and Next buttons on the bottom of the screen to scroll through the questions.** After you finish skimming, answer all the questions you know first; that way, you leave yourself much more time for the difficult questions. Check out the later section "Addressing and answering questions" for tips on how to answer questions.

- **Answer the easiest questions first.** You don't have to answer questions in order. Nobody except you will ever know, or care, in which order you answer the questions, so do the easiest questions first. You'll be able to answer them fastest, leaving more time for the other, harder questions.

- **Answer all questions.** No points are deducted for wrong answers. Look at the answer choices and discard any that are obviously wrong to improve your chances of guessing the correct answer. Guessing may mean getting the right answer; leaving the answer blank means a definite zero. And don't forget to go back for any harder questions you skipped earlier.

Knowing the question type can shape the way you think about the answer. Some questions ask you to analyze a passage or extract from a document, which means the information you need is in the source text. Others ask you to infer from the passage, which means that not all the information is in the passage. Although none of the tests are labeled with the following titles, the GED test questions assess your skills in these areas.

Analysis

Analysis questions require you to break down information and look at how the information bits are related to one another. Analyzing information in this way is part of reasoning and requires you to do the following:

- **Separate facts from opinions.** Unless the text you're reading gives evidence or "proof" to support statements, treat them as opinion.

- **Realize that when an assumption isn't stated that it may not necessarily be true.** Assumptions stated in the passage or question help you find the best answer.

- **Identify a cause-and-effect relationship.** For example, you have to eat an ice-cream cone quickly in hot weather. The cause is the hot weather and the effect is that the ice cream melts quickly.

- **Infer.** You may be asked to reach a conclusion based on evidence presented in the question. *Inferring* is a fancy way of saying that you'll reach a conclusion. In the preceding example, you can infer that you should stay in an air-conditioned space to eat your ice cream or eat it very quickly.

- ✔ **Compare.** If you consider the similarities between ideas or objects, you're *comparing* them. For example, the world is like a basketball because both are round.

- ✔ **Contrast.** If you consider the differences between ideas or objects, you're *contrasting* them. For example, the world isn't like a basketball because it's so much larger and has an irregular surface.

Relating to other people in social situations exposes most people to these skills. For example, in most sports-related conversations between friends (or rivals), you quickly figure out how to separate fact from opinion and how to infer, compare, contrast, and identify cause-and-effect relationships. In other social situations, you come to realize when an assumption isn't stated. For example, you likely assume that your best friend or significant other is going to join you for a late coffee the night before an important test, but, in reality, your friend may be planning to go to bed early. Unstated assumptions you make can get you into trouble, both in life and on the GED test.

Application

Application questions require you to use the information presented to you in one situation to help you in a different situation. You've been applying information left and right for most of your life, but you probably don't realize it. For example, when you use the information from the morning newspaper to make a point in an argument in the afternoon, you use your application skills.

Comprehension

A *comprehension* question asks whether you understand written material. The GED test-makers expect you to be able to state the info on the test in your own words, develop a summary of the ideas presented, discuss the implications of those ideas, and draw conclusions from those implications. You need to develop these comprehension skills to understand what the questions are asking you and to answer the questions quickly and accurately.

The best way to increase your comprehension is to read extensively and to have another person to ask you questions about what you read. You can also use commercial books that specifically help you with your comprehension by presenting you with written material and asking you questions about it. One of those books is in your hands. All the other *For Dummies* test-preparation books, as well as *AP English Literature & Composition For Dummies* by Geraldine Woods (Wiley), have reading comprehension as a major focus, too. Feel free to check out these books to improve your comprehension if you still have difficulty after using this book.

Synthesis

Synthesis questions require you to take apart blocks of information presented to you and put the pieces back together to form a hypothesis, theory, or story. Doing so gives you a new understanding or twist on the information that you didn't have before. Have you ever discussed something that happened, giving it your own twist and explanation to create a brand new narrative? If so, you've already put your synthesis skills to use.

Evaluation

Any time someone presents you with information or opinion, you judge it to make sure it rings true in your mind. This *evaluation* helps you make decisions about the information presented before you decide to use it. If the clerk behind the ice-cream counter suggests that you get a raspberry cone rather than the flavor you wanted because everyone knows that raspberry melts slower than all the other flavors, you may be a bit suspicious. If you notice that the clerk also has four containers of raspberry ice cream and only one of each other flavor, you may evaluate his comment as biased or even incorrect.

Cognitive skills

Mental skills that you use to get knowledge are called *cognitive skills* and include reasoning, perception, and intuition. They're particularly important in reading for understanding, which is what you're asked to do on the GED test. You can increase your knowledge and comprehension by reading books, researching on the web, or watching documentaries. After you read or watch something new, discuss it with others to make sure you understand it and can use the information in conversation.

Addressing and answering questions

When you start the test, you want to have a game plan in place for how to answer the questions. Keep the following tips in mind to help you address each question:

- ✔ **Whenever you read a question, ask yourself, "What am I being asked?"** Doing so helps you stay focused on what you need to find out to answer the question. You may even want to decide quickly what skills are required to answer the question (see the preceding section for more on these skills). Then try to answer it.

- ✔ **Try to eliminate some answers.** Even if you don't really know the answer, guessing can help. When you're offered four answer choices, some will be obviously wrong. Eliminate those choices, and you've already improved your odds of guessing a correct answer.

- ✔ **Don't overthink.** Because all the questions are straightforward, don't look for hidden or sneaky questions. The questions ask for an answer based on the information given. If you don't have enough information to answer the question, one of the answer choices will say so.

- ✔ **Find the answer choice you think is best and quickly verify that it answers the question.** If it does, click on that choice, and move on. If it doesn't, leave it and come back to it after you answer all the other questions, if you have time. *Remember:* You need to pick the *most* correct answer from the choices offered. It may not be the perfect answer.

Guess for success: Using intelligent guessing

The multiple-choice questions, regardless of the on-screen format, provide you with four possible answers. You get between one and three points for every correct answer. Nothing is subtracted for incorrect answers. That means you can guess on the items you don't know for sure without fear that you'll lose points if your guess is incorrect. Make educated guesses by eliminating as many obviously wrong choices as possible and choosing from just one or two remaining choices.

When the question gives you four possible answers and you randomly choose one, you have a 25 percent chance of guessing the correct answer without even reading the question. Of course, we don't recommend using this method during the test.

If you know that one of the answers is definitely wrong, you now have just three answers to choose from and have a 33 percent chance (1 in 3) of choosing the correct answer. If you know that two of the answers are wrong, you leave yourself only two possible answers to choose from, giving you a 50 percent (1 in 2) chance of guessing right — much better than 25 percent! Removing one or two choices you know are wrong makes choosing the correct answer much easier.

If you don't know the answer to a particular question, try to spot the wrong choices by following these tips:

- ✔ **Make sure your answer really answers the question.** Wrong choices usually don't answer the question — that is, they may sound good, but they answer a different question than the one the test asks.

- ✔ **When two answers seem very close, consider both answers carefully because they both can't be right — but they both *can* be wrong.** Some answer choices may be very close and all seem correct, but there's a fine line between completely correct and nearly correct. Be careful. These answer choices are sometimes given to see whether you really understand the material.

- ✔ **Look for opposite answers in the hopes that you can eliminate one.** If two answers contradict each other, both can't be right, but both can be wrong.

- ✔ **Trust your instincts.** Some wrong choices may just strike you as wrong when you first read them. If you spend time preparing for these exams, you probably know more than you think.

Leaving time for review

Having a few minutes at the end of a test to check your work is a great way to set your mind at ease. These few minutes give you a chance to look at any questions that may be troubling. If you've chosen an answer for every question, enjoy the last few minutes before time is called — without any panic. Keep the following tips in mind as you review your answers:

- ✔ **After you know how much time you have per item, try to answer each item in a little less than that time.** The extra seconds you don't use the first time through the test add up to time at the end of the test for review. Some questions require more thought and decision making than others. Use your extra seconds to answer those questions.

- ✔ **Don't try to change a lot of answers at the last minute.** Second-guessing yourself can lead to trouble. Often, second-guessing leads you to changing correct answers to incorrect ones. If you've prepared well and worked numerous sample questions, then you're likely to get the correct answers the first time. Ignoring all your preparation and knowledge to play a hunch isn't a good idea, either at the race track or on a test.

- ✔ **If you have time left after writing your Extended Response, use any extra time to reread and review your final essay.** You may have written a good essay, but you always need to check for typos and grammar mistakes. The essay is evaluated for style, content, and proper English. That includes spelling and grammar.

Sharpening Your Mental Focus

To succeed in taking the GED RLA test, you need to be prepared. In addition to studying the content and honing the skills required, you also want to be mentally prepared. Although you may be nervous, you can't let your nerves get the best of you. Stay calm and take a deep breath. Here are a few pointers to help you stay focused on the task at hand:

- ✔ **Take time to rest and relax.** Rest and relaxation are restorative, revitalizing your body and providing your brain with the downtime it needs to digest all the information you've been feeding it.

✔ **Make sure you know the rules of the room before you begin.** If you have questions about using the bathroom during the test or what to do if you finish early, ask the proctor before you begin. If you don't want to ask these questions in public, call the GED office in your area before test day, and ask your questions over the telephone. For general GED questions, call 877-EXAM-GED (877-392-6433) or check out www. gedtestingservice.com. This site has many pages, but the FAQ page is always a good place to start.

✔ **Keep your eyes on your computer screen.** Everybody knows not to look at other people's work during the test, but, to be on the safe side, don't stretch, roll your eyes, or do anything else that may be mistaken for looking at another test. Most of the tests will be different, so looking around is futile, but doing so can get you into a lot of trouble.

✔ **Stay calm.** Your nerves can use up a lot of energy needed for the test. Concentrate on the job at hand. You can always be nervous or panicky some other time.

Because taking standardized tests probably isn't a usual situation for you, you may feel nervous. This feeling is perfectly normal. Just try to focus on answering one question at a time and push any other thoughts to the back of your mind. Sometimes taking a few deep breaths can clear your mind; just don't spend a lot of time focusing on your breath. After all, your main job is to pass this test.

Part II
Enhancing Your RLA Skills

Five Tips for Improving Reading Comprehension

- **Skim first.** Read quickly through the passage to get the gist of what the passage is about. Doing so helps you identify the main point and gives you a framework on which to hang the details.

- **Silently ask questions as you read.** What's the point? What's the writer's purpose? Why am I reading this? Well-written passages often raise questions and answer them. As you read a passage, what questions arise? How are they answered?

- **Take notes.** As you read, jot down the main idea and a list of supporting details. This technique is especially useful for the Extended Response item, where you're asked to support your position with evidence from the passage(s).

- **Use context to construe the meaning of unfamiliar words.** If you don't know the meaning of a word, you can often guess its definition by the context in which it's used.

- **Reread.** If you read some text that doesn't make sense to you at first, read it again with a greater focus.

- **Keep track of time**. You're going to be taking a time-limited test, so you need to balance skimming versus reading in depth so that you have sufficient time to finish.

Head to www.dummies.com/extras/gedrlatest for even more tips to improve reading speed and comprehension.

In this part . . .

✔ Discover techniques for improving your reading comprehension and analyzing passages on a deeper level.

✔ Find out how to pick apart arguments, spot faulty logic and assumptions, and decide which of two sides of an argument is better supported in any two passages.

✔ Take a quick primer on English grammar and usage so you can easily identify and correct the most common errors and eliminate errors in your own writing.

✔ Get the lowdown on what evaluators look for when scoring the Extended Response essay and find out how to nail the essay writing portion of the test.

Chapter 5

Understanding the Written Word

. . . .

In This Chapter

▶ Putting events in chronological order and drawing conclusions from details

▶ Recognizing how ideas are related and extracting meaning from context

▶ Digging into the details and comparing points of view

▶ Tuning in to subtle differences in meaning and flow

▶ Comparing and contrasting various aspects of two passages

. . . .

The written word is one of the wonders of life. It communicates joys and sorrows, histories and futures, plans and outcomes, and even tell you how to get there from here. It can tell you the meaning of life and how to stop the DVD player from blinking 12:00. It entertains and sustains people and spreads knowledge from person to person and generation to generation. It can persuade as well as clarify, or even confuse.

The GED Reasoning Through Language Arts (RLA) test uses the written word to evaluate your ability to read, understand, and analyze meaning. In this chapter, we show you some of the tools you can use to analyze the written word.

Recognizing and Ordering the Sequence of Events

In any story, the events in the story form the *plot*. The events happen in a sequence, a logical order that makes sense. In instructional materials such as manuals, actions have to occur in the proper sequence so that the user gets the proper results. In newspaper articles, editorials, or history texts, events happen in a specific order, but the writer may place them in a different sequence for effect. As a reader, you must be able to correctly order events even when the piece doesn't explicitly state them.

In most text, the order of events in pretty clear, even when the author doesn't state, "this first, then that," as in the following passage:

The sound of the pull-tab was followed by a flurry of soft footsteps. First, Helga greeted Midnight, a big, black tom. Immediately behind him was Merlin, rubbing his black and tan body against her legs while talking to her, as Siamese are wont to do, never taking his blue eyes off the counter, where the food dishes were being filled. Not to be left out, Tristan and Isolde, the yellow tom and his sister, ran in, impatiently waiting for their food. Mildly exasperated, Helga portioned out the food and put the appropriate dish in front of each cat. A pill mixed into the food for this one, a special diet for that one, other meds here and there; it all needed care.

In Helga's story, which sequence of events is correct?

(A) the cat food tab is pulled, Merlin talks to Helga, the food is given to the cats

(B) Merlin talks to Helga, the cats are fed, Midnight arrives in the kitchen

(C) the cat food tab is pulled, Tristan and Isolde arrive, Merlin talks

(D) Merlin talks, the medication is added to the food, Tristan and Isolde arrive

From the context of the story, you know that the pull-tab is the first event and that the feeding the last. You know that the cats arrive in a particular order: Midnight, Merlin, and Tristan and Isolde. That means the only correct choice is Choice (A). The main point to note is that you're asked to verify the order of events, not to give a complete list of events in order. Choice (A) omits some events, such as Midnight's arrival, but the events listed are in the correct order.

Try working with this story from the December 2014 issue of *Soldiers,* the official U.S. Army Magazine:

Gabe was a puppy when I met him. He was just getting started. So a lot of times we would take him to crowded events or places to make sure that he stayed calm and that his attention was focused on me and my needs so he would be that way with other veterans.

We did this every day. I'd take him around to my appointments with me or around town if I needed to.

We used treats and praise as methods to train and reward. We trained him how to open doors; how to pick up artificial limbs; how to bark on command; how to remind people to take medication; how to take their socks off; how to pay a cashier; if someone started to fall, how to brace for them — anything you can think of. It's really quite amazing what these animals are capable of.

A lot of times what we'll do is we'll show the dog where whatever we want is and we'll walk them back and forth and back and forth so they know that's what we want. We'll teach them, and with praise and treats say, "Look!" And once we have their attention we'll say, "Find it." And then they'll go and grab it and we'll have them bring it to you.

Eventually you start hiding it and putting it in different places. You'll put it somewhere where it's harder to reach until they understand that when I say "Look for this," that's what their mission is. They need to find this. Give them a task. The dogs in the program are all Labrador and golden retrievers. They're working breeds. They want to please. They want to work. So eventually, when you get to the point where they can do that, you teach them a command for it and they'll go and get it for you.

Eventually, they're just like us. They're creatures of habit. If every single morning at 8:00 for six months or six weeks they've been going and getting this item, come 8:00, if it's not around, they're wondering why they're not going to look for it. They'll start looking to you and that's where we as their partners, we say, "Oh, I've already got it," or "Don't worry," and you'll give them a treat anyway. Or they'll give you a sign as if to say, "Remember I'm supposed to go get this?" "Oh, yeah, go find it," and they'll go find it and bring it back.

Source: http://soldiers.dodlive.mil/2014/12/how-to-train-a-service-dog/

What is the final stage in the dog training sequence mentioned in this article?

(A) The dogs want to work.

(B) The dogs work for treats.

(C) The trainer takes them for walks in crowded places.

(D) The work the dogs perform becomes habit.

Choice (A) is wrong because it's merely a statement that the dogs are willing to be trained. Choice (B) simply indicates how the dogs are trained. Choice (C) is one of the events, but it occurs early in the sequence. The only correct choice is Choice (D). The last paragraph states, "Eventually, they're just like us. They're creatures of habit," which indicates that the dogs have reached the final stage of their training; the work they perform becomes habit.

Drawing Inferences

To infer means to conclude, deduce, suppose, hypothesize, or speculate. An *inference* is a conjecture, an assumption, a suspicion, an extrapolation, or a guess. When you infer, you read between the lines, deriving information that's not directly stated. Writers don't always tell readers everything about their characters, the plots, or other aspects of the story. They provide clues and hints, making the reader do some of the work. As a reader, you need to combine what the author states with your own knowledge and logic to fill in the details.

Reread the passage in the previous section about Helga and her cats. What does this passage suggest about Helga?

(A) She has an astronomical cat food bill.

(B) She needs to get rid of a few cats.

(C) She loves cats.

(D) She is allergic to dogs.

All the listed choices are possible deductions or inferences. On the GED test, your task is to select the most correct answer from the choices given based on the given text. Choice (A) is a possibility. The text does suggest that at least one cat needs a special diet, which is potentially more costly. Feeding four cats is in itself possibly expensive. The text also states that others need medication and pills, but that has nothing to do with food bills. Getting rid of a few cats, Choice (B), is a possible deduction, but nothing in the passage suggests that she thinks in those terms; that conclusion would be the reader's value judgment. Choice (D) isn't a valid answer option; she may or may not be allergic to dogs, but the passage provides no clue to allow such a deduction. It mentions neither dogs nor allergies. Choice (C), She loves cats, is the only choice that is strongly supported. Consider the expense of feeding and medicating four cats and the effort in keeping all their individual needs straight. Choice (C) is the only strong and logical conclusion.

Plot

The author of Helga's story (see the passage in the earlier section "Recognizing and Ordering the Sequence of Events") doesn't tell you everything about the situation of the story; you have to read between the lines, which means making inferences. You start from what you know and make logical deductions to fill in the blanks. Try a couple of sample questions.

What started the action in this story?

(A) opening a can of cat food

(B) Midnight's arrival in the kitchen

(C) the Siamese cat's head butting Helga's leg

(D) none of the above

The correct answer is obviously Choice (A). You can infer from the situation that Helga was about to feed the cats, and that the pulling of a tab on a can of cat food signaled the event. The passage never states that the pull-tab was on a can of cat food, but you can infer that from context. Choices (B) and (C) are subsequent events. Choice (D) is wrong because you *are* able to infer the cause from the paragraph.

What can you tell about the general health of Helga's cats?

(A) They're all well fed.

(B) They're all seriously ill.

(C) The Siamese cat is ill.

(D) At least two of the cats have health problems.

More than one answer here has some basis in the text, but remember: You need to choose the *most* correct answer. Choices (A) and (B) are reasonable but aren't the best choices based on the text. Nothing in the story or the quoted line suggests all the cats are ill or that the illnesses are serious. Similarly, nothing indicates that the Siamese cat is the ill one. That leaves Choice (D), which is the correct answer. From the quoted line, you know that at least two cats are ill to some extent: "a special diet for that one, other meds here and there."

Setting

Setting is where the story takes place — for example, an apartment in New York City or a space station orbiting Mars. Often, readers must make inferences about the setting based on details provided. Reread the story of Helga and her cats in the earlier section "Recognizing and Ordering the Sequence of Events."

Where is the action in the passage taking place?

(A) a cat shelter

(B) a private home

(C) Helga's kitchen

(D) the vet's office

You can make a logical deduction based on the information presented; however, you need to read between the lines. You can quickly eliminate Choices (A) and (D). Nothing in the text suggests that it has an institutional setting, and these settings most likely would have more than four cats. Choice (B) is a logical deduction, but you can narrow it down to the most correct answer by selecting Choice (C), Helga's kitchen.

Characters

Characters are the people or other beings described in the story who typically perform the actions that keep the reader engaged. As a reader, you draw inferences about the characters in the stories you read without ever realizing it. Although the author may explicitly state certain things about a character, such as that he was *frugal* (a good money manager), more often, the author conveys such meaning more subtly, such as by having the character shop only at discount stores or insist on getting separate checks at dinner. You can tell about a character from how he reacts to a situation, interacts with other characters, and even chooses his words. One aspect of reading for comprehension and understanding is to decode these clues and create an image of the characters in the story.

Read the following passage extracted from "Beyond the Door" by Philip K. Dick.

That night at the dinner table he brought it out and set it down beside her plate. Doris stared at it, her hand to her mouth. "My God, what is it?" She looked up at him, bright-eyed.

"Well, open it."

Doris tore the ribbon and paper from the square package with her sharp nails, her bosom rising and falling. Larry stood watching her as she lifted the lid. He lit a cigarette and leaned against the wall.

"A cuckoo clock!" Doris cried. "A real old cuckoo clock like my mother had." She turned the clock over and over. "Just like my mother had, when Pete was still alive." Her eyes sparkled with tears.

"It's made in Germany," Larry said. After a moment he added, "Carl got it for me wholesale. He knows some guy in the clock business. Otherwise I wouldn't have—" He stopped.

Doris made a funny little sound.

"I mean, otherwise I wouldn't have been able to afford it." He scowled. "What's the matter with you? You've got your clock, haven't you? Isn't that what you want?"

Doris sat holding onto the clock, her fingers pressed against the brown wood.

"Well," Larry said, "what's the matter?"

He watched in amazement as she leaped up and ran from the room, still clutching the clock. He shook his head. "Never satisfied. They're all that way. Never get enough."

He sat down at the table and finished his meal.

The cuckoo clock was not very large. It was hand-made, however, and there were countless frets on it, little indentations and ornaments scored in the soft wood. Doris sat on the bed drying her eyes and winding the clock. She set the hands by her wristwatch. Presently she carefully moved the hands to two minutes of ten. She carried the clock over to the dresser and propped it up.

Then she sat waiting, her hands twisted together in her lap — waiting for the cuckoo to come out, for the hour to strike.

As she sat she thought about Larry and what he had said. And what she had said, too, for that matter — not that she could be blamed for any of it. After all, she couldn't keep listening to him forever without defending herself; you had to blow your own trumpet in the world.

She touched her handkerchief to her eyes suddenly. Why did he have to say that, about getting it wholesale? Why did he have to spoil it all? If he felt that way he needn't have got it in the first place. She clenched her fists.

Source: www.gutenberg.org/files/28644/28644-h/28644-h.htm

How does the author show Larry's mean personality when he presents the gift to Doris?

(A) He expresses concern that the clock is indeed what she wanted.

(B) He finishes his meal when an upset Doris runs away.

(C) He explains he got the clock at a discount.

(D) None of the above

The author doesn't come right out and state that Larry is mean, or worse. He allows the actions and dialogue to do that. Choice (A) is wrong; Larry's dialogue shows he is somewhat concerned that this clock is the right gift, but the concern is presented in a short-tempered manner. Choices (B) and (C) are possible, but they aren't the strongest clues. The strongest clue is the implicit, unfinished sentence "'Otherwise I wouldn't have —' He stopped." The fact that he was being stingy, especially when the text also shows the clock is something Doris really wanted, shows the meanness best. Doris's reaction when he makes that statement — she makes "a funny little sound" — confirms that interpretation.

The author shows Doris's feelings evolving in this short text. Which of these best captures that change?

(A) Doris starts happy and then goes through anger and then sadness.

(B) Doris's emotions go from sadness to joy to anger.

(C) Doris is quiet and compliant at the beginning and ends up sad.

(D) Doris starts happy and excited, is then crushed and sad, and ends angry.

The correct choice is Choice (D). Notice how the passage describes Doris. When she sees the present, she is described as "bright-eyed." When she opens the package and sees the clock, her eyes sparkle with tears of joy. When Larry makes the comment about buying the clock at a discount, she freezes and then runs from the room. The description indicates she is crushed. The end of the text shows her anger as she clenches her fists.

Choices (A) and (B) list the same emotions, but in the wrong order. Choice (C) doesn't apply because nothing suggests that Doris is compliant. Running from the room suggests she isn't prepared to put up with Larry's justifications, and the final description of clenched fists suggests anger, not sadness.

Ideas

Writers present ideas or insights. The language they use may be fairly dense; that is, the text uses relatively few words to convey deep meaning or complex ideas. Dense text requires interpretation to determine the author's meaning, especially true in older writings and government or legal documents. Although the writer expresses the ideas, you must extract the ideas through careful reading and analysis. In the following passage from *Beyond Good and Evil* by Friedrich Nietzsche, finding the key idea takes careful analysis.

231. Learning alters us, it does what all nourishment does that does not merely "conserve" — as the physiologist knows. But at the bottom of our souls, quite "down below," there is certainly something unteachable, a granite of spiritual fate, of predetermined decision and answer to predetermined, chosen questions. In each cardinal problem there speaks an unchangeable "I am this"; a thinker cannot learn anew about man and woman, for instance, but can only learn fully — he can only follow to the end what is "fixed" about them in himself.

Source: www.gutenberg.org/files/4363/4363-h/4363-h.htm

Which of these statements reflects the key idea in this text?

(A) Mankind's fate is built on a granite foundation.

(B) People's learning is limited by their basic internal beliefs.

(C) Everything in life is predetermined.

(D) Learning nourishes and alters us.

Nietzsche was a German philosopher who wrote dense text. The easiest way to decipher such text is to turn it into bullet points in simpler English:

✔ Learning alters us.

✔ At the bottom of our souls is something unteachable.

✔ Our souls rest on a foundation of predetermined decisions and answers to predetermined questions.

✔ A thinker can only reach for answers based on what is already in this foundation.

Based on this rewrite, you can easily see that the key idea in Nietzsche's text is Choice (B), People's learning is limited by their basic internal beliefs. Choices (A) and (D) simply echo statements in the text. Choice (C) is true but only presents part of the key idea.

Analyzing Relationships among Ideas

On the RLA test, you're expected to identify and analyze the relationships between ideas. When two or more ideas are presented in a text, they're related by sequence, connection, or cause and effect and ultimately lead you to arrive at a certain conclusion, as explained in the following sections.

Sequence

Ideas or events are related by *sequence* when one idea comes before or after the other or the two ideas exist at the same time. To identify ideas related by sequence, look for words such as *before, during,* and *after.* The following passage serves as an example of events related by sequence.

There was a major snowfall in Buffalo yesterday. Because of a gas shortage, many people were clearing snow by hand. The next day, local hospitals reported a significant increase in the number of heart attacks.

This passage relates a clear sequence of events: a snowfall, a shortage of gasoline, clearing snow by hand, and an increase in heart attacks. Determining whether the events prove a true causal relationship is more difficult; the clearing of snow by hand and the increase in heart attacks may be a coincidence. You need further information to draw such a conclusion. All that is clear here is that the events occurred in a sequential order.

Connection

Ideas or events are related by *connection* when they're presented as being like or unlike one another or are both relevant to whatever is being described or analyzed. To identify ideas and events related by connection, look for words and phrases such as *and, but,* and *as well.* Here's an example in which the word *and* is used to connect the characteristics of a certain task:

Changing settings on an onboard computer can be both complicated and time-consuming. If the work is not handled carefully, it could result in a complete crash of the system.

The first sentence clearly shows the connection: Changing settings is both complicated and time-consuming. The two ideas are linked in one sentence.

Here's an example in which the ideas are connected in a way that highlights their differences:

Lord Fontleroy was very generous in his giving to philanthropic organizations but stingy when asked by family members for any sort of financial assistance.

Cause and effect

Ideas and events are related by *cause and effect* when one idea or event gives rise to the other. To identify passages that contain cause-and-effect relationships, look for words and phrases such as *because, as a result,* and *outcome.* Keep in mind, however, that causes and their effects may be implied rather than explicitly stated. Here's an example of a cause-and-effect relationship that's clearly stated:

Due to the increasing frequency and duration of droughts in California, wildfires have become much more common and devastating.

The use of the *due to* establishes the cause-and-effect relationship: the increasing frequency and duration of droughts causes wildfires that are more common and devastating.

Correlation or coincidence isn't necessarily proof of causation. For example, in the earlier section "Sequence," the fact that the increase in heart attacks occurred after folks cleared the Buffalo snowfall doesn't mean the latter caused the former. Other explanations are possible.

Here's a passage from *The Prince* by Nicolo Machiavelli in which the cause-and-effect relationship is less obvious:

But let us come to Commodus, to whom it should have been very easy to hold the empire, for, being the son of Marcus, he had inherited it, and he had only to follow in the footsteps of his father to please his people and soldiers; but, being by nature cruel and brutal, he gave himself up to amusing the soldiers and corrupting them, so that he might indulge his rapacity upon the people; on the other hand, not maintaining his dignity, often descending to the theatre to compete with gladiators, and doing other vile things, little worthy of the imperial majesty, he fell into contempt with the soldiers, and being hated by one party and despised by the other, he was conspired against and was killed.

Source: www.gutenberg.org/files/1232/1232-h/1232-h.htm

Why was Commodus assassinated?

(A) He corrupted his soldiers.

(B) He was cruel and brutal.

(C) He didn't maintain his imperial majesty.

(D) all of the above

The correct answer is Choice (D), all of the above. The text presents a clear linkage showing that Commodus' brutal nature, lack of dignity, and other vile actions led to his being despised and eventually assassinated.

Conclusion

Ideas and events that are related ultimately lead you to draw a certain conclusion, the final step in the analytical process. The author may state the conclusion directly, making your job as reader easy, or more subtly present details that lead you to draw the conclusion for yourself.

The passage from *The Prince* in the preceding section presents the conclusion more or less directly, a variation of cause and effect. In other instances, you must come to a conclusion based on information presented. Often, text has an unstated underlying message, as in the following passage from "History of the CIA" at the CIA's website:

In July 1941, [President] Roosevelt appointed Donovan as the Coordinator of Information (COI) to direct the nation's first peacetime, nondepartmental intelligence organization. But America's entry into World War II that same December prompted new thinking about the role of the COI. The result was the formation of the Office of Strategic Services (OSS) in June 1942. The mandate of the OSS was to collect and analyze strategic information required by the Joint Chiefs of Staff and to conduct special operations not assigned to other agencies.

During the war, the OSS supplied policymakers with intelligence that played an important role in positively aiding military campaigns. The OSS shared jurisdiction over foreign intelligence activities with the FBI. (The FBI had been responsible for this work in Latin America since 1940.) Meanwhile, the military branches conducted intelligence operations in their areas of responsibility.

As World War II wound down with the American and allied victory, there was sentiment throughout the United States to return to normalcy and demobilize wartime agencies quickly, agencies like the OSS. Donovan's civilian and military rivals feared he might win his campaign to create a peacetime intelligence service modeled on the OSS. But President Harry S. Truman, who succeeded Roosevelt in April 1945, felt no obligation to the OSS after the war.

Technically abolished in October 1945, the OSS's analysis, collection, and counterintelligence services were transferred to the State and War departments, but on a much smaller scale.

Source: www.cia.gov/kids-page/6-12th-grade/operation-history/history-of-the-cia.html

Which of these conclusions is the most accurate?

(A) The OSS wasn't an effective espionage agency.

(B) The decision of one president isn't binding on another.

(C) Politicians feared spy agencies.

(D) When WWII ended, the OSS was no longer needed.

The best conclusion to draw from this example is Choice (B). The passage states that Truman felt no obligation to the OSS even though the previous president had established it. Choice (A) is incorrect because nothing suggests that the OSS was ineffective. Choice (C) may be partially true, but the text states that rivals, not politicians in general, feared the continuation of the OSS. Finally, nothing in the text either refutes or supports Choice (D), so it too is unacceptable.

Deriving Meaning from Context

The GED RLA test features some questions that challenge your ability to derive meaning from *context* — the situation or setting in which a statement is made or a word or phrase is used. For example, the word *around* may be used to describe people gathering *around* (near) the town square or meeting *around* (approximately) 7:00 p.m. The word has a very different meaning depending on the context in which it's used. Context also often provides the clues you need to figure out the meaning of an unfamiliar word. For example, suppose you encounter the following sentence in a passage about the honesty of politicians: "At a political rally, voters need to carefully question the veracity of any candidate's statements." Even if you don't know what the word *veracity* means, you can figure out from the context that it probably means something along the lines of "truthfulness." Here's another example:

When the shooting started, the troops ran for cover in a nearby bunker. Ducking bullets, they ran for the doorway, and the last man slammed the steel doors shut. Shells pounded the roof, and machine gunfire rang off the door, but they were safe inside.

What is a *bunker*?

(A) a building that has been around for a long time

(B) a fireproof shelter

(C) a building constructed to resist shelling and gunfire

(D) a central building in a military compound

From the context, you can easily figure out that a bunker is some sort of shelter designed to resist shelling and gun fire. It may have been around for a long time or be fireproof, but the context is enemy fire, so neither is of prime importance. Choice (D) isn't the best answer either; whether a bunker is a central building in a compound has no relevance to protection against enemy fire. Based on the context in which the passage uses *bunker*, Choice (C) is the correct answer.

You can also detect bias in the way information is presented — the context of the presentation. If someone prefaces a statement with "In my opinion. . ." or "All XYZ are. . ." you should question what follows. In the first instance, the mere use of the word *opinion* warns you that the facts may have been selected to present a particular point of view. The second example contains the word *all*, which often signals the beginning of an *overgeneralization* — a conclusion about something that claims more than the limited evidence supports. For example, claiming that all pit bulls are vicious dogs is an overgeneralization because some are very gentle. As you analyze passages on the GED test, watch out for words such as *all, none, everybody, nobody, always,* and *never,* which often introduce overgeneralizations and an opportunity for you to pick apart the argument.

Figuring Out the Function of Details

"The devil is in the details" is an old saying that means the details of any proposal or plan are what often cause it to fail. This saying also applies to writing. Details can add mood, feeling, and impact to settings, create an impression of personality in individuals, and generally highlight something about the nature of the subject of the writing. The details may also support or undermine an argument, making details a very important area of focus when the test asks you to analyze an argument.

On the GED RLA test, you may be presented with two versions of a passage, one with plenty of details and one without, and challenged to figure out the function of the details in the passage. Here's an example from *Pebbles on the Shore*, by Alpha of the Plough (Alfred George Gardiner):

The invitation reaches me in a tiny village on a spur of a range of beech clad hills, whither I have fled for a breathing space from the nightmare of the war and the menacing gloom of the London streets at night. Here the darkness has no terrors. In the wide arch of the sky our lamps are lit nightly as the sun sinks down far over the great plain that stretches at our feet. None of the palpitations of Fleet Street disturb us, and the rumours of the war come to us like far-off echoes from another world. The only sensation of our day is when, just after darkness has fallen, the sound of a whistle in the tiny street of thatched cottages announces that the postman has called to collect letters.

Source: www.gutenberg.org/cache/epub/10675/pg10675.html

Now consider this paraphrase:

I was living in a tiny village where I was taking a break from London, and the war, when the invitation reached me. Nothing disturbs us, neither newspapers nor rumours of war, and the only sensation of the day comes when the mailman picks up our letters.

The second version includes all the basic facts but omits details.

What effect does the detail in the first paragraph have on the feeling created by the passage?

(A) It makes the paragraph harder to read.

(B) It makes the paragraph more precise.

(C) It makes little difference.

(D) It creates a feeling or mood.

The detail certainly has little effect on the degree of difficulty in reading the paragraph (though some of the old-fashioned language may), so Choice (A) is wrong. The detail may make the paragraph more precise, but that's not its most important function. Choice (C) is wrong because the details do make a difference. Choice (D) is correct. Details in the first paragraph convey a sense of darkness and dread — "the nightmare of war" and the "menacing gloom" — in contrast to feelings of brightness and peace in the new setting — "the wide arch of the sky" illuminated by "lamps" and mere "rumours" of war sounding like "far-off echoes."

Sensory details add a great deal to writing because they draw the reader in and create images that the reader can feel, smell, touch, see, and hear, as in the following passage from *The Works of Guy de Maupassant, Volume III, The Viaticum and Other Stories:*

The bright night seemed to be scattering handfuls of stars into the placid sea, which was as calm as a blue pond, slumbering in the depths of a forest. Among the tall climbing roses, which hung a mantle of yellow flowers to the fretted baluster of the terrace, there stood out in the distance the illuminated fronts of the hotels and villas, and occasionally women's laughter was heard above the dull, monotonous sound of surf and the noise of the fog-horns.

www.gutenberg.org/files/17376/17376-h/17376-h.htm

What is the setting described here?

(A) terrace, quiet night, summer, overlooking sea

(B) terrace, hotel, foggy night

(C) rose garden, hotel, foggy night

(D) villa, water's edge, terrace, rose garden

The correct answer is Choice (A). The setting can't be a hotel, rose garden, or villa because the text describes hotels and villas "in the distance" and climbing roses on a terrace (but not a rose garden). The details describe the setting as peaceful. The night is described as "bright" with "handfuls of stars," and although the setting seems to get a little loud at the end with the women's laughter, the sound of the surf, and the fog-horns, even the "noise" is soothing in its monotony and joy.

In other cases, the details reinforce the idea of the paragraph. This is a description of trenches in WWI from the history of a Canadian regiment from *The 116th Battalion in France* by E. P. S. Allen:

The condition of the trenches in this sector was the worst imaginable. The mud was not only knee deep but like glue, and it was not at all an unusual occurrence for a man to lose his boots and socks in his endeavours to extricate himself. One of the smallest of our officers, Capt. Hughes, was heard to remark that it was a good thing for him that his colours were painted on his helmet.

Source: www.gutenberg.org/files/45860/45860-h/45860-h.htm .

The paragraph starts with a straightforward statement: The conditions in the trenches were the worst. The rest of the paragraph then provides the details to reinforce that image. The purpose of the details here is to reinforce the opening sentence.

Sometimes, other details in text can give you unexpected information. You can tell that this description from WWI wasn't written by Americans. Two words give it away: *endeavours* and *colours*. Why? Because the "ou" spelling is British and used by the English, Australians, and Canadians but not Americans.

Comparing Points of View

In literature, short stories, novels, and the like, *point of view* refers to how the author brings you into the story. Usually authors write in one of two forms, first-person and third-person. In a first-person story, the narrator will say "I did this" or "I felt that." You get a direct look at the narrator's feelings, motivations, and reactions. More commonly, authors write in the third-person. The characters in the story, including the main characters, are all presented as he, she, or it. In effect, the narrator has you looking in on the story. This approach allows the author to present information and insights to the reader that the characters may not know or be able to convey, including their own motivation and inner feelings. It also allows the author to drop hints to reveal insights into where the story is going before the characters themselves know. Here's an example:

Ripley could not know the alien was right around the corner. She stepped warily toward the bulkhead, watching her scanner for any signs of life. Abandoned by the rest of her crew, Ripley was well aware that her life was in her own hands.

From whose point of view is this paragraph written?

(A) Ripley's

(B) the alien's

(C) a crew member's

(D) someone else's

This question refers to the narrator's point of view. The narrator is describing Ripley's actions and feeling. Choice (A) is correct.

Point of view also comes into play in persuasive writing, as explained in the following sections.

Determining the author's point of view

Some writing is aimed at persuading the reader or presenting different points of view. Sometimes the points of view are very clear in opening statements; other times the point(s) of view are less obvious. Editorials and columns, both in print and in electronic media are certainly designed to promote a particular point of view. When reading such material, ask yourself, "What is the author trying to accomplish?" or "What side of this issue is the author trying to convince me to agree with?" Here's an example from a statement by President Harry S. Truman, August 6, 1945, after the dropping of the atomic bomb in Hiroshima.

Sixteen hours ago an American airplane dropped one bomb on [Hiroshima]and destroyed its usefulness to the enemy. That bomb had more power than 20,000 tons of TNT. It had more than 20,000 times the blast power of the British "Grand Slam," which is the largest bomb ever yet used in the history of warfare.

The Japanese began the war from the air at Pearl Harbor. They have been repaid many fold. And the end is not yet. With this bomb we have now added a new and revolutionary increase in destruction to supplement the growing power of our armed forces. In their present form these bombs are now in production and even more powerful forms are in development.

It is an atomic bomb. It is a harnessing of the basic power of the universe. The force from which the sun draws its power has been loosed against those who brought war to the Far East.

Before 1939, it was the accepted belief of scientists that it was theoretically possible to release atomic energy. But no one knew any practical method of doing it. By 1942, however, we knew that the Germans were working feverishly to find a way to add atomic energy to the other engines of war with which they hoped to enslave the world. But they failed. We may be grateful to Providence that the Germans got the V-1s and the V-2s late and in limited quantities and even more grateful that they did not get the atomic bomb at all.

At first reading, this memo is a straightforward account of the use and utility of the atomic bomb. Upon a second, closer reading, however, you may begin to see that this passage is actually trying subtly to persuade you of a certain point of view.

What is the implication of the sentences "They have been repaid many fold. And the end is not yet."?

(A) America is more powerful than Japan.

(B) If Japan doesn't surrender, America will continue its assault.

(C) It all started with Pearl Harbor.

(D) America is getting even with Japan.

Choices (A), (B), and (C) may all be considered correct; however, Choice (B) is the most correct answer because the two sentences quoted imply that even though America has gotten the upper hand, it will continue to attack Japan as long as the war continues. Choice (A) is questionable because although the passage supports that America has a more powerful weapon, it doesn't necessarily prove that America is more powerful overall. Choice (C) is a true statement but an incorrect answer because the passage *states* that Japan started the war by attacking Pearl Harbor; the sentences quoted in the question don't imply so. Choice (D) is incorrect because the sentences quoted indicate that America has already gotten more than even with Japan. Though the bombing itself may be considered payback, the sentence "And the end is not yet" implies that more is to come. (And it did. Three days after the bombing of Hiroshima, the United States dropped another atomic bomb on Nagasaki, prompting Japan's unconditional surrender.)

Analyzing the author's response to opposing viewpoints

Authors often have to respond to opposing viewpoints, and they have numerous tools at their disposal to do so. They can question or disprove the logic used to arrive at the opposing viewpoint or present evidence that challenges or undermines the evidence used to support the opposing viewpoint. Writers can also use deceitful practices and logical fallacies to argue their point, such as personally attacking anyone who disagrees with them, using emotional language to drown out logic and facts, selecting only facts that support their position and ignoring data that challenges it, and distorting facts to support their point of view.

Whenever a question on the GED test challenges you to analyze a response to an opposing viewpoint, ask the following questions and jot down your answers:

✔ Does the author address the opposing viewpoint?

✔ What evidence does the author present to counter the opposing viewpoint?

✔ Is the evidence used appropriate?

✔ Does the author use emotional language to sway the argument?

✔ Does the argument support the conclusion?

If your answer to any one of these questions is "no," then you've found a weakness in the argument or the response to the opposing viewpoint that you may want to explore more deeply in your analysis.

Consider these two passages:

Passage One

Some youth deliberately set out to harm others; this act is called bullying. However, when it happens by using social media, texting, and other technologies, it is called cyberbullying. That, too, should be a crime, especially because the intent to hurt and harm is there. Worse, considering how pervasive media technology is today, the bullying never stops; it follows the victims wherever and whenever they try to escape. The resulting evidence of the harm is also clear. The number of young people who have in desperation committed suicide after months and years of horrific abuse shows that.

Cyberbullying is a form of abuse, just like cyberstalking. It relentlessly hounds a designated target, even following the victim when he or she moves or changes schools. In a recent case, a teen was raped, and photographs of the rape were distributed to classmates in her school. Comments that followed taunted her as a slut — it was her fault; she was asking for it — to the point that she transferred schools. The teen reported the rape to the police who took little action, and the perps remained free. She received an endless stream of abusive e-mails and texts. Meetings with the principal of both high schools and parents of the bullies solved nothing. Even after transferring, the bullies found her again and the harassment started again. Only after being faced with community outrage did the police take action, and then only after the teen had committed suicide.

This was not an isolated case. Nearly half of all teens report they have been victims of cyber-bullying. There have been multiple suicides in many countries. The police are often unwilling or unable to take action, claiming that cyberbullying itself does not constitute a crime.

Education programs don't work, either. Virtually all schools these days have anti-bullying programs. Even grade-school children are taught about bullying and to show respect for others. They are also educated on how to be safe online. Yet the cyberbullying continues.

The threat of a criminal record is a deterrent and, at the very least, will give the police a tool with which to fight cyberbullying. Arresting bullies will certainly stop them in their tracks. It might also give the victims a tool for seeking redress. All the other initiatives have failed, so what choice is left?

Passage Two

Why criminalize cyberbullying? There are already laws that can be used against cyberbullies if the issue becomes serious. Cyberbullying may be crude and rude, but it is not a crime unless it becomes slanderous or libelous. If there is no physical harm done and no intent to drive someone to self-harm, why treat verbal abuse as a crime? If it continues and crosses into destruction of reputation, then it is criminal harassment, a chargeable offense.

If the cyberbullying is not serious enough for criminal charges, victims and their parents have other tools available. They can approach the school or parents of the perpetrators. They can ask websites to take down offensive materials. Parents can deal directly with each other.

Newspapers have stories about victims who have been driven to suicide or attempts at self-harm. But what proof is there that the cyberbullying was the sole cause? Were the victims already suffering from depression? Were there other issues in their lives that made them unstable and prone to self-harm?

Proponents argue that the fear of a criminal charge will be a deterrent. But if that is the case, why do so many people still drive drunk or continue to indulge in recreational drugs? There are clear consequences for these acts if caught, but they certainly do not stop these incidents. Teens are not the most rational beings, and the idea that their actions might result in criminal charges is not really foremost in their minds.

There are other tools available. Making someone into a criminal should be the last resort.

When analyzing the second essay, which is a response to the opposing viewpoint presented in the first essay, ask the questions we present earlier in the section and jot down your answers, as in the following example:

- ✔ **Does the author address the opposing viewpoint?** Yes. The author discusses the issue and expands on it by differentiating between cyberbullying that becomes criminal and cyberbullying that is merely name-calling.

- ✔ **What evidence does the author present to counter the opposing viewpoint?** By differentiating between minor and major cyberbullying, the author points out that criminal charges are available where required and that other solutions are available for lesser offenses.

- ✔ **Is the evidence used appropriate?** Yes. The information presented seems credible. The case study, in particular, is presented like a news story, merely stating the facts.

- ✔ **Did the passage include emotional language?** Yes and no. The last statement, "What choice is left?" is certainly emotional, but that is the only place where it's used.

- ✔ **Does the argument support the conclusion?** Yes. The argument and the evidence used to back it all build to support the position. Whether the reader agrees with the position is a personal issue. In this instance, the argument is meant to sway the reader.

Appreciating the Importance of Word Choice

The developers of the RLA test want to make sure you're sensitive to language and the subtle variations in meaning between similar words and phrases. They also need to assess your ability to understand *figurative language* — text written to stimulate the reader's senses and make the reader see and feel a part of what is happening or being described. The RLA test may present you with questions that challenge your ability to explain why a certain word was chosen or explain the effect that a particular word has in a passage. In addition, when you write your Extended Response, you need to demonstrate your command of the language, and part of that involves choosing just the right words to express yourself.

In the following sections, we focus in on word choice (often referred to as *diction*) to make you more conscious of words and their meanings.

Tuning in to variations in meaning and tone

Using a thesaurus, you can look up most words and find words with similar meanings. However, these similar words typically differ to some degree in meaning and tone. For example, "afraid" and "cowardly" convey a similar meaning, but the latter has a more judgmental feel; you wouldn't think of calling a child who's afraid of the dark "cowardly."

In your own writing, choose your words carefully and according to the following guidelines:

- ✔ Use words deliberately and carefully for effect.

- ✔ Use words that come naturally to the way you speak. Don't make a forced effort to impress readers with sophisticated words.

- ✔ As you practice writing outside of the testing environment, use a thesaurus and dictionary in tandem to find the word that most precisely expresses the desired meaning and tone.

Word choice for overall effect

Choosing the right words can have an amazing impact on the effectiveness of any writing. Read Abraham Lincoln's Gettysburg Address. It is a great example of using just the right words.

Four score and seven years ago our fathers brought forth, upon this continent, a new nation, conceived in liberty, and dedicated to the proposition that all men are created equal.

Now we are engaged in a great civil war, testing whether that nation, or any nation so conceived, and so dedicated, can long endure. We are met on a great battlefield of that war. We have come to dedicate a portion of it, as a final resting place for those who died here, that the nation might live. This we may, in all propriety do. But, in a larger sense, we cannot dedicate — we cannot consecrate — we cannot hallow, this ground. The brave men, living and dead, who struggled here, have hallowed it, far above our poor power to add or detract. The world will little note, nor long remember what we say here; while it can never forget what they did here.

It is rather for us, the living, to stand here, we here be dedicated to the great task remaining before us — that, from these honored dead we take increased devotion to that cause for which they here, gave the last full measure of devotion — that we here highly resolve these dead shall not have died in vain; that the nation, shall have a new birth of freedom, and that government of the people by the people for the people, shall not perish from the earth.

Source: www.ourdocuments.gov/doc.php?doc=36&page=transcript

One rule of good writing is to keep the writing simple, but Lincoln ignores that rule. He uses the phrase "four score and seven years ago" when he could just have said "87 years ago." It works because it sounds much deeper. The choice of wording is almost poetic, giving a rhythm to the reading of this speech. Lincoln repeats that turn of phrase in the last paragraph, using parallel phrasing: "government of the people, by the people, for the people. . ."

Lincoln also uses contrast to make his points. Look how he writes that few will remember this speech but that what the soldiers did will be remembered forever. He repeats that when he writes that the audience can't hallow (honor as holy) the ground of the battlefield; those who fought and died have done that. These contrasts create a powerful, emotional image.

Meaning and tone

Words have specific meanings, but authors often use words in a way that alters their meaning. This tendency is especially true in humorous, satirical writings and persuasive writings. Authors can use exaggeration or overuse words to create a different meaning or *tone* (overall point of view) in a written passage. The tone of a passage can be described in many ways, from sarcastic to confident, arrogant to simplistic. To determine the tone and meaning of a passage, you need to read it carefully because meaning is often implied rather than stated. Here's an example:

I just knew it was a great idea. Plunging head first into a canyon with a rubber band tied to my ankles had to be one of the greatest ideas I ever had. What could be more reasonable and logical than to trust my life to that silly little rubber band as the boulder-strewn bottom of the canyon approached and the wind ripped the screams from my throat?

Suddenly the rubber band grabbed tight. I felt a delicious feeling of security as those oh-so-lovely thick and reliable flexible steel cables brought me to a safe halt, and I gently bounced around, blissfully enjoying the magnificent canyon scenery.

Did the subject really think that plunging head first into a canyon tethered only by a bungee cord was a great idea? Did he or she really think that it was reasonable and logical to trust a life to a "silly little rubber band"? Of course not. But note how the author uses words that have a specific meaning to convey a meaning opposite of the dictionary definition of the chosen words. Without specifically saying it, the author implies how the subject feels about his or her actions.

Tone isn't the same as mood. Tone is the character of or attitude toward the subject or situation. *Mood* is how the passage makes the reader feel about the subject or situation.

How does tone of the passage change?

(A) from enthusiasm to terror

(B) from sarcasm to terror

(C) from sarcasm to contentment

(D) from enthusiasm to boredom

The subject is certainly not feeling any enthusiasm as the passage starts. The wording in fact creates the exact opposite feeling. That means Choices (A) and (D) are wrong. You can eliminate Choice (B) because nothing suggests the subject is still feeling terror at the end.

That leaves Choice (C). The passage begins with sarcasm (ridiculing the narrator's decision to bungee jump into a canyon) and ends with bliss and feelings of security (contentment). Choice (C) is your best option.

In the following passage from *Pride and Prejudice* by Jane Austen, a group has just had tea and is now sitting in the library after turning down a suggestion to play cards:

Miss Bingley's attention was quite as much engaged in watching Mr. Darcy's progress through his book, as in reading her own; and she was perpetually either making some inquiry, or looking at his page. She could not win him, however, to any conversation; he merely answered her question, and read on. At length, quite exhausted by the attempt to be amused with her own book, which she had only chosen because it was the second volume of his, she gave a great yawn and said, "How pleasant it is to spend an evening in this way! I declare after all there is no enjoyment like reading! How much sooner one tires of anything than of a book! When I have a house of my own, I shall be miserable if I have not an excellent library."

Source: www.gutenberg.org/files/1342/1342-h/1342-h.htm

What is the tone of this passage?

(A) arrogant

(B) boastful

(C) humorous

(D) sarcastic

The passage is about Miss Bingley and her reaction to the situation. You can eliminate the first two choices quickly because nothing about the passage is arrogant or boastful. The situation contains an element of humor as Miss Bingley is increasingly bored. But the clue is in her quoted speech. She yawns loudly and proclaims how pleasant reading like this is and how she would be lost without a large library. You can tell from the context that she feels the exact opposite, so sarcastic, Choice (D), is an appropriate tone for this passage.

Interpreting figurative language

Writers use language either literally or figuratively. A NASA scientist can describe an asteroid very literally: composed largely of water, mixed with some rocks and smaller solid fragments. Or, he or she may write figuratively, describing it as a dirty snowball — a somewhat more dramatic image that conveys the meaning accurately enough for the layperson.

Figurative language compares two things in a sentence, with the purpose of creating a clear image; writers use it in various forms:

- *Simile* uses the word *like* or *as* to compare two unlike objects. For example the phrases like "sleek as a panther" or "bright as the sun" are all a form of simile.

- *Metaphor* is a comparison of two unlike objects without using *as* or *like*. Jaques' claim in Shakespeare's *As You Like It* that "All the world's a stage" is a metaphor comparing the world to a stage in a theater.

- *Hyperbole* is a wild exaggeration. Think of how often your mom said to you, "I've told you a million times not to jump on the bed." You know she hasn't really made that statement a million times, but that number creates an effect by showing both impatience and exasperation and providing urgency. The common phrase "You could have knocked me over with a feather" is another example of hyperbole.

✔ *Personification* turns a nonhuman subject into something with human characteristics. You see it every day in the world of children's literature. Dancing donkeys and talking crickets don't exist in real life, but they're useful tools for engaging children in stories. Personification is often used in more mature forms of literature as a powerful descriptive tool.

✔ *Onomatopoeia* is the use of words that sound like what they're being used to describe. Think of the cereal that goes snap, crackle, and pop. Cereals don't make sounds themselves, but certainly that is what most people hear when milk poured onto a bowl of cereal. Or think of bees buzzing or cats hissing.

✔ *Alliteration* is the repetition of sounds, such as in the expressions "wild and wooly" and "vim and vigor," to reinforce the image being described. Here are a couple examples of alliteration used on context: "An angry actress awkwardly accepts an award after an awful appearance." "Critics condemn crass commercialism."

✔ *Idiomatic expressions* are phrases that mean something very different from their literal meaning. When you say that someone let the cat out of the bag, you usually don't mean a real cat and a real bag. Most people know from common usage that this phrase means disclosing a secret unintentionally. Expressions such as "face like thunder" or "raining cats and dogs" are part of everyday usage.

These devices shape the reader's understanding of, and reaction to, something they're reading. It can be for humor or persuasion, or to create any desired effect.

Here are a couple of questions that challenge your ability to identify various types of figurative language:

Identify the figurative language used in the following sentence: "She ran like the wind across the meadow."

(A) hyperbole

(B) personification

(C) simile

(D) idiomatic expression

The correct answer is Choice (C) because the sentence compares two unlike things (a girl and the wind) by using the word *like*.

Identify the figurative language used in the following sentence: "The teapot happily whistled a cheery tune as the water boiled."

(A) hyperbole

(B) personification

(C) simile

(D) idiomatic expression

Personification, Choice (B), is the device used here. Inanimate objects don't whistle happy tunes; people do. The use of the word *as* later has no bearing because it's not used as part of the comparison.

Extracting Meaning from Flow

The flow of a passage, determined by how the passage is structured and by the transition from one idea to the next, is often useful in interpreting the meaning of a passage. For example, if instructions are presented sequentially from step one to step ten, you know that the purpose of the passage is to instruct you on how to perform a certain task. If two systems of governance are compared and contrasted, then the purpose of the passage may be to educate the reader on the two systems of governance or persuade the reader that one system is better than the other.

In the following sections, we explain how to interpret passages by examining their structure and how they flow. First, we examine a speech to illustrate how flow works to help convey meaning. Then we look at the overall structure of the passage and how the parts contribute to the whole. Finally, we explore various methods for transitioning from one idea to the next.

Taking a big picture look at meaning and flow

Any written document has a natural flow, whether that document is literature or an instruction manual, poem, or contract. One of the best ways to get a feel for how flow helps to convey meaning is to look closely at a passage that flows well and uses rhythm and other rhetorical devices to express a certain point of view. Here is an excerpt of a speech by Barack Obama in Selma on the 50th anniversary of the Montgomery marches:

[T]here are places and moments in America where this nation's destiny has been decided. Many are sites of war — Concord and Lexington, Appomattox, Gettysburg. Others are sites that symbolize the daring of America's character — Independence Hall and Seneca Falls, Kitty Hawk and Cape Canaveral.

Selma is such a place. In one afternoon 50 years ago, so much of our turbulent history — the stain of slavery and anguish of civil war; the yoke of segregation and tyranny of Jim Crow; the death of four little girls in Birmingham; and the dream of a Baptist preacher — all that history met on this bridge.

It was not a clash of armies, but a clash of wills; a contest to determine the true meaning of America. And because of men and women like John Lewis, Joseph Lowery, Hosea Williams, Amelia Boynton, Diane Nash, Ralph Abernathy, C.T. Vivian, Andrew Young, Fred Shuttlesworth, Dr. Martin Luther King, Jr., and so many others, the idea of a just America and a fair America, an inclusive America, and a generous America — that idea ultimately triumphed.

As is true across the landscape of American history, we cannot examine this moment in isolation. The march on Selma was part of a broader campaign that spanned generations; the leaders that day part of a long line of heroes.

We gather here to celebrate them. We gather here to honor the courage of ordinary Americans willing to endure billy clubs and the chastening rod; tear gas and the trampling hoof; men and women who despite the gush of blood and splintered bone would stay true to their North Star and keep marching towards justice.

They did as scripture instructed: "Rejoice in hope, be patient in tribulation, be constant in prayer." And in the days to come, they went back again and again. When the trumpet call sounded for more to join, the people came — black and white, young and old, Christian and Jew, waving the American flag and singing the same anthems full of faith and hope. A white newsman, Bill Plante, who covered the marches then and who is with us here today, quipped that the growing number of white people lowered the quality of the singing. (Laughter.) To those who marched, though, those old gospel songs must have never sounded so sweet.

This speech flows. It's clear and rhythmical, uses plain language, and makes its points. The language is varied, interesting, and descriptive without being flowery. The overall flow of the passage contributes to the meaning it conveys: that America is greatest when heroic individuals work together to promote American justice and ideals.

Recognizing the parts of the whole

In writing, every sentence and every paragraph is, or should be, chosen for a particular purpose and effect. In a newspaper story, the first sentence must contain the entire story in a nutshell. The first paragraph expands that slightly, and the rest of the story presents the details. If it's properly written, the headline and the first paragraph relate nearly all the essentials.

In the Obama speech in the previous section, every paragraph contributes to the meaning and impact of the speech. One of the best ways to recognize how the parts contribute to the whole of any brief passage is to describe the purpose of each paragraph. Here's an example applied to Obama's speech:

- **Paragraph 1:** Name places of historical significance in America.
- **Paragraph 2:** Add Selma to the list and explain why it belongs on that list.
- **Paragraph 3:** Describe the heroes of Selma and what they accomplished — making America just, inclusive, and generous.
- **Paragraph 4:** Expand the march on Selma to include the broader campaign for justice.
- **Paragraph 5:** Bring the struggle into this moment and paint a vivid picture of the sacrifice its heroes endured.
- **Paragraph 6:** Build to a strong conclusion of hope and inclusion to inspire the crowd.

Don't be surprised on the RLA test if you encounter a question asking you the purpose of a specific paragraph in a passage or the role a single sentence plays in a paragraph. When you encounter such a question, simply summarize the paragraph or rephrase the sentence in your own words, and you'll usually arrive at the correct answer.

Analyzing the transitions that tie it all together

In a well-written passage, sentences and paragraphs flow smoothly and logically from one to the next. Writers establish flow by using various techniques along with transitional words and phrases, including the following:

- **Organization:** Organization is the single most important factor in establishing a smooth flow. A passage can be organized in several ways: chronologically (a sequence of events or steps in a process), logically (clear reasoning), spatially (describing parts of a machine, for example), cause and effect, comparison and contrast, and so on.
- **Repetition of key phrases:** Ending a paragraph with key word and starting the next paragraph with a sentence that contains the same word or a related word helps to stitch the two paragraphs together.
- **Transition words and phrases:** These include "however," "therefore," "concurrently," "furthermore," "moreover," and "finally." These are the heavy-hitters that writers call into action when they can't find a way to transition more subtly.

Transitions are powerful tools that can do far more than simply connect sentences and paragraphs. Compare the first and second paragraphs of the Obama speech in the earlier section "Taking a big picture look at meaning and flow." The first paragraph consists of two long sentences, naming places in America of historic significance. The phrases "destiny has been decided" and "symbolize the daring" reinforce their significance. These places aren't just important; they stand as icons of American vision, sacrifice, and daring.

That sets up the next paragraph. Note the contrast. After a paragraph of two long and elaborate sentences that carry the weight of history, the next paragraph starts with a sentence of only five words: "Selma is such a place." That brief sentence brings all that historical weight to bear down on one small southern town, Selma. A single word, "such," serves as the transition from the first to the second paragraph. It links all of the heroics and symbolism established in the first paragraph to the subject of that first sentence, Selma.

Now look at the fourth and fifth paragraphs. How is the fifth paragraph linked to the fourth?

(A) long sentences in the fourth paragraph contrast short introductory sentence in the fifth

(B) "them" in the first sentence of the fifth paragraph refers to "heroes" in the last sentence of the fourth paragraph

(C) it reads well

(D) thematically; no link in terms of language

The correct answer is Choice (B). The opening sentence of the fifth paragraph uses the word "them" as a clear link to the word "heroes" in the last sentence of the previous paragraph. Linkages don't have to be connecting words or phrase such as *and, for example,* or *furthermore;* they can be implied by the choice of wording.

Here's an excerpt from later in the same speech:

As we commemorate their achievement, we are well-served to remember that at the time of the marches, many in power condemned rather than praised them. Back then, they were called Communists, or half-breeds, or outside agitators, sexual and moral degenerates, and worse — they were called everything but the name their parents gave them. Their faith was questioned. Their lives were threatened. Their patriotism challenged.

And yet, what could be more American than what happened in this place? What could more profoundly vindicate the idea of America than plain and humble people — unsung, the downtrodden, the dreamers not of high station, not born to wealth or privilege, not of one religious tradition but many, coming together to shape their country's course?

What greater expression of faith in the American experiment than this, what greater form of patriotism is there than the belief that America is not yet finished, that we are strong enough to be self-critical, that each successive generation can look upon our imperfections and decide that it is in our power to remake this nation to more closely align with our highest ideals?

Look at the second and third paragraphs. How are paragraphs two and three in this extract linked?

(A) a transitional phrase

(B) repetition of a key term

(C) no linkage

(D) through a rhetorical question

No transitional phrase is used to link paragraphs two and three, so Choice (A) is incorrect. The two paragraphs are clearly linked, so Choice (C) is wrong. The last paragraph is a rhetorical question, one to which the answer is already known, but that has nothing to do with linkage, so it's not the correct choice. The answer is Choice (B), repetition of a key term. Note that the middle paragraph talks about the idea of the nature of the American people and how they come together to shape the American dream. The first sentence of the next paragraph refers to that American dream with the phrase "the American experiment," thereby linking the two paragraphs.

Here's an example from a newspaper column:

Canada has seen a number of recent outbreaks. There was one in Quebec in 2007, another in Ontario, especially Toronto in 2008. Many outbreaks in the Toronto area are linked to unvaccinated travelers returning from Mexico or Europe, where the risk of exposure is higher. Outbreaks continue in the prairie provinces where vaccination rates are lower. There was a 2010 outbreak in British Columbia, affecting some 82 people. This year, there have been at least seven confirmed cases in Toronto so far.

Nevertheless, outbreaks have been relative small in Canada so far. There is a sort of "herd immunity." Measles is spread by proximity. If 95 percent of the population has been vaccinated, the chances of spreading the infection are significantly reduced. The bulk of the "herd" has been inoculated. However, the rate of immunization has dropped for the last decade. Now measles is making a comeback.

What links these two paragraphs?

(A) a transitional word

(B) no linkage

(C) a rhetorical question

(D) none of the above

In this case, the transitional word "nevertheless" provides a clear transition from the first to the second paragraph. It signals a shift from a discussion of the increasing prevalence of measles to the contrasting fact that Canada has so far seen relatively few and small outbreaks. The correct choice is (A).

Transitions are also used between sentences, sometimes to create a stronger effect, as in the second paragraph: "The bulk of the 'herd' has been inoculated. However, the rate of immunization has dropped for the last decade. Now measles is making a comeback."

The use of the conjunction "however" sets the reader up to expect a contrast. The first sentence establishes that most people have been immunized but the second indicates that fewer people will be inoculated moving forward.

Comparing Two Passages

Some questions on the GED RLA test instruct you to compare two passages and analyze their similarities and differences in respect to a specific characteristic, such as style, purpose, or the ideas or issues they address. In the following sections, we introduce you to the characteristics in written passages you're likely to be asked to compare, offer guidance on making such comparisons, and provide you with example questions, so you can practice those skills.

Analyzing differences in perspective, tone, style, structure, purpose, and impact

Written passages are more than mere content. They often present a perspective on an issue and set a tone that engages the reader emotionally. Passages are structured a certain way to deliver the content effectively and efficiently. Authors adopt a certain writing style to communicate in a certain way, and the passage is always written to serve a specific purpose; for example, to inform, persuade, or entertain. And each passage has a unique impact on the reader.

In the following sections, we explain each of these qualities in greater detail and challenge you to compare their differences in these two passages:

Yesterday — would you believe it? — I heard *Bizet's* masterpiece for the twentieth time. Once more I attended with the same gentle reverence; once again I did not run away. This triumph over my impatience surprises me. How such a work completes one! Through it one almost becomes a "masterpiece" oneself — And, as a matter of fact, each time I heard *Carmen* it seemed to me that I was more of a philosopher, a better philosopher than at other times: I became so forbearing, so happy, so Indian, so *settled*. . . To sit for five hours: the first step to holiness! — May I be allowed to say that Bizet's orchestration is the only one that I can endure now? That other orchestration which is all the rage at present — the Wagnerian — is brutal, artificial and "unsophisticated" withal, hence its appeal to all the three senses of the modern soul at once. How terribly Wagnerian orchestration affects me! I call it the *Sirocco*. A disagreeable sweat breaks out all over me. All my fine weather vanishes.

From *The Case of Wagner, Nietzsche Contra Wagner, and Selected Aphorisms*, by Friedrich Nietzsche

Certain foods and beverages affect your cognitive ability, so avoid highly processed foods and foods high in processed sugars, starch, or fat. These foods tend to make you feel sluggish or result in brief highs followed by prolonged crashes. Lean more towards veggies and foods that are high in protein. When it comes to carbohydrates, opt for complex over simple. Complex carbohydrates are typically in fresh fruits, veggies, and whole grain products. Simple carbohydrates are in candy, soda, anything made with white flour, and most junk foods. And forget those energy drinks that combine huge amounts of caffeine sure to get you to a state of heightened tension.

If you plan on taking an energy drink, or anything else unusual, on the day of the test, here's the best advice I can offer: try it out on a practice test first. If the drink gives you the jitters or upsets your stomach, you won't want to discover this on the day of the test.

From *GRE For Dummies*, by Ron Woldoff with Joe Kraynak (Wiley)

Perspective

Perspective is the author's point of view and it usually comes on one of the following forms:

- ✔ **First person:** The author writes from his or her own perspective, using "I" (or "we," for coauthors) to identify him- or herself.

- ✔ **Second person:** The author addresses the reader directly as "you," as is commonly done in instructional writing.

- ✔ **Third person:** The author describes others as "he," "she," "it," and "they," as is commonly done in stories, novels, and other literary pieces.

The perspectives in the two passages presented in the earlier section "Analyzing differences in perspective, tone, style, structure, purpose, and impact" are vastly different. In the first passage, Nietzsche writes from his own, first-person perspective in describing his experience of listening to the opera *Carmen* by Georges Bizet. In the extract from *GRE For Dummies*, author Woldoff is speaking directly to the reader, in the second person, as an instructor.

We cover differences in purpose later in this section, but as you can see in this example, purpose may influence perspective. Here, Nietzsche's purpose is to express his appreciation for Bizet's music and perhaps convince the reader that Bizet is a better composer than Wagner, so a first-person perspective is ideally suited to his purpose. Likewise, in the second piece, addressing the reader is well suited for the purpose of instructing readers.

Tone

Tone is the writer's attitude toward the topic. The tone in the Nietzsche passage is obviously more passionate than the tone in the Woldoff piece, which is more objective. From the very first sentence of the Nietzsche passage, in which he mentions just having listened to Carmen for the 20th time, you can see that he is very excited. He uses several upbeat words, including "reverence," "triumph," "happy," and "holiness," and ends several sentences with exclamation points. Woldoff's tone is much more subdued.

Style

Style refers to the way something is written rather than to its content, and it can be difficult to pin down. Style involves word choice, sentence variety and complexity, and fluidity or choppiness. In the passages presented earlier, Nietzsche's style is the more complex, containing a blend of brief sentences and phrases along with longer, more complex sentences. The short sentences and phrases convey a sense of excitement, while the longer sentences demonstrate his complexity of thought and reason. Nietzsche's word choice ranges from elevated in the first half of the passage to critical in the second half.

Woldoff exhibits a more muted, informal, and balanced style that is conducive to instructing the reader. Although Woldoff varies his sentence structure and uses concrete language, none of the language is as emotionally charged as in Nietzsche's passage, and you don't find a single exclamation point!

You can't do this during the test, but to become more sensitive to a writer's style, read passages out loud so you can hear the differences. Also try reading different types of publications. For example, an article in *Sports Illustrated* is likely to be written in a very different style than an article in *Vanity Fair* or *U.S. News and World Report*.

Purpose

Purpose has to do with what the writer intends the writing to accomplish; for example, to inform, persuade, or entertain the reader.

What is the primary purpose of Nietzsche's writing?

(A) To describe

(B) To explain

(C) To tell a story

(D) To persuade

Certainly, Nietzsche's passage is descriptive, but because it also contains an emotional element and opinion, Choice (A) isn't your best choice. Likewise, although Nietzsche does explain his reason for preferring Bizet over Wagner, the explanation isn't the purpose of the passage, so you can rule out Choice (B). Except for the first sentence, the passage contains no elements of story-telling or dialogue, so Choice (C) doesn't apply. Nietzsche's writing is persuasive, so Choice (D) is the answer you're after. Nietzsche applauds Bizet and condemns Wagner in an attempt to prove the previous composer's superiority.

What is the purpose of Woldoff's writing?

(A) To describe

(B) To instruct

(C) To persuade

(D) To demonstrate

Woldoff's purpose is clearly to guide (instruct) the reader, so Choice (B) is correct. Woldoff wants the reader to know how to prepare for a test and states that very plainly. The passage contains no emotional words, no phrases to suggest the author's feelings or preferences — only information.

The purpose of a written passage isn't always clear. For example, factual and informational writing can also be persuasive, intended to change readers' minds. Persuasive writing can be entertaining or amusing. When reading a passage on the test, always ask yourself, "What is the main goal the writer is trying to accomplish in this passage?" Answer that question, and you've identified the purpose of the passage.

Structure

Structure is the framework that organizes a written passage. Common structures include the following:

- **Categorical:** Two or more topics are addressed in turn. Such a structure can be useful, for example, to organize a letter to your boss explaining issues in the workplace that you think can be improved.

- **Causal:** A passage may present a cause-and-effect relationship or reverse the organization to describe a certain condition and then analyze possible contributing causes.

- **Chronological or sequential:** Chronological order is ideal for narrating a story or providing step-by-step instructions to perform a task.

- **Comparative:** The comparative structure is used to compare and/or contrast two things. In one of the passages presented earlier in this section, Nietzsche contrasts Bizet's composition against that of Wagner.

- **Evaluative:** Evaluative writing typically states a problem or describes an issue and then presents and evaluates possible solutions or choices, weighing the potential benefits and drawbacks of each.

A passage may blend two or more structural elements. For example, an evaluative essay may include sections that compare and contrast different solutions. When you encounter a structure question on the GED test, read the question closely to identify the section of the passage you're being asked about.

Impact

Impact in writing refers to the effect the writing has on the reader. When you read or listen to Obama's Selma speech, a portion of which is presented earlier in this chapter, you can't help but feel inspired and perhaps even proud. This speech, like other effective political speeches, has a strong emotional impact.

On the GED test, you may encounter one or more questions that challenge you to identify the impact a passage has on the reader. Here's an example:

In what way is Nietzsche's passage likely to affect the reader?

(A) Inspire the reader to listen to Bizet's masterpiece

(B) Inspire the reader to think deeply about music

(C) Make the reader laugh

(D) Make the reader feel proud

Although Nietzsche's passage is probably intended to discourage people from listening to Wagner (due to the title *Nietzsche Contra Wagner*), that's not one of the choices, so Choice (A) is best. You can make a case for Choice (B), but Choice (A) is more specific. Neither Choice (C) nor Choice (D) is supported in the passage.

When writing your Extended Response, consider the impact you want your essay to have on the reader, the person who's scoring you. Here are some techniques for maximizing the impact of your writing:

- **Keep it simple — mostly:** Choose the most precise word so you don't have to use additional words to clarify what you mean.

- **Vary sentence structure:** Alternating shorter and longer sentences and simple and complex sentences adds interest. By varying your sentence structure, you can change the pace and rhythm of your writing to change the way your writing impacts the reader.

- **Write in active voice:** Place your noun before your verb, the actor before the action. For example, write "Linda encouraged her employees to relax on the weekends" rather than "The employees were encouraged by Linda, their supervisor, to relax on weekends." (For more about writing effectively, see Chapter 8.)

- **Avoid "it is" and "there are" constructions:** Start with a descriptive noun rather than a vague pronoun, such as *it* or *there,* and follow up with an action verb rather than a weak verb such as *is* or *are.*

Analyzing passages that present related ideas or themes

The GED RLA test expects you to be able to analyze passages based on similar ideas or themes. Questions that challenge your skills may focus on any of five ways in which two passages may differ: scope, purpose, emphasis, audience, and impact. In the following sections, we describe these qualities of written passages in greater detail as they pertain to the following two passages that present different viewpoints on a similar topic: the benefits of higher education.

Passage One

Earning a post-secondary degree or credential is no longer just a pathway to opportunity for a talented few; rather, it is a prerequisite for the growing jobs of the new economy. Over this decade, employment in jobs requiring education beyond a high school diploma will grow more rapidly than employment in jobs that do not: Of the 30 fastest growing occupations, more than half require postsecondary education. With the average earnings of college graduates at a level that is twice as high as that of workers with only a high school diploma, higher education is now the clearest pathway into the middle class.

In higher education, the U.S. has been outpaced internationally. In 1990, the U.S. ranked first in the world in four-year degree attainment among 25–34 year olds; today, the U.S. ranks 12th. We also suffer from a college attainment gap, as high-school graduates from the wealthiest families in our nation are almost certain to continue on to higher education, while just over half of our high school graduates in the poorest quarter of families attend college. And while more than half of college students graduate within six years, the completion rate for low-income students is around 25 percent.

Acknowledging these factors early in his administration, President Obama challenged every American to commit to at least one year of higher education or post-secondary training. The president has also set a new goal for the country: that by 2020, America would once again have the highest proportion of college graduates in the world.

Source: the White House Support for Higher Ed website (www.whitehouse.gov)

Passage Two

Not everyone needs a postsecondary education. Numerous pathways lead to fulfilling employment and financial success and do not require years of college or university education. Whether through apprenticeships in trades, training through the military, or entrepreneurial initiative, these approaches work. Moreover, people acquire a position without the huge debts incurred in formal postsecondary education.

It is true that unemployment rates decrease with educational attainment. The rate for people with only a high-school diploma is about 25 percent higher than that of people with a completed university degree. After they start working, however, that scenario changes. High-school graduates enter the workforce four years earlier than college graduates. The median income for a high-school graduate is about $35,000, while the university graduate's is $54,000. At a median income difference of about $20,000 a year, it will take the college graduate's total earnings at least seven years to catch up to those of the high-school graduate, based on lost income alone. But then you need to consider the cost of going to college. In 2010–2011, private colleges and universities in the United States cost an average of $36,000 annually (including residence fees), while public institutions cost about $13,000. In the meantime, fees have continued to increase. When you include the cost of education for those four years, it now would take the college graduate from public institutions another two years of employment to catch up to the high-school graduate. If the student went to a private college, it would take an additional seven years.

Scope

Scope refers to the range of information covered in the passage. For example, a passage may cover all the ins and outs of a particular issue or focus on one specific detailed point and examine that in depth. In the two passages presented in this section, the first passage has a broader scope, comparing the United States to other countries around the world in terms of percentage of the student-aged population attaining a four-year college degree. The scope of the second passage is narrower, focusing on the financial benefits and drawbacks of attaining a four-year college degree.

Purpose

The purpose of any written passage is to inform or persuade, but you can break down each of those categories into smaller categories. For example, a persuasive essay may strive to convince or influence the reader's choice, present and defend a certain point of view, recommend a product, advocate or support a certain policy, or justify a course of action. Likewise, an informative piece may set out to describe an object or a place, define a term, review a product or technology, instruct the reader on how to perform a task, or demonstrate how something works.

The purpose of both passages presented in the earlier section "Analyzing passages that present related ideas or themes" is to persuade. The first passage sets out to convince the reader to pursue a post-secondary education, while the second passage tries to persuade the reader to reconsider that option.

Emphasis

Emphasis is the boldface, underlining, italics, and exclamation points of writing. It enables the writer to stress certain points and take the focus off of others. Emphasis in a passage can be in two separate areas. The passage can focus on why one area of interest is more important than another within the scope of the passage. The writer may also use emphatic language, such as words that have an emotional weight or bias, to elicit a response from the readers. Questions on the GED RLA test may ask you to compare the difference in emphasis in two passages, as in the following question:

In what way is the emphasis in the two higher-education passages the same or different?

(A) Both passages stress the importance of a college education.

(B) The first passage places more emphasis on the global importance of having a college degree.

(C) The first passage stresses the importance of education in achieving personal fulfillment.

(D) The second passage emphasizes the costs of pursuing a post-secondary education.

You can rule out Choice (A) because only the first passage stresses the importance of a college education. Choices (B) and (C) are also wrong because the first passage claims nothing about the global importance of a college degree or its role in helping individuals achieve personal fulfillment. Choice (D) is correct because the second passage clearly emphasizes the costs of pursuing a college degree.

Audience

The *audience* consists of whoever is reading the passage. Writers must consider their audiences before they begin writing so they have a clear idea of how to communicate effectively with a given audience. An article trying to convince parents to send their children to college is going to be very different from an article trying to convince high school students to pursue a secondary education. Everything about a written passage is influenced by the intended audience, from the structure of the passage and the content it presents to the word choice and style used to communicate the ideas and information. On the GED RLA test, you may be asked to analyze how audience has likely influenced the differences in two passages. Here's an example:

In what way(s) does/do the audiences in the higher-education passages differ?

(A) The audience for the first passage is broader.

(B) The audience for the second passage is broader.

(C) The audience for the first passage is comprised mostly of high school students.

(D) The audience for the second passage is comprised exclusively of parents.

Choice (A) is the correct answer because the purpose of the White House passage is to convince voters, students, parents, and all other stakeholders of the value of a secondary education in order to gain support for any policies that help achieve the goal of improving the level of education in the workforce. The second passage is directed more at students and parents (the consumers of higher education) who need to weigh the costs and benefits for themselves and who may be less concerned about America's standing in the world or weaknesses in the workforce.

Impact

As explained earlier in this chapter, *impact* refers to the effect the writing has on the reader. In some ways, impact is subjective, but writers have several tools at their disposal to impact the audience in different ways. A writer, for example, may want to make the audience laugh or cry or feel shocked and dismayed.

In the two passages presented in the earlier section "Analyzing passages that present related ideas or themes," the impact on the reader is similar; both cause you to ponder the value of higher education. The impact is more cerebral than emotional, but that still counts.

Chapter 6

Analyzing Arguments and Weighing Evidence

· ·

In This Chapter

▶ Grasping the main idea of a written passage

▶ Analyzing the logic and evidence that support a claim

▶ Spotting assumptions and the underlying premise

▶ Evaluating two arguments side-by-side

· ·

A key skill for getting good marks on the GED RLA test is the ability to analyze arguments. An *argument* states and supports an opinion regarding an issue that has opposing views. Evidence can be used to both support the stated opinion and call opposing viewpoints into question. Questions on the GED RLA test may ask you to identify or summarize the point the author is trying to make, analyze the logic and evidence used to support the author's viewpoint, identify an assumption or premise on which the article is based, or compare a certain aspect of two arguments presented side-by-side. Whatever the question may be, it requires you to read a passage closely, extract key concepts, and identify strengths and weaknesses in the argument. In this chapter, we provide the insight and guidance you need to pick apart arguments along with plenty of practice to hone your skills.

Identifying and Summarizing the Main Idea

The *main idea* of a passage is the central or most important point. In an argument, the main idea is whatever the author of the passage is trying to convince you, the reader, to believe or the action the author wants you to take. To identify the main idea of the passage that presents a certain point of view, take the following steps:

1. **Read the passage from beginning to end.**

2. **Write down the main points stated or implied.**

3. **Write a list of evidence used to support each point.**

4. **Decide which is the main point and which points are used to expand on the main point.**

Your finished product provides a bird's eye view of the passage, which typically reveals the main idea and provides everything you need to summarize the main idea.

Questions on the GED RLA test may not ask you specifically to identify the main idea of a passage. Instead, they may ask what the passage builds up to or ask you to choose the best headline for the passage. Although they don't ask for the main idea of the passage directly, that's exactly what they're after.

Read the following extract from a speech by Barack Obama on March 7, 2015, about the importance of higher education and the Student Aid Bill of Rights:

. . . In an economy increasingly built on innovation, the most important skill you can sell is your knowledge. That's why higher education is, more than ever, the surest ticket to the middle class.

But just when it's never been more important, it's also never been more expensive. The average undergrad who borrows to pay for college ends up graduating with about $28,000 in student loan debt.

That's why my administration has worked hard to make college more affordable. We expanded tax credits and Pell Grants, enacted the largest reform to student loan programs in history, and fought to keep interest rates on student loans low. We've acted to let millions of graduates cap loan payments at 10 percent of their income so they don't have to choose between paying the rent and paying back their debt. I've sent Congress my plan to bring the cost of community college down to zero — because two years of higher education should be as free and universal as high school is today.

But all of us — elected officials, universities, business leaders, everybody — need to do more to bring down college costs. Which is why this week, I unveiled another way that we can help more Americans afford college. It doesn't involve any new spending or bureaucracy. It's a simple declaration of values — what I call a Student Aid Bill of Rights. It says that every student deserves access to a quality, affordable education. Every student should be able to access the resources to pay for college. Every borrower has the right to an affordable repayment plan. And every borrower has the right to quality customer service, reliable information, and fair treatment, even if they struggle to repay their loans.

That's it. Just a few simple principles. But if we all rally around these principles, there's a lot that colleges, lenders, and the people you sent to Washington and to your state legislatures can do to realize them across the country.

So if you believe in a Student Aid Bill of Rights that will help more Americans pay for a quality education, I'm asking you to visit WhiteHouse.gov/CollegeOpportunity. Sign your name to this declaration. Tell your families, and your friends, and fellow students. I'm going to ask Members of Congress, and lenders, and as many business leaders as I can find. Because making sure that students aren't saddled with debt before they even get started in life is in all our interests.

In America, a higher education cannot be a privilege reserved for only the few. It has to be available to everybody who's willing to work for it. . . .

Source: www.whitehouse.gov/the-press-office/2015/03/14/weekly-address-student-aid-bill-rights

If you write down the key points made in this speech, your list should look something like this:

- ✔ The administration has been working hard to make college more affordable.

- ✔ Everybody needs to do more to bring down college costs.

- ✔ You should demonstrate your support for the Student Aid Bill of Rights.

This form of analysis requires you to isolate the points in a text, decide whether they're main points or expand on other points, and then list them accordingly. You can make the case that two other points in the speech are that 1) higher education is the surest ticket to the middle class, and 2) students are graduating with too much debt. However, these are merely statements — assumptions or premises on which the passage is based. For additional details on identifying the assumptions or premises on which a passage is based, see "Rooting Out Assumptions and the Underlying Premise" later in this chapter. Main points typically have more details to support them.

After identifying the key points, write down the details used to support each point:

🗸 The administration has been working hard to make college more affordable:

- expanded tax credits and Pell Grants
- enacted reforms to the student loan programs
- kept interest rates low
- helped students cap loan payments
- sent Congress plans for zero cost community college education

🗸 Everybody needs to do more to bring down college costs:

- Elected officials in federal and state government
- Universities
- Business leaders
- Lenders
- Student Aid Bill of Rights, four principles
    - Every student deserves access to quality, affordable education.
    - Every student should have access to resources to pay for college.
    - Every borrower has a right to an affordable repayment plan.
    - Every borrower has a right to quality customer service from his or her lender.

🗸 You should demonstrate your support for the Student Aid Bill of Rights:

- Go to WhiteHouse.gov/CollegeOpportunity.
- Sign your name.
- Tell others.

The three main points give an overview of what the text argues: The administration worked to make college more affordable; everyone needs to do more; you should demonstrate your support for the principles in the Student Aid Bill of Rights (SABR).

Now you can go back over the information and decide on the main idea of the text.

What does all the information in the text build up to?

(A) Lenders need to treat borrowers fairly.

(B) The cost of higher education is too high.

(C) The Student Aid Bill of Rights (SABR) will help more Americans pay for quality education

(D) Higher education cannot be a privilege

Choices (A) and (B) are both correct, but they're not the key points. Choice (D) is a key point, but the passage argues it only implicitly, not directly. The main thrust of the text is to ask for support for the SABR because of what it will do. That means the best choice is Choice (C), The Student Aid Bill of Rights (SABR) will help more Americans pay for quality education.

Inferring the main idea from details

The main idea isn't always stated explicitly in a passage. Sometimes, you need to infer it from details in the text. To do so, reduce the text to a series of points and then decide where these points lead. That will be the main idea, stated or not.

Read this excerpt from NASA's "Climate change: How do we know?"

The Earth's climate has changed throughout history. Just in the last 650,000 years there have been seven cycles of glacial advance and retreat, with the abrupt end of the last ice age about 7,000 years ago marking the beginning of the modern climate era — and of human civilization. Most of these climate changes are attributed to very small variations in Earth's orbit that change the amount of solar energy our planet receives. The current warming trend is of particular significance because most of it is very likely human-induced and proceeding at a rate that is unprecedented in the past 1,300 years.

Source: `climate.nasa.gov/evidence`

Reduce the passage to a series of points:

- ✔ Climate has changed throughout history.
- ✔ Earth has had seven glacial cycles in 650,000 years.
- ✔ Six of those seven are attributed to orbital variations.
- ✔ Current global warming trend is unique because it's likely human-induced.
- ✔ Current warming is happening at unprecedented rate.

The article builds up to the last two points. The order here is important. The idea that climate change is nothing new is part of the passage, but the flow of ideas moves away from that starting point toward the last two points — the current warming is probably caused by humans and is occurring at an unprecedented rate. The last two then have to be key.

What would be a good headline for this passage?

(A) Climate Change: Nothing New

(B) Rate of Modern Climate Change Unprecedented

(C) Current Climate Change Caused by Humans

(D) New Technology Studies Climate Change

Choice (A) is true but doesn't present the whole story. Choice (B) is supported in the passage. Although the passage mentions that the current warming trend is *probably* caused by human activities, the passage doesn't say that human activity has been proven to be the cause, so you can rule out Choice (C). You can also rule out Choice (D), which may be correct but isn't supported in the passage. The best choice is Choice (B); it's one of the two main points and the only option in the answer choices supported by evidence in the passage.

Drawing generalizations and hypotheses from the evidence

A *generalization* is a broad conclusion drawn from evidence presented. A conclusion based on limited or unsupported evidence is called a *hypothesis*, which is essentially an educated guess. The GED RLA test expects you to be able to extract information from passages and turn that information into a general statement. The good news is that the test provides you with a passage that contains all of the information you need to draw your conclusion and formulate a fitting generalization or hypothesis. To answer such a question, read the passage closely and jot down the main ideas. One of the main ideas should guide you to the correct answer choice. Here's an example from the Environmental Protection Agency's "Emergency Disinfection of Drinking Water:"

1. Use bottled water that has not been exposed to flood waters if it is available.

2. If you don't have bottled water, you should boil water to make it safe. Boiling water will kill most types of disease-causing organisms that may be present. If the water is cloudy, filter it through clean cloths or allow it to settle, and draw off the clear water for boiling. Boil the water for one minute, let it cool, and store it in clean containers with covers.

3. If you can't boil water, you can disinfect it using household bleach. Bleach will kill some, but not all, types of disease-causing organisms that may be in the water. If the water is cloudy, filter it through clean cloths or allow it to settle, and draw off the clear water for disinfection. Add ⅛ teaspoon (or 8 drops) of regular, unscented, liquid household bleach for each gallon of water, stir it well and let it stand for 30 minutes before you use it. Store disinfected water in clean containers with covers.

4. If you have a well that has been flooded, the water should be tested and disinfected after flood waters recede. If you suspect that your well may be contaminated, contact your local or state health department or agriculture extension agent for specific advice.

Source: water.epa.gov/drink/emerprep/emergencydisinfection.cfm

Review this passage and list the key points:

1. _____
2. _____
3. _____
4. _____
5. _____

The idea of making generalizations from evidence is more than simply making one or two statements that sum up the information presented. The passage is about making water safe to drink, but what is the aim of all that information? What one phrase would summarize the purpose of all these basic points? Try answering the following question:

Which of the following statements most accurately summarizes this passage?

(A) Water must always be purified to make it suitable for drinking.

(B) In an emergency, tap water is not safe to drink.

(C) There are various ways to obtain safe drinking water when tap water is contaminated.

(D) You can make contaminated water safe by boiling it or adding bleach.

The first generalization to draw from all this information is that untreated water isn't safe to drink. The second generalization is that contaminated water can be made safe, or at least safer, to drink. Choice (C) is the only choice that is both supported in the passage and broad enough to summarize the entire passage. Choice (A) isn't supported in the passage because the passage discusses drinking water safety only in the context of an emergency, not "always." Choice (B) is implied in the passage and serves more as an assumption on which the passage is based. Although Choice (D) is true and supported in the passage, it doesn't accommodate the fact that bottled water is also an option. Choice (C) is the best answer.

Have a look at this passage from *An Unsinkable Titanic* by John Bernard Walker (CreateSpace Independent Publishing Platform):

. . . she [the Titanic] was supposed to be the "last word" in first-class steamship construction, the culmination of three-quarters of a century of experience in building safe and stanch vessels. In the official descriptions of the ship, widely distributed at the time of her launching, the safety elements of her construction were freely dwelt upon. This literature rang the changes on stout bulkheads, watertight compartments, automatic, self-closing bulkhead doors, etc., — and honestly so. There is every reason to believe that the celebrated firm who built the ship, renowned the world over for the high character of their work; the powerful company whose flag she carried; aye, and even her talented designer, who was the first to pronounce the Titanic a doomed vessel and went down with the ship, were united in the belief that the size of the Titanic and her construction were such that she was unsinkable by any of the ordinary accidents to which the transatlantic liner is liable.

Source: www.gutenberg.org/files/46219/46219-h/46219-h.htm

Which of the following conclusions can you most reasonably draw from the evidence presented in this passage?

(A) People had good reason to believe that the Titanic was unsinkable.

(B) People were misled to believe that the Titanic was unsinkable.

(C) The person who designed the ship was wrong.

(D) The Titanic was a well-built sea vessel.

To answer this question, first jot down the evidence presented in the passage:

1. _____

2. _____

3. _____

4. _____

5. _____

Use your evidence list to test the answer choices. Based on the evidence, which is the most valid conclusion you can draw from the passage?

The evidence presented backs up the idea that *confidence* in the unsinkability of the Titanic was perfectly justified. Remember, the hypothesis is based on the evidence; history proved that the Titanic wasn't safe, not unsinkable. However, based on this passage, people had good reasons for their confidence in the Titanic. Choice (A) is best. Nothing in the passage supports the notion that reports at the time were intended to mislead people about the Titanic's safety, so rule out Choice (B). Although the designer of the ship may have made mistakes, nothing in the passages supports this theory, so Choice (C) is wrong. You can also rule out Choice (D), because even though the Titanic may have been a well-built sea vessel, that's not the main point of the passage; the main point has more to do with people's confidence in it.

Digging into the Details

Whether an RLA test reading passage tells a story, describes a scene, provides instructions, or presents a certain point of view, it contains details or evidence that you may be asked to summarize or analyze. To answer such questions correctly, you must be able to read closely and with a critical eye on the details. A close look at the details may reveal how effective the passage is at conveying an idea or expressing or supporting a particular point of view.

In this section, we offer guidance to help you read more closely and spot strengths and weaknesses in reading passages.

Summarizing details

Regardless of what type of reading passage you encounter, you're often required to summarize details to identify the correct answer. Two approaches work well:

- Write a list of details presented and then write one sentence that describes them all.

- Draw a picture with the main point in the middle surrounded by the details that support it. Figure 6-1 shows a diagram of the main idea and supporting details for the Titanic passage presented in the earlier section "Drawing generalizations and hypotheses from the evidence."

Figure 6-1:
Draw a diagram of the main idea with supporting details.

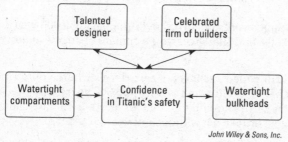

John Wiley & Sons, Inc.

If you're a visual learner, opt for the diagram over the numbered list. Although both approaches can be considered visual, the diagram is more effective at producing a mental image.

Following the train of thought

When writers present an opinion or argument regarding an issue, they typically do so in steps or by introducing one or more main points. Questions on the GED require an ability to read and follow an argument from beginning to end and identify the steps in that argument. To identify the correct response to train of thought questions, jot down the progression of ideas in the passage. You may want to number the steps or use a ladder diagram or flowchart to trace the progression of the argument.

Look again at the NASA passage on climate change presented earlier in this chapter:

The Earth's climate has changed throughout history. Just in the last 650,000 years there have been seven cycles of glacial advance and retreat, with the abrupt end of the last ice age about 7,000 years ago marking the beginning of the modern climate era — and of human civilization. Most of these climate changes are attributed to very small variations in Earth's orbit that change the amount of solar energy our planet receives. The current warming trend is of particular significance because most of it is very likely human-induced and proceeding at a rate that is unprecedented in the past 1,300 years.

Which of the following statements does not follow logically from the argument presented in the passage?

(A) The Earth's climate has changed throughout history.

(B) The current climate trend is of particular significance.

(C) The current climate trend is likely human-induced.

(D) None of the above.

To answer this question, draw a flowchart like the one shown in Figure 6-2.

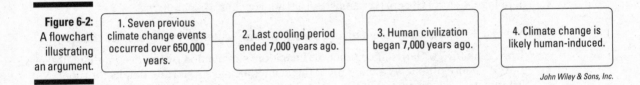

Figure 6-2: A flowchart illustrating an argument.

1. Seven previous climate change events occurred over 650,000 years.

2. Last cooling period ended 7,000 years ago.

3. Human civilization began 7,000 years ago.

4. Climate change is likely human-induced.

John Wiley & Sons, Inc.

When you map the argument and do a little math, the author's train of thought becomes clearer; however, you still need to do some work as a reader to make the connection:

✔ Seven previous climate change events occurred over the past 650,000 years. Round the number of years up to 700,000, and that gives you a climate change event every 100,000 years or so.

✔ The last climate change event ended 7,000 years ago. Here's where your critical thinking comes in. If a climate change event occurs every 100,000 years, and the last event ended 7,000 years ago, then Earth shouldn't be due for another climate change event for another 93,000 years, give or take a few thousand years.

✔ Human civilization started about 7,000 years ago, coinciding with the "abrupt end" of the previous global cooling event and the start of the current global warming period. This line of reasoning leads logically to the conclusion that the current climate trend is likely to be caused by human activity. Of course, "likely" doesn't mean that current global warming is caused by human activity, only that the possibility exists.

So the correct answer to the question is Choice (D), none of the above. Choice (A) follows logically from the argument, because the argument states that climate change events have occurred over the past 650,000 years. Choice (B) is also logical because the passage points out two reasons why the current trend is of particular significance: 1) It's likely to be human induced, and 2) The warming is occurring more rapidly than during past events. You already determined by mapping the argument that Choice (C) follows logically from the argument.

Distinguishing between supported and unsupported claims

Assessing the validity of evidence is a critical skill on the RLA test. Newspapers, speeches, and other media constantly bombard people with information and opinions. To formulate a thoughtful opinion on any issue, you must be able to distinguish between supported and unsupported claims. Evidence needs to be more than just a list of statements — it must be clear, detailed, and proven.

You're likely to encounter questions on the RLA test that challenge your ability to distinguish the difference between supported and unsupported claims. To do so, write down a list of claims made in the passage. Below or next to each claim, write down the evidence given to support it; write "No evidence" if none is provided.

The following passage contains a mixture of supported and unsupported claims:

The union movement has outlived its usefulness. It is based on a model of confrontation suitable for the 19th century but no longer needed in the 21st. The movement assumes that all employers are determined and able to increase their profits at the expense of workers. Whether they are keeping wages low or stripping workers of benefits, the employers are out to get the workers.

However, today labor laws provide protection against corporate excesses. Minimum wage standards, pensions, health insurance managed by the government, and laws governing safety in the workplace are all in place to protect workers. Laws against discrimination and legal procedures for firing workers restrict an employer's ability to terminate employment unjustly. Laws are even in place to protect workers who file complaints with government agencies against employers.

With all these protections, unionization does little for workers other than add to the workers' expenses as they support a bloated union bureaucracy.

Which of the following claims has the most support in this passage?

(A) The union movement is based on an outdated model.

(B) Current labor laws protect workers.

(C) Unions do little for workers other than take their money.

(D) Laws protect workers who file complaints against their employers.

To answer this question, write down the list of claims presented in this passage. Your job is half done here, because the answer choices present the claims you need to evaluate:

Claim	*Support*
The union movement is based on an outdated model.	_____
Current labor laws protect workers.	_____
Unions do little for workers other than take their money.	_____
Laws protect workers who file complaints against their employers.	_____

After reviewing the support for each claim, you should be able to easily narrow down your options to Choices (A) and (B). Choice (C) is an unsupported claim. Choice (D) is evidence to support the claim that current labor laws protect workers. Comparing Choices (A) and (B), you should see that more evidence is presented to support the claim that current labor laws protect workers. Choice (B) is the best answer.

While you're at it, give yourself some additional practice in analyzing the progression of this argument. The passage opens with the author's thesis: Unions are no longer needed. The author explains that the union movement is based on a premise that was true in the past but is no longer true.

Note that the wording "out to get the workers" is clearly *loaded*. It aims to elicit an emotional response rather than convey a reasoned argument, and it reveals the author's bias against this attitude in those that support modern-day unions.

The second paragraph is accurate. This information is presented in a newspaper style, without bias. Readers can argue whether these government requirements are sufficient, but they do exist. Union members would perhaps add that unions provide protection above what the government agencies provide. The statement that there are minimum wage laws doesn't address the issue of whether those wages are suitable or adequate, or that unions work to improve wages above the minimum standards set by government.

The final paragraph restates the thesis. However, the last sentence in that paragraph again uses loaded words to denigrate unions — "bloated union bureaucracy" — and phrasing to suggest that workers receive nothing in exchange for the union dues they pay. This biased language may win points with less careful readers, but for sophisticated readers like you, they actually weaken the argument.

Spotting valid and invalid reasoning

On the RLA test, some questions test your ability to identify valid and invalid reasoning. In order for reasoning to be valid, it must lead logically from the premise to the conclusion. Common types of invalid reasoning include the following:

- **Overgeneralization:** An *overgeneralization* draws a broad conclusion from a limited amount of evidence; for example, "Global warming can't possibly be caused by humans, because over the past 650,000 years, long before humans started burning fossil fuels, the earth has experienced seven periods of global warming and cooling."

- **Illogical conclusion:** Correlation doesn't prove causation. In other words, a conclusion that doesn't necessarily follow based on the evidence provided is illogical. For example, consider the statement "Since standardized testing became widely used in schools to evaluate academic achievement, classroom performance has declined." Just because classroom performance started to decline at the same time standardized testing was implemented doesn't necessarily prove that standardized testing caused the decline.

- **Personal bias:** Personal bias results when a writer bases conclusions on opinion rather than on evidence. For example, "I'm noticing more and more SUVs on the road than ever before. It seems as though people have given up on the idea of conserving energy and reducing pollution." This particular bias is called *selection bias*. The writer may have noticed more SUVs on the road because, whether she realizes it or not, she may have become more conscious of them for some reason, perhaps looking for proof to support her belief.

Valid reasoning draws conclusions based on fact. On the test, you may need to spend a few moments thinking about an argument and the evidence used to support it to figure out whether the argument is logical.

To identify faulty reasoning, look for the following common signs:

- A claim made with few or no facts to support it

- A broad conclusion based on too few examples

- Correlated events in which the cause-and-effect relationship is claimed but not proven

- Statements presented as truths with little or no clear evidence to support them as facts

- A statement of opinion presented as a fact

- Words such as *all*, *every*, *none*, and *nobody*, which commonly indicate an overgeneralization

Use an Euler (pronounced "oiler") diagram to test the validity of any *deductive argument* (a line of reasoning that leads from premise(s) to a conclusion); for example: "Dogs have four legs. My cat has four legs. Therefore, my cat is a dog." Obviously, the two premises are correct: Dogs have four legs, and my cat has four legs. Just as obviously, the conclusion is wrong, but why? Use an Euler diagram to find out. Here's how:

1. **Write down all premises on which the argument is based.**

2. **Diagram the premises, using circles to illustrate the groups defined in the premises and/or assumptions of the argument.**

   See Figure 6-3 for examples.

3. **If a conclusion is being drawn about an individual in one or both groups, draw an X to mark in which group(s) the individual belongs.**

4. **Compare your Euler diagram to the conclusion.**

   The Euler diagram for the dog and cat argument presented earlier looks like the Euler diagram in upper left of Figure 6-3. The diagram shows that although both dogs and cats fit into the same group of Animals with Four Legs, my cat is clearly not a dog.

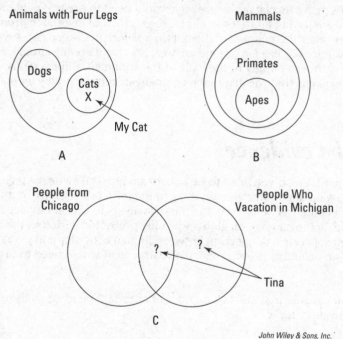

Figure 6-3:
Euler
diagrams.

John Wiley & Sons, Inc.

The Euler diagram in the upper right of Figure 6-3 proves the following argument: "All primates are mammals. An ape is a primate. Therefore, all apes are mammals."

The Euler diagram at the bottom of Figure 6-3 disproves this argument: "Some people from Chicago vacation in Michigan. Tina vacations in Michigan, so she must be from Chicago." In this case, Tina may or may not be from Chicago, so "must be" makes the conclusion wrong.

Euler diagrams are useful only for arguments that take the form of "All Xs have a specific feature. My Y has that feature. Therefore, my Y is an X.

Practice spotting faulty reasoning by looking for it in the following passage:

The Affordable Care Act should be repealed on the grounds that it's not affordable. Soon after passage of the act, my catastrophic healthcare policy that I was paying $247 a month for was canceled. My insurance company informed me that my policy did not comply with Affordable Care Act regulations. The company offered to upgrade my plan to an affordable option that would cost me $479 a month.

Which of the following statements most accurately assesses the validity of the logic in this argument?

(A) The argument provides sufficient evidence to prove its claim.

(B) The argument fails to define "affordable healthcare."

(C) The argument is based on an overgeneralization.

(D) The argument incorrectly ties the rise in premium to the passage of the Affordable Care Act.

The correct answer is Choice (C). The writer concludes that the Affordable Care Act has made healthcare unaffordable based on a single incident in which his insurance company raised his premium. To prove its claim, the passage would need to present evidence showing that most people were paying more for healthcare, as a total of insurance premiums and out-of-pocket expenses, after the passage of the bill than before it. Choice (A) is wrong; this argument isn't solid. Choice (B) is a fairly good answer; arguments really should define key terms, but this guideline doesn't apply to the logic of the argument. Choice (D) is wrong because the passage explains that the insurance company linked the policy increase to the Affordable Care Act.

Analyzing the evidence

To perform well on the RLA test, you need to be able to analyze the evidence presented to support an argument. A passage can claim anything in the form of a premise, but unless that premise is generally accepted as being true, the passage needs to present evidence that proves it. For example, in the passage on global warming presented earlier in the chapter, the evidence provided suggests a connection between human activities and global warming. However, it provides no definitive proof; a conclusive argument would need to present additional evidence.

Evidence is simply information that meets a number of criteria. You must analyze the evidence, using the following criteria:

- ✔ Relevance to the point being argued
- ✔ Sufficiency to prove the stated claim
- ✔ Consideration of evidence that may prove the contrary

The following sections address each of these criteria in turn.

Is the evidence relevant?

For evidence to count as proof, it must be relevant to the claim. Writers may use irrelevant evidence intentionally (to mislead the audience) or unintentionally (in the case of poorly written passages). Either way, irrelevant evidence doesn't count. Here's a passage that contains both relevant and irrelevant evidence:

We should really do away with daylight saving time (DST). It was started by the Kaiser during WWI as a wartime energy savings measure. The idea was adopted by many countries around the world. Today, it hardly matters. Though giving us an hour more daylight in the evenings is nice, lighting is not the largest component of energy use. We continue to use air conditioning, cook meals, and drive regardless of DST. Factories and offices continue to operate. Large malls and small stores operate with artificial light all the time. Few rely on daylight for illumination. DST saves very little energy. And DST has some downsides. Many people have a hard time adjusting to the time change. For the first week after the time change, accidents of all kinds, especially traffic accidents, increase.

A good way to analyze the evidence is to make a two-column list or table (perhaps similar to Table 6-1) with claims/evidence on the left and relevance of those claims and evidence used to support the argument on the right. Take a few minutes to complete the table below:

Table 6-1	Argument: DST Should Be Abolished	
Point	*Claim/Evidence*	*Relevance*
1		
2		
3		
4		
5		
6		
7		

Table 6-2 shows an example of a completed version.

Table 6-2	Argument: DST Should Be Abolished	
Point	*Claim/Evidence*	*Relevance*
1	Started by Kaiser	Irrelevant
2	WWI energy saving measure	May or may not be partially relevant
3	Lighting no longer large component of energy use	Valid consideration
4	Other energy uses unaffected by DST	Valid consideration
5	Businesses don't depend on daylight	Valid consideration
6	Shops use artificial illumination	Valid but subset of point 5
7	Increase in accidents	Valid if verifiable

The list also shows an additional fact: Points 5 and 6 are really the same point. Businesses in general don't depend on daylight for illumination.

That is the summary of the evidence, most of it verifiable from the readers' own knowledge or verifiable outside sources.

Is the evidence sufficient?

To be convincing, evidence must be necessary and sufficient:

- ✔ Necessary in terms of being relevant and essential to prove the claim
- ✔ Sufficient in terms of being enough to convince a reasonable person that the claim is true or valid

What constitutes "sufficient evidence"? Whether evidence is sufficient to prove a point is somewhat subjective. The argument presented in the previous section in favor of abolishing daylight saving time is certainly sufficient for supporting the author's opinion. However, additional evidence may be required to convince readers who have a strong reason to support DST.

Here's a sample question that tests your ability to determine whether the evidence is sufficient for convincing the reader of the need to abolish DST:

Which of the following statements, if true, would be most likely to undermine the argument presented in the passage?

(A) Daylight saving time extends darkness in the morning hours, making it unsafe for children heading off to school.

(B) Most crimes occur at night, under the cloak of darkness.

(C) Daylight saving time increases revenue for the outdoor sports and recreation industries.

(D) People get confused the two times a year they need to reset their clocks.

To answer this question, you can immediately rule out answer Choice (A), because it supports the argument for abolishing DST. Choice (B) may be true, but without additional details, it's not very relevant; DST doesn't change the total number of hours of lightness and darkness. The last two choices both have merit, but Choice (D) is unlikely to be sufficient to convince most people. Choice (C) is the better choice.

What evidence was ignored?

When presenting an argument, the evidence omitted can be as important as the evidence presented. For example, scientists have presented much evidence supporting the climate change hypothesis. Over the last century, ocean temperatures have risen, summer temperatures worldwide have risen, and the Arctic and Antarctic icecaps have shrunk. More extreme weather events, from strong storms to periods of unseasonal cold, have also occurred. All this evidence supports the climate change hypothesis. However, the extreme cold winters recently in some locations has caused doubt. Excluding that fact would certainly raise questions in a reader's mind. Ideally, such evidence would be included and refuted in order to overcome potential objections in the reader's mind.

Here's an example:

A few progressive states, including Colorado and Washington, have legalized the recreational use of marijuana. Legalizing marijuana makes a lot of sense. It increases state revenue while reducing law enforcement and court costs related to enforcing marijuana laws. As legitimate businesses start producing and selling marijuana, less money flows to drug cartels and other crime organizations. In addition, regulations provide for a safer, more uniform product, keeping more dangerous forms of marijuana off the streets and providing easier access for people who use marijuana for medicinal purposes.

Yes, marijuana has proven to be addictive, but it's not nearly as addictive as alcohol, heroin, cocaine, or even nicotine cigarettes. Although it does alter perception and leads to increases in vehicle accidents, this particular issue can be addressed, as it is in the case of alcohol, without making marijuana illegal. Some addiction specialists argue that marijuana is a common gateway drug that leads to the use of more serious substances, including cocaine, heroin, and prescription medications, but in some studies, the results are inconclusive. I see absolutely no other reason any intelligent person could possibly think that marijuana should be illegal.

Which of the following is a possible objection to the argument presented in the passage that isn't addressed in the passage?

(A) Marijuana is the most prevalent illegal drug found in impaired drivers.

(B) Ten percent of marijuana users develop a marijuana dependency.

(C) Marijuana users are 2.5 times more likely to abuse prescription medications.

(D) Marijuana use restricts blood flow to the brain and continues to do so for up to seven months of abstinence.

Choices (A), (B), and (C) are all addressed to some degree in the passage, but the passage never mentions any possible health effects on the human body, as presented in Choice (D); therefore, Choice (D) is the only correct answer.

Analyze data, graphs, and pictures used as evidence

The RLA test expects you to be able to extract and analyze information from data, graphs, and pictures. This analysis involves making deductions or inferences from these sources. (A *deduction* is a logical conclusion that follows from a given set of data. An *inference* is a generalization that describes a set of data.) Numerical data is often presented in a table, as shown in Figure 6-4, followed by a question that challenges your ability to extract or interpret data presented in the table.

Figure 6-4: Data to be analyzed presented in a table.

Table 1. Projections of the Population and Components of Change for the United States: 2015 to 2060							
(Resident population as of July 1. Numbers in thousands)							
Year	Population	Numeric Change	Percent Change	Natural Increase	Vital Events		Net International Migration[1]
					Births	Deaths	
2015	321,369	2,621	0.82	1,380	3,999	2,619	1,241
2016	323,996	2,627	0.82	1,377	4,027	2,650	1,250
2017	326,626	2,630	0.81	1,374	4,055	2,681	1,256
2018	329,256	2,631	0.81	1,369	4,080	2,712	1,262
2019	331,884	2,628	0.80	1,361	4,104	2,743	1,267
2020	334,503	2,619	0.79	1,349	4,125	2,777	1,271
2021	337,109	2,606	0.78	1,331	4,142	2,811	1,275
2022	339,698	2,589	0.77	1,307	4,155	2,848	1,282
2023	342,267	2,569	0.76	1,279	4,165	2,887	1,291
2024	344,814	2,547	0.74	1,246	4,174	2,927	1,301
2025	347,335	2,521	0.73	1,210	4,181	2,971	1,310

John Wiley & Sons, Inc. (Info used in table from U.S. Census Bureau, Population Projections, 2014, table 1.)

What is the projected population of the United States for 2020?

(A) 334,503

(B) 334,503,000

(C) 337,109

(D) 337,698,000

Reading the table isn't as easy as it first appears. Choice (A) is tempting. If you go to the Year column and find 2020 and then follow it across to the number in the Population column, you get 334,503. Unfortunately, the fine print near the top of the table indicates that the population numbers, including Natural Increase, Vital Events, and Net International Migration, represent thousands, so 334,503 actually represents 334,503,000, which is answer Choice (B), the correct answer. Choices (C) and (D) are also wrong; the data has been selected from the wrong line or missed a significant detail.

How does the source of population growth change between 2015 and 2025?

(A) The number of deaths declines.

(B) Net international migration is a larger source than natural increase.

(C) Natural increase declines.

(D) Births are the largest single source of population growth.

The table projects that the population of the U.S. will increase between 2015 and 2025. Two elements that make up population growth: natural increase and net international migration. *Natural increase* is the population increase that comes as a result of the existing population producing more births than deaths. If you subtract births from deaths in any given year, you see that the result is the number in the natural increase column. The table shows deaths increasing, so Choice (A) is wrong. It's also wrong because it doesn't answer the question; if deaths increase, they can't possibly be a source of population *growth*. Choice (C) is true, but again, because natural increase declines, it can't be a source of population *growth*. Choice (D) is wrong because births aren't the same as natural increase. Births contribute to population growth only to the degree in which they exceed deaths and result in a natural increase. The correct answer is Choice (B): Natural increase (net births minus deaths) is declining while net international migration is increasing.

Information is also presented visually, in the form of graphs, as shown in Figure 6-5. Graphs allow the reader to see trends more easily than when data is presented numerically, especially when comparing several items.

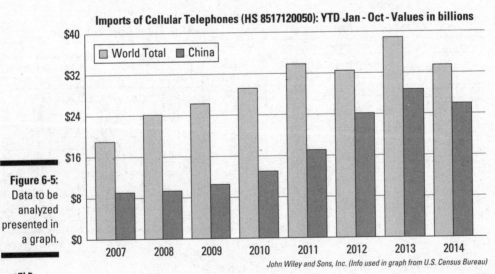

Figure 6-5: Data to be analyzed presented in a graph.

John Wiley and Sons, Inc. (Info used in graph from U.S. Census Bureau)

How has the number of phones imported from China changed in the years 2007 to 2014?

(A) increased

(B) decreased

(C) no change

(D) cannot be determined

The graph shows several trends. The first is that imports of cellular phones climbed steadily from 2007 to 2011, declined slightly in 2012, rose again in 2013, and dropped in 2014. It shows a steady increase in imports from China from 2007 to 2013 and then a slight decline in 2014. Determining China's proportion of the trade requires more interpretation. In the year 2008, imports of cellular telephones amounted to about $24 billion. Of that, about $9 billion was from China. China's proportion of the imports was $9/24$, or 37.5 percent of the total. By 2014, the total imports amounted to about $34 billion. China was the source of about $26 billion of that total. China's proportion of the trade was $26/34$, or 76.5 percent of the total. A few more calculations would better reflect the changes over time, but even this limited view shows a trend, making Choice (D) incorrect. The correct answer is Choice (A). China's proportion of the trade hasn't declined, so Choice (B) is wrong. A change has occurred, so Choice (C) doesn't work.

The GED test may also present illustrations or photographs that convey information and challenge you to extract that information from the graphic. A picture is worth a thousand words. That may not literally be true, but pictures certainly add to informational text by providing a great deal of information that can be used as evidence to support arguments.

The photographs shown in Figure 6-6 are of the Elephant Butte Reservoir in New Mexico. The image on the left is from June 2, 1994, and the image on the right is from July 8, 2013. The dark area is the lake. The color of the water also is an indicator of the depth; the darker the color, the deeper the water.

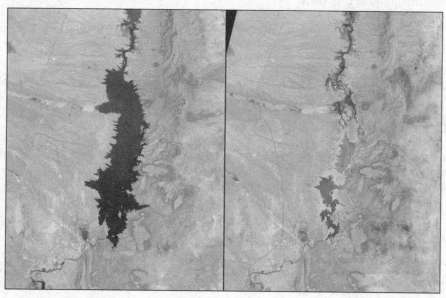

Figure 6-6:
The GED test challenges you to obtain information from images.

Images courtesy of NASA Earth Observatory

What conclusion does this set of images support?

(A) Satellite images provide excellent overviews of landscape.

(B) Relying on reservoirs for water is a bad idea.

(C) The reservoir has failed.

(D) Local agriculture that depends on irrigation is at risk.

The image clearly shows the reduction in the size of the reservoir. Choice (A) is correct but misses the key point. You could certainly conclude Choice (B) is correct, based on the photograph, but it isn't the best choice because it overgeneralizes, drawing a broad conclusion from a single instance. Choice (C) is possible, but nothing in the photos supports it; nothing suggests that the structures creating this reservoir failed. The best answer is an *extrapolation,* a deduction based on the size of the reservoir. Farmers who depend on this reservoir for irrigation water are in trouble, and Choice (D) is the answer you're after.

Rooting Out Premises and Assumptions

Arguments contain one or more premises on which the argument is based, and you need to be able to tell the difference between the two:

- ✔ A *premise* is a statement, presumed to be true, on which an argument is based. For example, "Freedom of speech is the most essential of all freedoms" establishes the writer's belief. For the argument to be convincing, the reader would need to accept this statement as true as well.

- ✔ An *assumption* is an unstated premise. For example, in the statement, "We have a global imperative to reverse global warming," the assumption is that global warming is harmful in some way, even though that premise isn't stated explicitly.

Whenever you're called on to analyze an argument or present an opposing viewpoint, look for the premise or assumption on which the argument is based. One very common and effective way to challenge an argument is to question the premise or assumption or, better yet, prove it to be wrong. It's the foundation of the argument. Take out the foundation, and the entire building crumbles.

In the following sections, we provide additional guidance and practice in identifying the premise(s) or assumption(s) on which an argument is based.

Finding the premise on which the argument is based

Finding a premise in an argument is easier than finding an assumption, because a premise is a statement included in the argument. It's even easier to locate if it's preceded by one of the following conditional words or phrases:

- ✔ because
- ✔ due to
- ✔ for
- ✔ given that
- ✔ in that
- ✔ on the basis of
- ✔ owning to
- ✔ since

For example, "Due to the likelihood of attracting biased jurors, the judge should move the trial to another county." The premise here is that by having the trial in this county, the court is likely to end up with jury members who are biased in favor of or against the person on trial. The conclusion — that the judge should move the trial to a different county — depends on how true the premise is.

Try your hand at identifying the premise in the following example:

Healthcare costs are out of control because doctors make too much money. According to an article in Forbes magazine, 21.5 percent of physicians in the United States are in the top 1 percent of income earners. In addition, the average physician in the United States earns $250,000 a year, while the average physician in the United Kingdom earns $114,000 annually.

Which of the following statements, if true, would work toward disproving the premise of this argument?

(A) Out of pocket expenses for people who enroll in Medicaid under the Affordable Care Act have dropped from $1,463 to $34 per year.

(B) Physicians in the Netherlands earn on average $286,000 annually.

(C) The Centers for Disease Control (CDC) estimates that 75 cents of every dollar spent on healthcare in the U.S. goes toward treating largely preventable chronic illnesses.

(D) In the healthcare system, doctors are paid for doing more rather than having their compensation tied to how effective they are in treating patients.

Don't feel bad if you picked Choice (B), (C), or (D), which are all wrong. This is kind of a trick question. Remember, the premise is stated but *presumed* to be true. The premise in this passage is that healthcare costs are out of control, not that doctors make too much money. If the fact that doctors make too much money were presumed to be true, the writer would not have given evidence to try to support that conclusion. Correct answer: Choice (A), the only evidence that challenges the premise that healthcare costs are out of control.

Identifying assumptions

Spotting assumptions is a little more difficult than spotting premises because you're asked to see what's *not* there, what's *not* stated. To find the hidden assumption, look between the conclusion and the evidence used to support the conclusion. The assumption usually requires the reader to make a leap from evidence to conclusion without providing any rational link between the two. Consider the following argument:

She was a wonderful teacher. All of her students received As and Bs.

What is the underlying assumption?

(A) Students who receive high grades have effective teachers.

(B) Great teachers give great marks.

(C) Students learn better from great teachers.

(D) Student grades are an accurate indicator of a teacher's effectiveness.

Look for an "if–then" statement implicit in this sentence. The underlying assumption is that a connection exists between the teacher's status as wonderful and all students' receiving great marks. If the students received great marks, then the teacher is wonderful. Choice (A) is incorrect because although the passage implies a connection that a wonderful teacher improves student performance, it doesn't imply that students can't achieve high grades without an effective teacher. Choices (B) and (C) are general statements that may or not be correct, but they don't relate to this specific example. Choice (D) is correct because the passage assumes that high student grades reflect a teacher's performance. The only reason the teacher is wonderful is because she gave everyone great marks.

Here's another example:

Real men don't eat quiche, but Robert loves quiche and eats it at every opportunity.

What is the assumption in this sentence?

(A) Robert eats too much quiche.

(B) Quiche makes men.

(C) Quiche does not make real men.

(D) Robert is not a real man.

You can rephrase this info as an "if–then" statement. If Robert doesn't eat quiche, he is a real man, or if Robert eats quiche, he isn't a real man. Because Robert loves quiche, he isn't a real man (according to the example; we have nothing against quiche). Choice (D) is the correct answer. Choice (A) is irrelevant, and you can discard it. Choices (B) and (C) get no support from the text. Of course, if you were asked to provide an opposing view, your option would be to attack the premise. What's the premise? The premise is "Real men don't eat quiche."

Try your hand at one more sample question:

Many social workers and community groups have been urging employers in the service sector to increase the minimum wage to $15 an hour. The struggle has been largely unsuccessful. The only solution may be new government-enforced minimum wage laws.

Identify the underlying assumption.

(A) Only legislation will improve minimum wages.

(B) Community groups are largely ineffective.

(C) Service sector workers need unions.

(D) Employers have no desire to raise minimum wages.

This example is more complicated. The basis of this passage is that wages need to improve and laws may be the only solution. Community groups had no effect and laws may be required because why? That "why" is your underlying assumption. It comes in two possible variations: Employers have no desire to raise minimum wages, or employers have to be forced to raise minimum wages. The only option stated in the answer choices is "Employers have no desire to raise minimum wages," Choice (D) is the correct answer. You can ignore Choice (C) because no basis for that argument exists in the passage.

Comparing Two Arguments

When you're taking the RLA test, you can count on having at least one question that challenges you to compare two arguments, especially in the Extended Response portion of the test. The passages may use evidence in different ways, interpret the same evidence differently, or draw very different conclusions on the same issue. Specifically, questions that challenge you to compare two arguments expect you to be able to analyze the arguments in the following four ways:

 ✔ Analyze differences in interpretation and use of evidence

 ✔ Synthesize two arguments to formulate a third approach

✔ Draw new conclusions based on evidence provided in both arguments

✔ Take what you know from the two arguments and apply it to other situations

In the following sections, we introduce each skill and give you the opportunity to hone your skills through practice.

Analyzing differences in interpretation and use of evidence

Evidence is more than just a series of facts. It must be interpreted and linked to the claims in a passage. Authors often interpret the same evidence in different ways. For example, scientists often study identical twins to find out why they may have differing IQs as they grow up. Some argue that social factors in their development influence intellectual development. Others argue that cell mutation in life accounts for a large part of the difference. Read about a historical event in a book written right after the event and in one written several decades later. Between selecting different evidence and interpreting the same evidence differently, two very different stories emerge.

Consider this fact: According to the Bureau of Justice Statistics, African Americans make up nearly 40 percent of the total prison and jail population. African Americans comprised just over 17 percent of the general population in 2013.

These two facts can be used as evidence to arrive at two very different conclusions:

✔ African Americans are far more likely to commit crimes than are Americans of other races and ethnicities.

✔ The criminal justice system unjustly targets African Americans.

The evidence is open to interpretation. The passage doesn't link the percentage of African Americans in jail to the proportion of African Americans in the overall population. To make any reasonable argument and reach any reasonable conclusion, far more evidence is needed to explain any possible link or expose other issues, such as socioeconomic inequalities.

Here's another example of how you can draw very different conclusions from the same information:

I looked up at the sky. It was clouding over, so I decided to take my umbrella with me.

I looked up at the sky. It was clouding over. Now I didn't have to worry about getting sunburn.

Both of these statements start with the same evidence, the cloud cover, but end with very different conclusions. Based on the evidence presented, both conclusions are valid.

When an RLA question asks you to compare two passages, take the following steps:

1. **Read one passage.**

2. **Write down the main idea or the claim stated or implied in the passage.**

3. **Write down any other claims made in the passage.**

4. **For each claim, list the evidence provided to support it along with whether the evidence is true/valid.**

5. **Highlight any evidence that may be misinterpreted.**

6. **Repeat the process for the second passage.**

Your list of claims and evidence, and analysis of the validity of any evidence, help you make clear comparisons.

Any evidence that's misinterpreted or applied erroneously may create doubt about the validity of the conclusion. Further, some evidence may be coincidental; for example, the fact that the sky is clouding over doesn't necessarily mean that rain is imminent.

Consider the following two passages, both of which are about President Truman's decision to drop the atomic bomb on Japan.

Passage One

Truman decided to drop the atomic bomb on Japan. By the middle of 1945, Germany had been defeated, but the war in the Pacific continued. The U.S. government offered surrender terms to Japan, but the Japanese government rejected them. The American military had suffered heavy casualties in the island-to-island war—about one third of its forces. Japanese forces fought fiercely, often to the death. The military estimated that invading the main islands of Japan would involve nearly 2 million American casualties, including more than 350,000 deaths. Japanese military and civilian losses would be even higher. The government calculated that the use of the atomic bomb would actually save lives, so justifying its use.

Passage Two

America did not have to use the atomic bomb on Japan. Despite the heavy casualties America had suffered in the Pacific, the USSR had available manpower. With the war in Europe over, the Soviets had begun moving a large portion of their military eastward. The American conventional bombing campaign was working, too. By early 1945, Japan was experiencing great difficulties in manufacturing enough military supplies to continue the war. Continuing that bombing campaign and postponing any invasion would have saved American lives, and Japan eventually would have been forced to surrender. America could have invited Japanese observers to a demonstration atomic bomb test, showing them what they were facing. Any of these factors could have led to a Japanese surrender without the use of an atomic bomb.

The first passage argues that using the atomic bomb was justified because

1. Japan had rejected surrender terms.

2. America had already suffered massive casualties.

3. The invasion of Japan would cause even greater casualties.

The evidence in this passage is open to interpretation. The first evidence lists American casualties to that point in the Pacific. These are verifiable facts and can be accepted. However, the passage also lists huge casualties resulting from an invasion of Japan. The passage states that these were estimates. How much to believe this passage depends on the degree of reliability assigned to these estimates. That evaluation can put the entire conclusion in doubt.

The second passage offers reasons America didn't have to use the atomic bomb:

1. The USSR was a possible source of manpower to offset American casualties.

2. Conventional bombing was working.

3. A demonstration of the bomb may have led to surrender.

The second passage offers only one fact — that the conventional bombing campaign was working. The other evidence is based on supposition. The USSR forces may or may not have been available. It's not certain that a demonstration of the atomic bomb would have encouraged surrender. Even the more factual claim, that the conventional bombing campaign was working, isn't supported in the passage.

Synthesizing two arguments

One way to demonstrate your ability to compare arguments is to synthesize the two arguments — merge two or more ideas to create a new claim, connecting facts to each other and deriving new meaning. The skills presented earlier in this chapter — the use and evaluation of evidence, the assembly of that evidence in a logical order, and the identification of assumptions and premises — all prepare for this next step.

When you're asked to synthesize two arguments, jot down a list of the claims and evidence provided in the two passages. For example, suppose you're asked to synthesize the arguments presented in the previous two passages on the bombing of Japan. You may come up with a list that looks something like this:

- America had already suffered massive casualties trying to defeat Japan.
- Japan had rejected surrender terms.
- Invading Japan proper would entail even more massive casualties.
- More manpower was potentially available from the USSR.
- Japan was having trouble manufacturing sufficient military supplies to continue.
- U.S. government estimates showed that using the bomb would save more lives than would be lost.
- The conventional bombing campaign was working.

When you have two opposing arguments such as those presented in these two passages, one of the easiest ways to synthesize the two arguments is to aim somewhere in the middle. The first passage indicates that the U.S. was justified in dropping the bomb, while the second passage argues that this drastic action could have been avoided. Looking at the list, you can see that both passages mention the casualties of the war and considerations about reducing war casualties. A synthesis of the two arguments may lead to a third possibility that perhaps the United States could have dropped the bomb on less populated areas or focused the bombing on areas with higher military concentrations and fewer civilians.

Drawing new conclusions

When you encounter an RLA question that asks you to draw a new conclusion based on the arguments or evidence provided in two passages, follow the same procedure as presented in the preceding section. List the main ideas and evidence presented in the two passages and take a step back to see where it points. Chances are good that it will point you in the direction of the correct answer choice. Here's an example:

Passage One

Childhood vaccinations should not be mandatory. The Centers for Disease Control (CDC) recommends 49 doses of 14 different vaccines between the day of birth and the age of six and 69 doses of 16 vaccines between the day of birth and the age of 18 years. In some cases, numerous vaccines are given on the same day and sometimes in a combination vaccine, such as the measles, mumps, and rubella vaccine, further increasing the child's risk of experiencing a severe reaction. This aggressive vaccination schedule hasn't made children any healthier. In fact, children seem to be developing more chronic diseases as they receive more vaccines — illnesses such as autism, ADHD, allergies, asthma, and diabetes.

Passage Two

All parents should be required by law to vaccinate their children. Vaccination protects the child from serious illness, including measles and polio. Equally important is that vaccination prevents the spread of serious illnesses, even protecting those who aren't immunized. Studies show that when a certain percentage of a population is immunized against a contagious disease, the principle of *herd immunity* goes into effect, protecting even those who are ineligible to receive the vaccine, such as infants, pregnant women, and those whose immune systems have been compromised.

Which of the following statements represents a reasonable compromise between the two arguments presented in these passages?

(A) Vaccinations could be postponed when a child is ill.

(B) Vaccinations could be spaced four to six months apart.

(C) Vaccinations could be delayed until the age of one year old.

(D) All of the above.

Although the two sides of the vaccination debate are represented in the passages, they don't address a third option that would involve various ways to reduce the potential risks associated with childhood vaccinations. All the answer choices provide possible solutions to lower the risks while still ensuring that all children are vaccinated. Choice (D) is the best choice.

Applying information to other situations

One or more questions on the RLA test are likely to ask you to read one or two passages and apply what you learn from them to another situation or issue. We can't offer much guidance on how to develop this skill. It requires using your noodle and doing some practice. Here are two passages followed by a sample question so you know what to expect:

Passage One

In their book *Living Wheat Free For Dummies*, Rusty Gregory and Alan Chasen claim that consumption of wheat products triggers an immune response in many people who are sensitive to modern forms of wheat. The immune response causes systemic (throughout the body) inflammation, which is the root cause of many chronic illnesses, including allergies, asthma, arthritis, type 2 diabetes, cardiovascular disease, obesity, dementia, and some forms of cancer.

Passage Two

Several diets considered the healthiest involve increasing consumption of healthy proteins and fats and reducing or eliminating sugary and starchy foods, including breads and cereals. Diets that fall into this category include the Paleo diet, the Candida diet, and the Atkins diet. Some nutritionists, however, warn that these diets tend to be high in cholesterol and low in fiber and contribute to cardiovascular disease. They tend to recommend more balanced diets, such as the Mediterranean diet, the DASH diet, and the TLC diet, which promote moderate consumption of whole-grain products, including breads and cereals.

Which of the following diets is likely to be recommended for those with the inflammatory disease fibromyalgia?

(A) The Paleo diet

(B) The Mediterranean diet

(C) The DASH diet

(D) A low-fiber, high-cholesterol diet

Choice (A) is the correct answer because the second passage describes the Paleo diet as one that reduces consumption of breads and cereals, which primarily contain wheat. You can rule out Choices (B) and (C); both of these diets call for moderate consumption of whole-grain products, which the first passage claims contribute to inflammation. Neither passage claims that a low-fiber, high-cholesterol diet is healthy, so you can eliminate Choice (D).

Chapter 7

Mastering Language Conventions and Usage

● ●

In This Chapter

▶ Making subjects agree with verbs and pronouns agree with their antecedents

▶ Picking the best word for the job

▶ Correcting common errors in sentence structure

▶ Making minor edits in capitalization and punctuation

● ●

Although the GED test doesn't label question sets with the words *writing* or *grammar*, the concepts are worked into almost everything on the test. To pass this component of the RLA test, you need to demonstrate that you have a command of the conventions of Standard English. You need to know how to make the subject and verb in a sentence agree both in person and number, how to choose the right words and avoid slang, how to properly structure a sentence, and how to fix minor errors in capitalization and punctuation.

To help you succeed, we provide insightful information in this chapter about the skills that this part of the test covers, what you can do to brush up on those skills, and the general question format for this component. With this information in hand, you can be confident in your ability to tackle any type of Standard English question on test day.

Correcting Errors in Agreement

Subjects and verbs are either singular or plural. *The dog sees*, or *the dogs see*. When one is singular, the other must be too. Plural nouns require the plural form of the verb. Pronouns must also agree with the words they replace. A female pronoun (such as *she*) can't be used to replace a male noun. *Indefinite pronouns*, words such as *some, none*, and *many*, require singular or plural verbs, depending on their use. The situation gets even more complicated with pronouns such as *everybody*, which seem plural but are used in the singular form. Modifiers and phrases add to the complications. This section clarifies the concept of agreement and provides plenty of examples and practice to help you develop the requisite skills.

Addressing subject-verb agreement

The simplest form of subject-verb agreement deals with a clearly stated noun and verb.

> The boy bites the dog.

The word *boy* is singular; the verb *bites* is singular. Everything is fine.

> The boys bite the dog.

The word *boys* is plural; the verb *bite* is plural. Everything is fine here, too.

Conjunctions are used to join words, phrases and sentences. The conjunction *and* joins the two singular nouns and creates a plural. If "the boy and the girl" is the subject of the sentence, the conjunction *and* joins the two nouns and the sentence requires a plural verb.

> The boy and the girl are doing their homework.

Other conjunctions don't have that effect. *Either/or* and *neither/nor* don't join the nouns in a way that requires a plural verb. In context, they separate the nouns, and the subject becomes "this or that" or "not this, not that" as in these examples:

> Neither the senator nor the aide has read the report.

> Either the son or the daughter is making dinner.

If one of the two nouns in such a phrase is plural, the verb agrees with the noun closest to the verb. If the sentence is a question and the verb comes before the nouns, the same proximity rule applies. If both nouns are plural, the verb must be plural.

> Neither the teacher nor the students have read the report.

> Is either the teacher or the students going to read the report?

> Neither the children nor Mother has made dinner.

> Have either the children or Mother made dinner?

> Neither the students nor the teachers are here.

Note this important exception: Some nouns are *collective nouns,* such as *pride of lions, murder of crows* (yes, that is really the collective noun for a bunch of crows), *team of players,* and *group of people.* The words *pride, murder, team,* and *group* represent a collection of members, whether lions or basketball players. However because these nouns refer to a single collection, they require a singular verb form.

Here's a partial list of collective nouns, each of which is followed by one of its applications enclosed in parentheses:

assembly (of worshippers)	herd (of animals)
band (of monkeys)	litter (of pups)
bed (of mussels)	mob (of people)
brood (of chicks)	nest (of birds)
clan (of Scots)	pack (of wolves)
company (of soldiers)	run (of fish)
congress (of politicians)	school (of fish)
fleet (of ships)	swarm (of bees)
flock (of birds)	tribe (of baboons)
group (of anything)	troop (of Girl or Boy Scouts)

This isn't a complete list by any means. You can use a search engine with the keywords "collective nouns" to find more examples.

Collective nouns either stand alone or combine with the preposition *of,* as in "The band approaches the river" or "The band of monkeys approaches the river." A collective noun usually refers to a singular collection, as in "the school of fish" or "the fleet of destroyers," and so requires a singular verb. The school of fish *is fleeing* the sharks. The fleet of destroyers *is patrolling* the Caribbean.

However, collective nouns can be plural as well. When more than one group or collection is involved, plural verbs are required.

> Three bands of apes were competing for the bananas left by the zookeeper.

> Two litters of pups were born at the vet's at the same time.

Phrases that modify a subject can confuse the issue. These are common: *as well as, along with,* and other phrases that include *with*. They link to the subject but don't change the verb to plural.

> The teacher, along with her students, is visiting the White House.

> The students, along with their teacher, are visiting the White House.

Words such as *some of, all of,* and *a quarter of* are used to quantify nouns.

> a quarter of the school

> all of the bills

> some of the cats

In these cases, the verb takes its number from the word after *of,* as in these examples:

> A quarter of the school has the flu.

> A quarter of the dogs are Golden Retrievers.

> All of the bill is his responsibility.

> All of the bills are his responsibility.

> Some of the cats are rescue cats from the local shelter.

> Some of the cat's fur is purple.

You may also encounter a few special cases. When a sentence starts with a variation of *here* or *there,* the verb always takes its number from the nouns completing the sentence. The noun *pants,* and many others ending in *s,* such as *measles, physics,* and *billiards* are considered singular because they refer to one item: one particular disease, subject, or game. Sums and measurements are also treated as singular because they refer to a single item, even when the sum is many units. Others, including *pants* and *glasses,* are treated like plurals even though they refer to one object. Go figure. You just have to tune your ear to these exceptions and others like them:

> There are two cats in the room.

> There is no reason to behave that way.

> Here is the money I owe you.

> Here are the coupons you wanted.

> Measles is a dangerous disease.

> Social Studies is an interesting subject.

> My jeans are brand new. They are the only pair I bought.

> My glasses are always missing just when I need them most.

> Five hundred dollars a month is too much to pay for insurance.

Practicing subject-verb agreement

Try a few examples. Look at the sentence and write in the proper form of the verb.

1. The dogs (is running/are running) ☐ free.
2. The pride of lions (is/are) ☐ resting in the shade.
3. Neither the lions nor the hunter (like/likes) ☐ the heat.
4. A new pack of wolves (has/have) ☐ moved into the park.
5. The Girl Scouts (is/are) ☐ are well prepared. Their troop (has/have) ☐ set up camp nearby.
6. The writer and the editor (is/are) ☐ working on the manuscript.
7. There (is/are) ☐ several kinds of apples for sale.
8. Some of the apples (is/are) ☐ of the Granny Smith variety.
9. Physics (is/are) ☐ my favorite subject.
10. (Have/Has) ☐ either the teacher or the students seen that movie?

The answers:

1. Plural: Two or more dogs *are* running.

2. Singular: *Pride* is a collective noun acting as one unit.

3. Singular: *Hunter* is closer than *lions* to the verb, so it takes the singular verb.

4. Singular: *Pack* is a collective noun used as one unit.

5. Plural first instance, singular second instance: *Girl Scouts* is plural, but *troop* is collective noun acting as one unit.

6. Plural: The coordinating conjunction *and* makes the subject plural.

7. Plural: Reword the sentence to eliminate the "There is/are" construction, and you see that "Several kinds *are* available."

8. Plural: *Some* refers to apples, so it takes a plural verb.

9. Singular: Physics is the title of a course. Titles are treated as singulars.

10. Singular: Apply the proximity rule: *Teacher* is closer than *students* to the verb, so the verb takes the singular.

Making pronouns agree with their antecedents

A *pronoun* is a word that takes the place of a noun in a sentence, so you don't have to keep repeating the noun. Here's an example of a passage before and after pronouns:

Before: The <u>teacher</u> took the <u>teacher's</u> <u>students</u> to visit the White House. <u>The teacher</u> was amazed how well <u>the teacher's</u> <u>students</u> behaved. After the visit, <u>the teacher</u> praised <u>the students</u>.

After The teacher took <u>his</u> students to see the White House. <u>He</u> was amazed how well <u>they</u> behaved. After the visit, <u>he</u> praised <u>them</u>.

Pronouns take their meaning and their singular/plural status from an *antecedent,* the noun earlier in a sentence passage that the pronoun refers to. Personal pronouns, like nouns, must agree with their antecedents in person, gender, and number:

- ✔ **Person** is first (*I/we*), second (*you*), or third (*he, she, it,* or *they*).

- ✔ **Gender** is masculine or feminine and is relevant only to the pronouns *he* and *she.* Gender doesn't apply to *I, we, you, it,* or *they.*

- ✔ **Number** is singular or plural. First person singular is *I* and *mine,* whereas first person plural is *we* and *ours.* Second person singular and plural is *you* and *yours.* Third person singular is *he/him/his, she/her/hers,* or *it/its,* and third person plural is *they/them/ theirs.*

Pronouns also vary in terms of the role they play. For example, suppose you and Micah are playing baseball. He pitches, and you hit the ball to him. Two different pronouns, *he* and *him,* refer to the same person, Micah. Initially, he's performing the action, so *he* is the subject of the sentence. Later, the ball is coming to him, so *him* is the object of the action. Here are the various forms of the personal pronouns in a nutshell:

Person	*Case*		
Singular	*Nominative/Subject*	*Objective*	*Possessive*
First Person	I	me	mine, my
Second Person	you	you	yours
Third Person	he, she, it	him, her, it	his, hers, its
Plural			
First Person	we	us	our, ours
Second Person	you	you	yours
Third Person	they	them	their, theirs

Just remember to use the proper form of the pronoun. In the example presented earlier in this section, *teacher* is the antecedent. The teacher is a man, so you need to use masculine pronouns (*he* and *his*) to refer to him; the use of "*his* class" and "*he* was amazed" shows that. The word *students* is a plural antecedent, so the third person plural pronouns must be used to refer to them; "*they* behaved" and "he praised *them*" serve as examples.

Choosing the right verb when you have multiple pronouns

People often get confused when two or more pronouns appear in the same sentence as a subject or object, as in the following examples:

> Yesterday, you and me went to the movies.

> They saw you and I at the movies.

Both sentences use the wrong form of the first person pronoun. In the first sentence, "you and me" is the subject of the sentence, so both pronouns should be in the nominative case; however, *me* is the objective case. In the second sentence, *you* and *I* are objects of the verb *see,* so they should both be objective pronouns. *I* is in the nominative case and therefore should be *me.*

To clear up confusion about a pronoun when it appears with another pronoun, rephrase the sentence using only the pronoun you're confused about. When you do that, the error becomes obvious:

Yesterday, me went to the movies

They saw I at the movies.

The correct pronouns sound much better:

Yesterday, I went to the movies

They saw me at the movies.

The proper forms of the whole sentence should be these:

Yesterday, you and I went to the movies.

They saw you and me at the movies.

Giving yourself a refresher in reflexive pronouns

Pronouns that end in *self,* such as *myself* or *themselves,* are called *reflexive pronouns.* Reflexive pronouns are useful in two cases:

- ✔ **When a subject acts on itself:** For example, "My cat grooms itself daily."
- ✔ **To emphasize that the subject of the sentence, and nobody else, completed the action:** For example, "The king himself issued the order to surrender."

In either case, the pronoun must have a clear antecedent in the same clause:

The speaker introduced herself before delivering the keynote address.

We closed the store together, but I took the money to the bank myself.

Some people (we won't name names) use reflexive pronouns incorrectly, thinking the reflexive "sounds better," as in the following sentence:

They saw their friend and myself at the movies

This setup is wrong for two reasons. *Myself* is in the wrong case (it should be the objective *me*), and the pronoun has no clear antecedent to refer to. What does *myself* refer to? The proper form would be

They saw their friend and me at the movies.

Welcoming relative pronouns into the family

Relative pronouns also often cause issues. These are words such as *who* and *whom, which* and *that,* and variations with the intensifier *ever* (*whoever* or *whichever.*) These pronouns are usually used together with the noun to which they refer, so agreement isn't an issue.

The woman who just arrived and to whom the microphone was just handed is about to speak.

People commonly confuse *who* (nominative case) and *whom* (objective case). Just remember that *who* performs action and *whom* receives action.

Considering collective and proper pronouns

Pronouns indicating number, such as *everybody, few, some, many, all,* and (in some cases) *either* and *neither,* can also pose a problem. Treat these as collective nouns (described in the earlier section "Addressing subject-verb agreement"). If the pronoun refers to the antecedent as a single group, the pronoun is singular and takes a singular verb. If the antecedent is plural, then the pronoun is plural:

> None of the teachers are here.

> All of the teachers are here.

> Few have notebooks. (The subject *teachers* is understood.)

> Neither has a notebook. (The subject *teacher* is understood.)

The *proper pronouns, which* and *that,* are confusing because they were once used interchangeably. In modern American English, the usage has become more specific. The relative pronoun *which* is used in clauses describing a preceding noun and is set off with a comma.

> The car, which had just been painted, was totaled in an accident this morning.

The clause "which had just been painted" is used as an adjective clause to describe the car, but you can remove it without changing the meaning of the sentence. The premise remains: The car was totaled.

The word *that* makes the subsequent clause specific; removing it from the sentence does change the meaning.

> The car that had just been painted was totaled this morning.

The clause isn't set off by commas, and it tells the reader the specific car the sentence refers to. Removing the clause would change the meaning.

When a clause can be removed without changing the meaning of the sentence, use *which* and a comma. If removing the clause changes the meaning, use *that* with no comma.

Practicing your pronoun-antecedent agreement skills

Pick the correct pronoun for the underlined word or phrase in each of the following sentences:

1. The woman and <u>me</u> went shopping.

 (A) me

 (B) I

 (C) myself

 (D) mine

2. If you need help, contact either Technical Support or <u>myself</u>.

 (A) myself

 (B) us

 (C) ourselves

 (D) me

3. Everybody <u>works</u> here, ready for any emergency.

   (A) works

   (B) work

   (C) were working

   (D) were

4. The traffic police were examining the car, which had been in an accident, before making their report.

   (A) car, which had been in an accident,

   (B) car which had been in an accident,

   (C) car, that had been in an accident,

   (D) car that had been in an accident

Check your answers:

1. The correct answer is Choice (B). "The woman and me" is the subject of the sentence. Because the first person pronoun is part of the subject, it needs to be in the nominative case, *I,* not the objective case, *me;* the reflexive, *myself;* or the possessive, *mine.*

2. Drop the phrase "either Technical Support or" to clarify which form to use. The correct answer is Choice (D), *me.* Choice (B) would work more than two people were giving that instruction. Choices (A) and (C) are wrong because the sentence includes no subject for the pronoun to refer to, so you don't need a reflexive construction.

3. *Everybody* seems like a plural, but it's actually singular; it's a collective pronoun. *Everybody* is one singular group and needs the appropriate singular verb. The only singular verb offered is Choice (A).

4. The correct answer is Choice (D). The phrase "had been in an accident" is used to specify which car was being examined. Removing that phrase changes the meaning of the sentence. That means the proper use of *which/that* requires *that.* Choice (C) is wrong because no commas are used with a phrase started by *that.*

Choosing the Right Words

Given the fact that the English dictionary contains over one million words, it's not surprising that people get confused using them. Some words sound the same but are spelled differently and have entirely different meanings. Others are easy to distinguish in terms of appearance and sound but have slightly different meanings. And a few words and phrases are appropriate for use in conversations with your friends but ill-suited for more formal settings. In the following sections, we help you sort out any confusion you may have and improve your ability to spot word-choice errors and determine how to correct them on the test.

Tuning your ear to homonyms

Homonyms, words that sound the same but have different meanings, are a poet's and punster's delight. They may be identical or spelled differently, so their misuse causes problems for writers. Learning these words is important not only for proper communication but also for scoring well in English language usage on the RLA test.

When a sentence starts with "the tree's bark" or "the dog's bark," the meaning is clear. When a sentence starts with "A hare" or "A hair," that meaning may not be as obvious. The words sound alike and can be misused.

Here is a partial list of some of the most commonly confused homonyms and their meanings:

- **ad:** advertising

  add: arithmetic term
- **bare:** uncovered

  bear: the animal; endure
- **capital:** important, great, money

  capitol: government building or official seat of government
- **cereal:** grains or breakfast food

  serial: in a series
- **cite:** quote

  sight: to see; a scene

  site: location
- **complement:** go together with

  compliment: praise
- **ewe:** female sheep

  you: second person pronoun
- **flee:** to run away

  flea: the insect
- **flew:** past tense of *fly*

  flu: illness

  flue: part of a chimney
- **hare:** the bunny

  hair: what's on your head
- **here:** this place

  hear: take in a sound
- **its:** possessive pronoun

  it's: contraction of *it is*
- **lead:** the metal

  led: guided
- **male:** masculine

  mail: letter
- **marry:** wed

  merry: happy

- **not:** negative

  knot: to tie something; a nautical speed measure

  naught: nothing
- **peak:** top of something

  peek: take a quick look
- **peace:** absence of war

  piece: portion or part
- **prey:** to hunt; something being hunted

  pray: worship
- **principal:** head of the school; key item

  principle: important belief
- **rain:** wet weather

  reign: monarch's rule

  rein: horse guide
- **stationary:** not moving

  stationery: letterhead
- **their:** possessive pronoun

  there: location

  they're: contraction of *they are*
- **to:** direction

  too: as well

  two: number
- **weather:** atmospheric/climate conditions

  whether: indicates a choice
- **vice:** crime; bad habit

  vise: workshop clamp
- **your:** belonging to you

  you're: contraction of *you are*

Practice distinguishing homonyms by answering the following questions.

1. Supply the correct version of the missing phrase to complete the following sentence:

   We did not know [   ] was going to improve.

   (A) weather the weather

   (B) weather the whether

   (C) whether the whether

   (D) whether the weather

2. Tying the [   ] was for [   ], [   ] that we had expected anything different.

   First instance

   (A) knot

   (B) not

   (C) naught

   Second instance

   (A) knot

   (B) not

   (C) naught

   Third instance

   (A) knot

   (B) not

   (C) naught

3. Fill in the blanks:

   The school's principal/principle [   ] stood by the principal/principle [   ] that attendance was mandatory.

   1. The word *weather* refers to climate phenomena. *Whether* offers a choice — whether this or that — so Choice (D) is the correct answer.

   2. The word *knot* means "a tangle or connection." *Naught* means "nothing," and *not* means "no" or "negative." Look at the usage in the sentence. The first needs something that can be tied, so Choice (A), *knot*, is the correct word. The second occurs in the phrase "was for naught," meaning "was for nothing" or "did not work," so Choice (C), *naught*, is correct. The last use has the meaning of "no" or "negative," so the proper form is Choice (B), *not*.

   3. *Principal* refers to someone running a program or a main or key item. The word *principle* refers to an important philosophical or scientific idea, such as the principle of freedom of speech. In this sentence, the first blank refers to someone in charge, so *principal* is the proper usage. In the second blank, the word refers to an idea or belief in the importance of attendance, so *principle* is the appropriate word.

Correcting errors with frequently confused words

Here are some words that don't quite qualify as homonyms but confuse a lot of people just the same:

✔ **accept:** To receive or agree with: I *accept* the truth of that; she *accepts* the invitation.

except: To exclude: Everyone was invited *except* him.

✔ **advice:** A suggestion or recommendation: Mom always gives good *advice*.

advise: To offer advice: He *advised* the student to study for the GED test.

✔ **affect:** To make a difference to or touch the feelings of: Poor nutrition will negatively *affect* my health. Less commonly, *affect* means to put on a show of emotion: She *affected* disinterest in the whole spectacle.

effect: The result of an action: Poor nutrition has a negative *effect* on my health. In the plural, it can also mean property: They returned her *effects*.

✔ **assure:** To remove doubt: We were *assured* passing the GED test would improve our lives.

insure: To take out insurance: In most states, you must *insure* your cars.

ensure: To make sure, certain: The Affordable Care Act is an attempt *ensure* that all citizens have affordable health insurance.

✔ **borrow:** To take something with the intention of returning it: We all *borrow* tools.

lend: To give something temporarily: We *lend* tools but expect them back.

loan: Money lent at interest. The car *loan* was approved, and we paid it back over 48 months. (Technically speaking, you can use *loan* in place of *lend* when giving someone temporary use of something, but the words aren't interchangeable in figurative expressions such as "lend an ear.")

✔ **council:** An advisory or governing group: The town was run by a citizen's *council*.

counsel: To give advice as an authority: His friend *counseled* him to get legal advice.

✔ **desert:** To abandon in a negative way: The soldiers *deserted* their post. The word is also used to describe a very dry environment with little or no vegetation: Dad was worried we'd get lost in the *desert* on our trip to Arizona.

dessert: A treat after a meal: Ice cream is a popular *dessert*.

To tell the difference between desert (with one *s*) and dessert (with *ss*), keep in mind that you'd probably enjoy two *desserts* but only one *desert*.

✔ **emigrate:** To leave a country with no intention of returning: They *emigrated* from France to New Orleans.

immigrate: To enter another country with no intention of leaving: Victims from the war-torn region immigrated to America.

✔ **heroin:** The drug. *Heroin* is a highly addictive illegal narcotic.

heroine: A female hero: Wonder Woman is a comic book *heroine*.

✔ **gorilla:** A great ape with a large head and short neck that generally lives in the jungles of Africa: Dian Fossey worked with endangered *gorillas* in Africa.

guerilla: Soldier who isn't a member of a regular army: The U.S. Army faced a lot of Viet Cong *guerillas*.

✔ **irregardless:** No such word. Forget it.

regardless: Without regard to or for: We will go for a hike *regardless* of the weather.

irrespective: Regardless: We fly our kites irrespective of the weather. (This is where the confusion with *irregardless* originates. Here the *ir-* beginning is fine; it's absolutely wrong with *regardless*.)

✔ **lay:** To set something down: We *lay* the book on the table.

lie: To set oneself down: I *lie* down to take a nap; the book *lies* on the table. (Of course, *lie* also means to tell a fib, but that usage is rarely confused.)

Lie and *lay* commonly cause confusion. *Lie* (to rest or recline) is an *intransitive* verb, meaning it takes no object. The subject of the sentence is doing the lying. *Lay* is a *transitive* verb, meaning it requires an object. The subject of the sentence sets down something else. The confusion arises from the fact that the past tense of *lie* is *lay*: "The book *lay* on the table since yesterday."

✔ **like:** Similar to: The apple I just ate tasted *like* onion. *Like* implies that whatever follows is similar to but not the same as what follows. (Of course, *like* is also used as a verb to express a fondness for something or someone.)

such as: Including: I prefer fruit that grows on trees, *such as* apples, oranges, and cherries. Unlike the word *like,* the phrase *such as* implies inclusion. In this example, the speaker prefers all tree fruit, including apples, oranges, and cherries.

✔ **loose:** Not secure, able to move about: The engagement ring was *loose*.

lose: To have something or someone suddenly disappear: She was afraid she may *lose* the ill-fitting engagement ring. Don't *lose* your temper. Of course, *lose* is also commonly used to describe the outcome of a competitive event: to lose a game, for example.

For more, commonly confused words, search the web for "frequently confused words."

Also keep an eye and ear out for the following commonly misused words or phrases:

✔ **besides the point:** The proper use is *beside the point* — no *s*. The expression means "not relevant," and the word *beside* refers to *point,* which is singular.

✔ **can't hardly:** The correct phase is *can hardly;* it means to be unable to do something: I can hardly wait or I can hardly see. Using *can't* makes no sense.

✔ **could care less:** How little do you care? Well, if you could care less, that means you do care at least a little. When what you mean is "I don't care at all," the phrase you're looking for is *couldn't care less.*

✔ **could/should/would of:** The ungrammatical *could of* and its cousins stem from what's essentially a transcription error. The proper phrase *could have* has a contraction form: *could've.* In speech, *could've* sounds like *could of,* which is what people often write when they really need *could have.*

✔ **did good:** The expression *he did good* or *the team did good* has become idiomatic (widely used in everyday speech), but it's grammatically wrong. The word *good* is an adjective and can't be used to modify (describe) a verb. You can say something is good, but actions are done well: She played the game well. She is a good player. (The only exception is when someone actually does good, as in where *good* means "good deeds": Philanthropists are dedicated to doing good.)

✔ **literally:** Misuse of this word literally makes grammarians do a slow burn. Well, actually, no. They don't burn or smolder. They figuratively burn or smolder. This word gets thrown around as an intensifier, something to emphasize a statement. "The movie was so funny she was literally rolling on the floor with laughter." Of course, she probably was not actually rolling on the floor; the phrase was used to show just how funny the movie was. Avoid using *literally* unless it refers to something actually happening.

Eliminating informal language

Although you're free to use colloquial (informal) English when communicating with your pals, the RLA tests your knowledge of Standard English, so on the test, at least, you need to avoid writing anything like this:

> So anyways, I text him like what we were gonna do? He just totally blew me off, so I shot his text 2 his girlfriend. ROFL. U shoulda seen his face.

This may be perfectly fine when texting among friends but is unacceptable when writing an essay, an email to an employer, or even texting someone with whom you do business. When writing letters or essays, use formal, Standard English. Table 7-1 offers some guidelines.

Table 7-1	Avoiding Informal Words and Phrases
Informal	*Formal fix*
Vague language	*Use precise language*
The <u>thing</u> is	The issue is
The current policy is <u>bad</u>.	The current policy wastes taxpayer money.
She was bothered by a lot of <u>stuff</u>.	She had three major concerns.
I have a <u>couple of</u> ideas.	I have three solutions.
The impersonal you	*Address a specific person or group*
When <u>you</u> get anxious, <u>you're</u> likely to make mistakes.	When an individual becomes anxious, she is more prone to making mistakes.
When you talk with disgruntled customers, you need to listen.	When speaking with disgruntled customers, a customer service representative needs to listen.
Slang/colloquialisms	*Replace with formal words*
The couple had <u>a lot</u> of issues.	The couple was dealing with numerous marital issues.
I <u>got</u> an *A* in Spanish.	I earned an *A* in Spanish.
He <u>kinda</u> (or <u>kind of</u> or <u>sort of</u>) knows how to fix cars.	He somewhat knows how to fix cars.
<u>Let</u> me explain.	Permit me to explain.
Phrasal verbs	*Replace with a more precise verb*
bring up	raise (children) or introduce (topic or issue)
call off	cancel
decide on	choose
give back	return
hold up	delay
leave out	omit
look up	search
put off	postpone
set up	arrange
turn down	reject
Contractions	*Spell it out*
can't	cannot
I'm	I am
shouldn't	should not
won't	will not

At this point, we want to issue the following shameless disclaimer: Do as we say, not as we do. We wrote this book using a combination of Standard and non-Standard English per the request of our publisher (what's a *For Dummies* book if not informal?). You'll no doubt notice the use of phrasal verbs, contractions, colloquialisms, and other GED test faux pas.

Here's an example of a business letter that is far too informal:

> Hey John,
>
> Just so you know, my application is in the snail mail. I wanted to get in touch earlier, but I had some other stuff to deal with first. Anyway, I finally put my CV together, and it's on its way.
>
> So I hope you'll okay an interview for me. Call me if you need anything further.
>
> Looking forward to hearing from you,
>
> Ed.

A letter or email like this one regarding a job application would go straight into the recycling bin. It's full of informal language, which unacceptable in a business situation. After you know the people involved, a less formal style may be okay, but for most professional situations, this kind of writing is just wrong. Here is the same text in more formal language:

> Dear Mr. Smith,
>
> Since we spoke, I have organized my CV and forwarded it to your attention. You should receive my resume, job application, and CV shortly by postal mail.
>
> Please do not hesitate to contact me if you require any further information.
>
> I look forward to hearing from you.
>
> Sincerely,
>
> Ed Jones

Now for some practice: Here's a letter of complaint to the manufacturer of a defective product:

> Dear Sir,
>
> I'm writing to tell you your coffee maker died yesterday, barely a week after I got it home. I spoke to some dude on your help desk, but he did nothing for me. This is certainly totally wrong.
>
> I want this coffee maker replaced under warranty. Please call. I'm ready to take your call anytime.
>
> Yours,
>
> George Gently

How would you correct the underlined portion of each of these sentences? (Choice (A) means no change.)

1. <u>I'm writing to tell you your</u> coffee maker died yesterday, barely a week after I got it home.

   (A) I'm writing to tell you your

   (B) I am writing to inform you that your

   (C) I am writing to inform you your

   (D) This letter is to inform you that your

2. I'm writing to tell you your <u>coffee maker died yesterday, barely a week after I got it home</u>.

   (A) your coffee maker died yesterday, barely a week after I got it home

   (B) your coffee maker broke yesterday, barely a week after I got it home

   (C) your coffee maker broke within one week of the purchase date

   (D) your coffee maker is defective; it stopped working less than a week after I purchased it

3. I spoke <u>to some dude on your help desk</u>, but he did nothing for me.

   (A) to some dude on your help desk

   (B) to someone on your help desk

   (C) to one of your help desk representatives

   (D) to some staff

4. This <u>is certainly totally wrong</u>.

   (A) is certainly totally wrong

   (B) response is unacceptable

   (C) is certainly wrong

   (D) is totally wrong

5. <u>I'm ready to take your call anytime.</u>

   (A) I'm ready to take your call anytime.

   (B) Please do not hesitate to call.

   (C) Please call whenever.

   (D) I'm available for your call anytime.

Now, check your answers:

1. The best choice for formal English is Choice (D). Choice (A) is wrong because it uses a contraction (*I'm*) and drops the conjunction *that*. Choice (C) also omits the *that*. Choice (B) is much better, but not best.

2. The best choice is Choice (D). Although the language may seem stiff, it uses *defective* rather than *died* or *broke* and describes the problem in a civil tone. Using the word *died* for a defective product is slang (which you should avoid), so Choice (A) is wrong. Choices (B) and (C) make some improvements in phrasing, but *broke* is still informal.

3. The best option is Choice (C). Replacing "some dude on your help desk" with "one of your help desk representatives" communicates in a more formal manner. Using *dude* is inappropriate for a formal letter, and *someone* isn't much better.

4. Choice (B) is the best option. Choice (A) uses informal English and has no clear antecedent. The reader is uncertain of the nature of the wrong done. Is the reader upset that the machine malfunctioned or that the dude manning the help desk wasn't helpful? Choices (C) and (D) do nothing to clarify.

5. Choice (B) is your best option. Choices (A) and (D) use contractions, which is a bad idea on the GED test. "Call whenever" is very casual, so Choice (C) isn't a good choice.

Fixing Broken Sentences

As sentences become more complex, the room for errors increases. The simplest sentence has only one subject and one predicate — an actor and an action, a noun and a verb. For example, in the sentence "Jack runs," *Jack* is the subject, and *runs* is the predicate. When you start adding details, the subject and predicate become longer and more complex: "Jack, an athlete with a score to settle, runs furiously toward the finish line." "Jack, an athlete with a score to settle" is the subject, and "runs furiously toward the finish line" is the predicate.

Sentences become increasingly long and complex when you start adding independent and dependent clauses. An *independent* clause is one that can stand alone as a sentence, as in the case of "Jack runs." A *dependent* clause is one that must be joined to an independent clause, as in " because a dog was chasing him." You can join these independent and dependent clauses in various combinations to form the following three types of sentences:

- **Compound sentences** contain two independent clauses joined by a comma followed by a coordinating conjunction: *and, but, or, nor, for, so,* or *yet.* Alternatively, you can join the two clauses with a semicolon and no coordinating conjunction. Here's an example of each:

    The sailboats were racing down that channel, and they both reached the finish line at the same time.

    The sailboats were racing down that channel; they both reached the finish line at the same time.

- **Complex sentences** contain an independent clause plus one or more subordinate clauses, each introduced by a subordinating conjunction: *after, although, as, as if, because, before, even if, even though, if, if only, rather than, since, that, though, unless, until, when, where, whereas, wherever, whether, which,* or *while.* They're subordinate because they can't stand on their own. Here's an example:

    The sailor won the race, although his sailboat was not the best in the competition.

- **Compound-complex sentences** contain two or more independent clauses and at least one dependent clause. These sentences are usually long and unwieldy, so use them sparingly.

    Argentina's sailboat finished last; when the sudden squall hit, the crew was unprepared to lower the sails, and the sails were quickly shredded.

These complex structures create a great deal of room for errors. Here are some of the most common errors covered in the RLA test, along with ways to avoid and correct them.

Taking care of misplaced modifiers

Modifiers are words or phrases that enhance the meaning of the word they describe. Modifiers can be *adjectives* (words that describe nouns), or adverbs (words that describe verbs, adjectives, or other adverbs). They can be single words or longer phrases. In the sentence "The exhausted driver nearly fell asleep," *exhausted* is an adjective that modifies *driver,* and *nearly* is an adverb that modifies *fell asleep.*

Misplaced modifiers are descriptive words or phrases that aren't clearly linked to the words they describe. Look at the difference in meaning of these two examples:

She almost ran all the way to school.

She ran almost all the way to school.

In the first example, she came close to running but not quite. Maybe she jogged. In the second sentence she ran, but not quite all of the way to school. To prevent confusion, place the modifier closest to the verb or noun it modifies. Here's an example:

Misplaced: They were repairing the red car in the body shop with the dented fender. (In this example, it would be the body shop that had a dented fender.)

Corrected: They were repairing the red car with the dented fender in the body shop.

Dangling modifiers are descriptive words or phrases that have no noun or verb to describe.

Reading the test results, university acceptance was certain.

Who or what is reading the test results? As written, it's "university acceptance" (the noun closest to the modifier), but that doesn't make sense. That means you have a dangling modifier. The fix is easy:

Reading the test results, the applicant was certain of her university acceptance.

Here's another example of a misplaced modifier:

We smelled the odor of old socks and unwashed towels entering the gym.

Obviously, the socks and towels didn't enter the gym unless someone carried or wore them in, but "entering the gym" is so distant from the word it modifies the meaning is open to interpretation. Again, the fix is easy; move the modifier closer to the word it modifies:

Entering the gym, we smelled the odor of old socks and unwashed towels.

Now for some practice: Check the box next to each sentence that has a misplaced modifier.

❑ Sprinkled across the sky, the tourists admired the colorful macaws.

❑ Although still in high school, the professor thought Michael had great potential.

❑ Getting out of his car, the papers fell out of his bag.

❑ While running though the park, a big dog attacked James.

❑ Within minutes of seeing the stray dog, James was ready to adopt.

Check your answers. The modifier is placed correctly in only the last sentence. Changing the word order of the first four sentences would correct the problem.

Achieving parallelism, coordination, and subordination

Parallelism, subordination, and coordination all involve joining words and phrases together in ways that achieve clarity, balance, and fluidity. In the following sections, we explain parallelism, subordination, and coordination in more detail and provide guidance in identifying and correcting common errors.

Spotting and correcting faulty parallelism

Parallelism is the balance achieved when combining similar words or phrases in a sentence. More simply put, when you refer to two or more things in a sentence, use the same parts of speech in the same form. Here's an example of faulty parallelism followed by a corrected version of the same sentence:

Faulty: George likes cards, to play chess, and playing video games.

Corrected: George likes playing cards, chess, and video games.

Although you commonly encounter faulty parallelism in a series of items, it also crops up in other situations. Table 7-2 provides a bird's-eye view of the types of situations to look for along with an example of faulty parallelism and a corrected version for each.

Table 7-2	Common Parallelism Errors and Corrections	
Situation	**Faulty parallelism**	**Correct parallelism**
Items joined by a coordinating conjunction	Ace Manufacturing offers its workers higher pay and to take longer vacations.	Ace manufacturing offers its workers higher pay and longer vacations.
Items in a series	We love skiing, skating, and to watch sports.	We love skiing, skating, and watching sports.
Items being compared	Frogs spend more time swimming than they hop.	Frogs spend more time swimming than hopping.
Items joined by a form of the verb *to be*	What you see is the thing you get.	What you see is what you get.
Items joined by correlative conjunctions (*either/or, neither/nor, not only/but also, both/and,* and *whether/or*)	Earth revolves not only around the sun but also rotates on its own axis.	Earth not only revolves around the sun but also rotates on its own axis.

To determine whether parallelism exists, turn the sentence into a bulleted list. If each bullet item is in the same form, they're parallel. If not, you're looking at faulty parallelism.

Identifying and fixing faulty coordination

You use a coordinating conjunction, preceded by a comma, to combine two complete sentences into a longer compound sentence. Coordination problems arise when you use the wrong coordinating conjunction, creating confusion. Here's an example of faulty coordination followed by a corrected version:

Faulty: The restaurant was packed, and the parking lot was empty.

Corrected: The restaurant was packed, but the parking lot was empty.

The first sentence uses the coordinating conjunction *and* to connect two contrasting situations, which doesn't make sense. You'd expect that if the restaurant was packed, the parking lot would be full, but that's not the case. The coordinating conjunction *but* signals that a contrast is about to come.

Faulty coordination also occurs when a coordinating conjunction jams together two items or phrases that aren't closely related or equal in status, as in the following example:

Faulty: President Obama was awarded the Nobel Peace Prize and was born in Hawaii.

Corrected: President Obama, who was born in Hawaii, was awarded the Nobel Peace Prize.

Pinpointing and correcting faulty subordination

Subordination occurs in complex sentences, as described earlier in this chapter, when a sentence contains an independent and a dependent clause joined by a subordinating conjunction. The dependent clause is subordinate to the independent clause. Faulty subordination occurs when the sentence uses the wrong subordinating clause, resulting in confusion, as in the following example:

Faulty: Although pointillism was the most popular painting technique at the time, some of the most talented painters, including van Gogh and Seurat, embraced the technique.

Corrected: Because pointillism was the most popular painting technique at the time, some of the most talented painters, including van Gogh and Seurat, embraced the technique.

Faulty subordination also arises when the more important of the two clauses is subordinate to the less important clause, as in the following example:

Faulty: The hurricane threat had passed, although the travel bans in coastal areas remained in effect.

Corrected: Although the hurricane threat had passed, the travel bans in coastal areas remained in effect.

Testing your skills: Parallelism, coordination, and subordination

Practice your skills at identifying and repairing faulty parallelism, coordination, and subordination by correcting the following sentences:

1. The apartment was clean, affordable, and with lots of space.

   _____

   _____

2. Because most plants need plenty of water to grow, desert plants thrive in arid conditions.

   _____

   _____

3. William Faulkner was a Nobel Prize laureate, and he never graduated from high school.

   _____

   _____

4. Although some diets restrict fat consumption, several studies, however, show that certain fats are essential for good health.

   _____

   _____

5. World leaders should be held not only accountable to citizens in their own countries but also to citizens in other countries.

   _____

   _____

Check your answers against the following revisions, but keep in mind that your answer isn't necessarily wrong if it doesn't match the correction provided here. You usually have more than one option.

1. The apartment was clean, affordable, and spacious.

2. Although most plants need plenty of water to grow, desert plants thrive in arid conditions.

3. Although he never graduated from high school, William Faulkner became a Nobel Prize laureate.

4. Although some diets restrict fat consumption, several studies show that certain fats are essential for good health. (Another option would be to revise the sentence to remove *although* rather than *however,* but you'd also need to adjust the punctuation.)

5. World leaders should be held accountable not only to citizens in their own countries but also to citizens in other countries.

Tightening wordy sentences

Wordiness, in the spirit of good writing is, in the words of the great poet, something we should aim to eliminate so that the precision of our words shines through and illuminates the passage. You just suffered through an example of very wordy prose. People use interjections in spoken language all the time. They use vague words and then try to clarify with a lot of descriptive language. They throw in extra adjectives and adverbs that simply repeat what the noun or verb already states. Some writers feel it sounds more academic or educated, but it merely confuses and irritates.

On the RLA test, some questions may challenge you to identify wordy constructions and choose more succinct alternatives. You also need to avoid the pitfalls of wordiness when writing your Extended Response. In the following sections we introduce common sources of wordiness and explain how to tighten your prose.

Using precise language

The single most effective solution to pare down and strengthen your prose is to use the most precise words you can think of. Here are a couple of examples of wordy sentences, each of which is followed by a trimmed-down version:

> ✔ We thought long and deeply about sending our child to a private school.
>
> We deliberated sending our child to a private school.
>
> ✔ The group of angry protesters marched quickly to city hall and tried to break in.
>
> The mob stormed city hall.

Write with descriptive nouns and verbs, and you won't need so many additional words to clarify.

Opting for active over passive voice

In a typical sentence, the actor enters first and then performs. You know from the beginning who's doing what. Passive voice flips the order:

> ✔ **Passive:** The lesson was written on the blackboard by the teacher.
>
> **Active:** The teacher wrote the lesson on the blackboard.
>
> ✔ **Passive:** The cells were attacked by the virus.
>
> **Active:** The virus attacked the cells.

As you can see, the passive voice is indirect, unclear, and wordy. However, passive voice comes in handy at times, such as when a politician wants to distance herself from an unpopular decision; she can simply say, for example, "The decision was made to increase taxes." It's also helpful in formal essays or scientific writing, when the writer must shift the focus to the data.

Cutting out redundancy

Beware of phrases that state the same thing twice. Here are some common redundant phrases to avoid along with their succinct counterparts.

Redundant	Succinct
a total of a dozen eggs	a dozen eggs
briefly summarize	summarize
close proximity	close; nearby
cooperate together	cooperate
end result	result
exactly the same	identical; the same
future to come	future
period of two weeks	two weeks
revert back	revert

Avoiding overuse of be verbs

People who merely exist are boring, and so is the verb *to be* in all its forms: *be, being, been, is, am, are, was,* and *were.* Unless these verbs are accompanied by a real action verb, be on the lookout for a weak and/or wordy construction. Here are some examples, each of which is followed by a sample correction:

- ✔ The protesters were the people who looted the store.

  The protesters looted the store.
- ✔ Environmentalists were the major proponents of the new regulations.

  Environmentalists promoted the new regulations.
- ✔ There are many constituents who would disagree with the senator.

  Many constituents would disagree with the senator.
- ✔ It is obvious that sugar and starchy foods increase body fat.

  Obviously, sugar and starchy foods increase body fat.

Don't use expletives in your writing. No, we're not talking about swear words here; we want you to avoid the "it + be" and "there + be" constructions known as *expletives.* These setups, such as "It is important that" and "This is the person who," almost always produce weak, wordy sentences. (Definitely avoid the other kind of expletives on the RLA test, too.)

You can find entire websites devoted to concise writing, complete with plentiful examples, exercises, and even some sample questions. Search the web for "concise writing" or "eliminating wordiness."

Saying no to nominalizations

Nominalizatons are the noun forms of verbs. Here are a few examples:

Verb	Nominalization
Analyze	Analysis
Collect	Collection
Conclude	Conclusion
Demonstrate	Demonstration
Discover	Discovery
Fail	Failure
Indicate	Indication
Refuse	Refusal
Stabilize	Stabilization

You can slash word count while strengthening your prose by converting nominalizations back to their verb forms and, in the process, often remove a be verb. Here are a few examples of nominalizations and adjustments that eliminate them:

- The peace treaty led to a cessation of hostilities.

  The peace treaty ended the conflict.
- The police conducted their investigation of the crime scene.

  The police investigated the crime scene.
- As an indication of her dedication to the cause, Sally presented a donation of $10,000.

  Sally donated $10,000 to demonstrate her dedication to the cause.

Watching out for prepositions

Prepositions (*of, with, in, for,* and so on) are red flags for wordiness. You may have noticed this in the preceding section on nominalizations. When you convert a noun to a verb, you're forced to add a prepositional phrase, as in the case of "cessation *of* hostilities" and "investigation *of* the crime scene." Here are a few additional examples:

- The opinion of the court is that the defendant be released.

  The court decided to release the defendant.
- Please contact our office in a timely manner.

  Please contact our office promptly.

Purging phrasal verbs

Phrasal verbs are two or more words that function as a verb and can usually be replaced with a single verb. For example, you can replace the phrasal verb "pick up on" with "sense." See "Eliminating informal language" earlier in this chapter for a short list of phrasal verbs and their suitable replacements.

Replacing negatives with positive statements

You can often reduce wordiness simply by making a negative statement positive. Here's an example:

If players do not show up with their gear, they will not be allowed to play.

Players must show up with their gear in order to play.

Practicing your word-slashing skills

Here's a wordy passage to practice on. On a separate sheet of paper, cross out unnecessary words and phrases and write your revision.

> At any given moment, there are people who want to go for long drives and little automotive adventures on the weekend. It is obvious that this is something that car rental companies should exploit. We all know that rental companies can use all the extra revenues they can get, due to the fact that the economy has worsened, making renting a car a frivolous expense often cut.

When you're done, grade yourself. You can gauge your success by counting the number of words you eliminated or comparing your revision to the following version:

> Many people like long weekend drives. Because fewer people can afford to rent cars since the recession, car rental companies could use this market to improve revenues.

Evaluate your writing the same way. Does a particular word of phrase add anything to the text? Can it be replaced with simpler words or phrases?

Remember the KISS rule: Keep it simple, silly. Good writing is clear, simple, and direct.

Smoothing out awkward sentences

Awkward sentences are difficult to read and understand. They can be unnecessarily complex and may contain faulty parallelism, passive voice, misused words, and empty phrases. When you are presented with an awkward sentence to correct on the test, try to read it aloud in your inner voice. If the sentence trips you up as you read it or you have to read it several times to grasp its meaning, you're looking at an awkward sentence. Long sentences are easy to spot and correct: Remove any unnecessary words and phrases. Spotting and correcting other issues may be more challenging.

Practice your skills. Choose the correct version of each of the following sentences. Note that Choice (A) is the same as the original version.

1. You should take this test when you have finished studying and when feeling better.

   (A) You should take this test when you have finished studying and when feeling better.

   (B) You should take this test when you have finished studying and if feeling better.

   (C) You should take this test when you have finished studying and when you will feel better.

   (D) You should take this test when you have finished studying and are feeling better.

2. The girls loved reading, to dance, and the movies.

   (A) The girls loved reading, to dance, and the movies.

   (B) The girls loved to read, dance, and watch movies.

   (C) The girls loved reading, dancing, and watching movies.

   (D) Choices (B) and (C) are both correct.

3. It can be seen from the report that in this case repairs should be made with all due haste.

 (A) It can be seen from the report that in this case repairs should be made with all due haste.

 (B) It can be seen from this report that these repairs are urgent.

 (C) The report states that in this case repairs are needed urgently.

 (D) The report states these repairs are urgent.

4. Flying down the hill, the visitors admired the skiers.

 (A) Flying down the hill, the visitors admired the skiers.

 (B) The visitors admired the skiers flying down the hill.

 (C) The visitors, flying down the hill, admired the skiers.

 (D) none of the above

5. Recently, scientists stumbled upon a discovery of a virus that has a negative effect on human cognition.

 (A) Recently, scientists stumbled upon a discovery of a virus that has a negative effect on human cognition.

 (B) Scientists recently stumbled upon a discovery of a virus that negatively affects human cognition.

 (C) Recently, scientists discovered a virus that diminishes human cognition.

 (D) Scientists recently discovered a virus that has a negative effect on human cognition.

Check your answers:

1. The correct answer is Choice (D) because it creates two parallel clauses: "when you have finished studying" and "when [you] are feeling better." Choice (A) is the original, which is wrong because "you have finished studying" and "feeling better" aren't parallel. Choice (B) simply introduces a new error by changing *when* to *if*. Choice (C) introduces a new error by bringing in the future tense *(will)*.

2. Choice (D) is correct. The original sentence is an example of faulty parallelism because each item in the series is in a different form.

3. Choice (D) is your best choice. "It can be seen," "in this case," and "all due haste" are wordy and unnecessary. Choice (D) is the clearest, shortest, and most direct version of the sentence.

4. The best choice has to explain who or what was flying down the hill. Because the phrase refers to the skiers, not the visitors, that phrase needs to be closest to the noun *skiers*. Choice (B) is your best choice.

5. Choice (C) is best. Not surprisingly, it's also the shortest version.

Using transitional words and phrases effectively

Transitional words and phrases link paragraphs and sentences to the material that went before and make reading and understanding easier. They indicate how successive sentences or paragraphs connect. They show sequence, with words and phrases like *afterward, first of all, then, subsequently,* and so on. They highlight examples, using words and phrases like *for example* or *thus.* Words and phrases like *especially* and *above all* indicate something important is coming and add emphasis. Here's a list of commonly used transition words grouped by purpose:

Purpose	Transition words
Addition	also, again, as well as, besides, furthermore, in addition
Consequence	accordingly, as a result, consequently, hence, otherwise, so then, subsequently, therefore, thus,
Comparison	but, by the same token, conversely, however, in contrast, instead, likewise, nevertheless, on one hand, on the contrary, on the other hand, rather, similarly, still, yet
Emphasis	above all, chiefly, especially, particularly, singularly, with attention to
Exception	aside from, barring, beside, except, excepting, excluding, exclusive of, other than, outside of
Example	chiefly, especially, for example, for instance, in particular, including, namely, particularly, primarily, specifically, such as
Generalization	as a rule, as usual, for the most part, generally, generally speaking, ordinarily, usually
Restatement	in brief, in essence, in other words, in short, namely, that is, that is to say
Sequence	afterward, at first, at the same time, earlier, first of all, for now, for the time being, in the first place, in the meantime, in time, in turn, later, later on, meanwhile, next, simultaneously, soon, the next step, then, to begin with, while
Summary	after all, all in all, all things considered, briefly, by and large, finally, in any case, in any event, in brief, in conclusion, in short, in summary, in the final analysis, on balance, on the whole, to sum up, to summarize

For a complete list, search the web for "transitional words and phrases."

Here's a passage that shows transitional words (underlined) in action:

> They agreed to rent the apartment to the stranger. He paid the first month's rent on time, but <u>subsequently</u> the payments were either late or never made at all. <u>For example</u>, the May rent arrived two weeks late, and the June rent was not paid. <u>In other words</u>, the stranger proved to be a bad tenant. <u>Generally</u>, they checked their prospective tenants' backgrounds, but they forgot to in this case. They were able to evict him. <u>Subsequently</u>, they learned he had a long record of the same issues with previous landlords.

Don't overuse transitional words or phrases as we've done in this sample passage. We used an abundance here to illustrate their use.

Eliminating sentence fragments and run-on or fused sentences

The problem starts with spoken language. People often speak in *sentence fragments* (incomplete sentences lacking a subject or verb) because that's the nature of conversation:

Boy: What's up?

Girl: Just studying.

Boy: Why?

Girl: For a science test.

Boy: An important one?

Girl: Not really. Just term work.

You understand this conversation because you mentally insert the missing words. In writing, you're not having a conversation. You're presenting information and ideas. Communication is one way. Sentences without proper punctuation, sentences joined by commas, and sentences missing subjects or verbs are likely to confuse the reader, and you won't be there to answer questions and clarify statements. In this section, we describe two errors that plague sentences and explain how to fix them.

Detecting and fixing run-on or fused sentences

Run-on sentences or *fused sentences* occur when two or more independent clauses are jammed together with incorrect (or no) punctuation:

School was over for the day the kids all made a mad dash for the playground.

You have two complete sentences:

<u>School was over for the day</u> and <u>the kids all made a mad dash for the playground.</u>

Putting the two thoughts together is fine. The end of the school day and kids running to the playground are linked ideas. To repair the sentence, you have four options:

- **Make two separate sentences:**

    School was over for the day. The kids all made a mad dash for the playground.

- **Add a semicolon between the two clauses:**

    School was over for the day; the kids all made a mad dash for the playground.

- **Add a comma and a coordinating conjunction between the two clauses:**

    School was over for the day, so the kids all made a mad dash for the playground.

- **Revise the sentence to make one of the clauses subordinate to the other:**

    When school ended, the kids all made a mad dash for the playground.
    ("When school ended" is the subordinate clause.)

A run-on sentence commonly occurs in the form of a *comma splice*: two independent clauses joined by a comma. Commas can't link independent clauses:

Comma splice: The rain was just pouring, we quickly found shelter under an awning.

Correction: The rain was just pouring; we quickly found shelter under an awning.

Correction: The rain was just pouring, but we quickly found shelter under an awning.

You correct the sentence in the same way as the previous example: by inserting a semicolon after the word *pouring* or a coordinating conjunction after the comma.

Don't confuse coordinating conjunctions (*and, but, or, nor, for, so, yet*) and transition words, such as *therefore* and *otherwise*. You can use both words to join independent clauses, but use a comma before coordinating conjunctions and a semicolon before transitional words. Here's an example:

Incorrect: The rain was just pouring, however, we quickly found shelter under an awning.

Correct: The rain was just pouring; however, we quickly found shelter under an awning.

Use a semicolon before a transition word only if the word joins two independent clauses. Sometimes, transition words are embedded in sentences and set off by commas, as in the following example:

> To use your keycard, however, you must also enter your PIN.

In this example, "to use your keycard," isn't an independent clause, so you don't use a semicolon.

Comma-splice errors are fairly common on the RLA test.

Finding a home for sentence fragments

A sentence fragment is a sentence that's missing one of its parts — either the requisite the actor or action required to make it a fully formed sentence. It may look like a sentence, starting with a capital letter and ending in a period, but it's missing a subject or predicate. To fix a sentence fragment, supply the missing noun or verb or combine the fragment with another sentence. Here's a passage with several fragments:

> The lab was open all night. Jeff on Professor Faraday's experiment, running late. When the alarm sounded, he had no choice but to leave. Quickly covered the experiment and ran for the door.

Here's a corrected version:

> The lab was open all night. Jeff, <u>who was working</u> on Professor Faraday's experiment, <u>was</u> running late. When the alarm sounded, he had no choice but to leave. Quickly, <u>he</u> covered the experiment and ran for the door.

Providing a subject for each sentence fragment corrected the problem, but you can repair the fragments in other ways. On a sheet of paper, try rewriting this passage several different ways to eliminate the fragments.

Practicing your sentence repair skills

Try your hand at spotting the errors and selecting the correct repairs for the following sentences. Note that the first answer choice is the original sentence.

1. Most of the audience left before the concert ended, it was far too loud.

   (A) Most of the audience left before the concert ended, it was far too loud.

   (B) Most of the audience left before the concert ended; because it was far too loud.

   (C) Most of the audience left before the concert ended; therefore, it was far too loud.

   (D) Most of the audience left before the concert ended because it was far too loud.

2. The movie stirred the emotions. A story of a girl and her dog trekking across the country.

   (A) The movie stirred the emotions. A story of a girl and her dog trekking across the country.

   (B) The movie stirred the emotions. It was the story of a girl and her dog trekking across the country.

   (C) The movie stirred the emotions. A girl and her dog trekking across the country.

   (D) The movie stirred the emotions; a story of a girl and her dog trekking across the country.

3. With his driver's license suspended, Gary ran the red light, he sped past a squad car.

   (A) With his driver's license suspended, Gary ran the red light, he sped past a squad car.

   (B) With his driver's license suspended, Gary sped past a squad car and runs a red light.

   (C) With his driver's license suspended, Gary ran the red light and sped past a squad car.

   (D) With his driver's license suspended, Gary ran the red light and past a squad car.

   Check your answers:

   1. Choice (D) is best because it separates the two independent clauses with a comma followed by a subordinating conjunction. Choice (B) is wrong because the subordinating conjunction is preceded by a semicolon. Choice (C) is wrong because *therefore* is an illogical transition word for this sentence.

   2. Choice (B) is correct. This question is a classic example of a sentence fragment. Giving the second "sentence" a noun and a verb *(it is)* and separating the two clauses with a period repairs the fragment.

   3. Choice (C) is correct. Here's another example of a comma splice. You can't join two independent clauses with only a comma. Choice (C) fixes the problem simply by eliminating the subject of the second independent clause — *he*.

Tweaking the Text: Capitalization, Contractions, Possession, and Punctuation

You don't have to be a professional editor to answer questions involving capitalization, possession, and punctuation, but you do need to know the rules and how to apply them in context. The following sections bring you up to speed on these three areas.

Brushing up on capitalization rules

The GED RLA test expects you to be able to recognize which words should start with a capital letter and which words don't. In general, *initial cap* (capitalize the first letter of) the following items:

- The first word of every sentence
- Every word in a person's title, such as *Miss, President,* and *Senator,* when the title is followed by the person's name
- Multiword titles, as in Minister of Defense, when followed by the person's name
- The names of cities, states, and countries; for example, Chicago, California, and China.
- Names of languages and nationalities
- Religious names such as God, Allah, Buddha, and other specific gods such as Ra or Zeus
- Company names
- The first and last words in the title of a book, song, movie or other creation, as well as any other major words, as in *The Night of the Living Dead.*

Don't capitalize these nouns:

- ✔ Titles when they follow a name, as in Ronald Reagan, former president of the United States
- ✔ Titles when not attached to a name but used as a general term: the kings, the pastor, and the professor
- ✔ *Moon, sun,* or other bodies in the solar system besides planets
- ✔ General references to foods, animals, and plants, such as "We saw a bear in the blueberry bushes"

Telling the difference between contractions and possessives

Verb contractions and possessive nouns each use apostrophes, but each does so for a different purpose. You need to know the difference:

- ✔ **Contractions:** This area of writing mechanics has nothing to do with those painful moments before childbirth! Instead, *contractions* are what you get when you shorten a word by leaving out a letter or a sound. For example, when you write *can't,* you're using a shortened form of *cannot.* In this example, *can't* is the contraction.

  The important thing to remember about contractions is that the *apostrophe* (that's a single quotation mark) takes the place of the letter or letters that are omitted.

- ✔ **Possessives:** Do you know people who are possessive? They're all about ownership, right? So is the grammar form of possessives. *Possessives* are words that show owner-ship or possession, usually by adding an apostrophe to a person's or object's name. If Marcia owns a car, that car is *Marcia's* car. The word *Marcia's* is a possessive. Make sure you know the difference between singular and plural possessives. For example: "The girl's coat is torn." (*Girl* and *coat* are singular, so the apostrophe goes before the *s.*) "The girls' coats are torn." (*Girls* and coats are plural, so the apostrophe goes after the *s.*) When working with plural possessives, form the plural first and then add the apostrophe.

Don't make the most common mistake of confusing the contraction *it's* with the possessive *its.* The contraction *it's* stands for *it is.* The possessive uses no apostrophe.

Fine-tuning your punctuation skills

Punctuation includes periods, commas, semicolons, colons. Follow these punctuation do's and don'ts.

Do

- ✔ Use a period to end a complete sentence.
- ✔ Use a comma to
  - Separate items in a series, such as apples, bananas, and oranges.
  - Separate two complete sentences that are joined by a coordinating conjunction, such as *and, but, or, for, nor, so,* or *yet:* "Patty enjoyed going to the movies, but she hated having to spend so much on concessions."

- Separate an introductory clause or phrase from the main clause: "Whenever I go to the store, I buy fresh bananas." Introductory clauses typically begin with adverbs or subordinating conjunctions, such as *after, although, because, even though, if, since, than, though, unless, when, where, whether,* and *while.*

- Set off a clause, phrase, or word that's not essential to the meaning of the sentence: "My dog, sensing danger, ran to the front door and snarled."

✔ Use a semicolon to

- Separate two complete sentences that are related: "Sometimes, you separate two sentences with a period; other times, you use a semicolon."

- Separate two complete sentences connected with *however, therefore,* or some other transition word or phrase: "I usually have eggs for breakfast; however, I often order a BLT for breakfast when eating out."

- Separate items in a series when one or more of the items contains a comma: "We visited several cities along the way, including Paris, Texas; New Orleans, Louisiana; and Biloxi, Mississippi."

✔ Use a colon after an independent introductory clause and the phrase or clause that extends, illustrates, or amplifies the introductory statement: "The workers agreed on their demands: higher pay and a four-day workweek."

Don't

✔ Use a comma without a coordinating conjunction to separate two independent clauses: "Nobody came to the game, it was too cold out." (That's a comma splice.)

✔ Use a comma to separate two verbs or phrases that apply to the same subject: "The car packed with hooligans sped through the busy intersection, and nearly ran into a pickup truck full of watermelons."

✔ Use a comma after the main clause when a restrictive clause, usually starting with *that* follows it; for example, remove the comma before *that* in the following sentence: "The license, that I need to operate this vehicle, is nowhere to be found." (The phrase "that I need to operate this vehicle" is essential for specifying which license the person is talking about, so it isn't set off from the main clause by commas; in this case, you also remove the comma after *vehicle.*)

✔ Use a semicolon to introduce a list: "I bought three things for our camping trip; insect repellant, sunscreen, and boots." (The semicolon in this case should be a colon because it introduces words that extend the independent introductory clause.)

✔ Use a semicolon before a coordinating conjunction: "I avoided getting the flu this winter; but I did have a bad case of the sniffles." (The semicolon should be a comma.)

Practicing with capitalization, contractions, possessives, and punctuation

Challenge your newly acquired skills by answering the following sample questions. Note that the first answer choice repeats the original sentence.

1. People flew in to oaxaca, Mexico, from around the world to watch the total eclipse of the Sun.

   (A) People flew in to oaxaca, Mexico, from around the world to watch the total eclipse of the Sun.

   (B) People flew in to Oaxaca, Mexico, from around the world to watch the total eclipse of the Sun.

   (C) People flew in to Oaxaca, Mexico, from around the world to watch the total eclipse of the sun.

   (D) People flew in to oaxaca, Mexico, from around the world to watch the total eclipse of the sun.

2. We loved that movie with the penguins, but we can never remember it's name.

   (A) We loved that movie with the penguins, but we can never remember it's name.

   (B) We loved that movie with the penguins, but we can never remember its name.

   (C) We loved that movie with the penguins, but we can never remember it is name.

   (D) We loved that movie with the Penguins, but we can never remember it's name.

3. Unaware of the impending danger, the couple entered the vacant home.

   (A) Unaware of the impending danger, the couple entered the vacant home.

   (B) Unaware of the impending danger the couple entered the vacant home.

   (C) Unaware, of the impending danger, the couple entered the vacant home.

   (D) Unaware of the impending danger, the couple, entered the vacant home.

4. George Washington was the first President of the United States, Andrew Jackson was the seventh.

   (A) George Washington was the first President of the United States, Andrew Jackson was the seventh.

   (B) George Washington was the first president of the united states, Andrew Jackson was the seventh.

   (C) George Washington was the first president of the United States; Andrew Jackson was the seventh.

   (D) George Washington was the first President of the United States; Andrew Jackson was the seventh.

Check your answers:

   1. The correct answer is Choice (C). *Oaxaca* and *Mexico* must both be capitalized, and *sun* is lowercase unless it's at the beginning of a sentence.

   2. Choice (B) is correct because it's the only sentence that that has the correct possessive form of the word *it*.

   3. The correct answer is Choice (A). "Unaware of the impending danger" is an introductory phrase that requires a comma after it. All the other choices either have no comma or use superfluous (unnecessary) commas.

   4. The correct answer is Choice (C). You can rule out Choices (A) and (B) because they both have a comma splice. That narrows it down to Choices (C) and (D). Choice (C) wins out because *president* is lowercase when placed after the president's name.

Chapter 8

Penning Powerful Prose for the Extended Response

- -

In This Chapter

▶ Knowing how the Extended Response essay is scored

▶ Picking the side of the issue you can argue most effectively

▶ Collecting details and organizing your thoughts

▶ Tailoring your message to your audience and purpose

▶ Putting your thoughts into words and eliminating errors

- -

The RLA Extended Response item asks you to write an essay in 45 minutes on an assigned topic. This part of the test assesses your literacy and understanding. Even if you can understand the essay topic, you must now demonstrate that you're thoroughly familiar with the process of writing an essay and know correct spelling and the grammar and language usage rules (see Chapter 7). You're asked to read one or two source texts that present different viewpoints on an issue. You must determine which argument is better supported and write an essay supporting your position.

Keep in mind that writing this essay isn't that different from writing a letter or a blog post, except that you must explain and clarify the subject for the reader without rambling on until you run out of space.

In this chapter, we explain the criteria used to score the Extended Response essay and step you through the process to ensure that your essay meets the guidelines. Although writing isn't necessarily a linear process, we present a sequential approach to writing the Extended Response Essay. As you revise your essay, you may need or want to revisit earlier steps in the process.

Wrapping Your Brain around the Extended Response Guidelines

In spite of its name, the Extended Response doesn't consist of a real research essay so much as a series of related paragraphs. You aren't expected to produce a book-length opus complete with documented research. Rather, you're expected to write a coherent series of interrelated paragraphs on a given topic and use correct grammar, punctuation, and spelling. Your score is based partially on how effectively you analyze the argument and evidence presented in the passage(s), and partially on how effectively you present your own argument and evidence. Examiners look for an essay that's well organized and sticks to the topic given. Specifically, to write a top notch essay, here's what you need to do:

- **Choose the position in the passage(s) that's supported best.** Whether you agree or disagree with the issue presented is immaterial. The essay doesn't test your knowledge of a given topic or the validity of your personal opinions. Rather, it tests your ability to analyze the source documents and express and support your position using evidence from the passage(s).

- **State your position clearly and forcefully.** Don't mince words. Early in your essay, possibly as early as in the first sentence, state your position on the issue.

- **Support your position with plenty of evidence from the passage(s).** The reading passage(s) contain(s) all the evidence you need to support your claim. Don't introduce any evidence from your personal experience, reading you've done outside the test, or anywhere else.

- **Fully develop your main points.** Whenever you make a point, back it up with evidence from the passage(s). Stating a claim doesn't cut it; you have to develop and support those claims.

- **Present your thoughts and support in logical order.** Your essay must progress smoothly and logically from point A to point B, and you must tie all your supporting detail into your main points. Most importantly, stick to the topic.

- **Write a clear message with a specific purpose to convince a particular audience.** Your purpose is to convince an audience who may disagree with your position or be undecided. Your message must be clear and direct.

- **Transition smoothly throughout your essay.** Use transitional words and phrases as needed to tie paragraphs, sentences, and ideas together in a way that lets the reader easily follow your train of thought. Keep in mind, however, that transitional phrases can't overcome the weaknesses of a poorly organized essay. One of the best ways to transition smoothly from one idea to the next is to organize your essay so it follows a logical progression.

- **Choose precise words.** The best word is the clearest.

- **Vary your sentence structure.** Demonstrate your mastery of the language by composing sentences of varying length and complexity.

- **Avoid mistakes.** Spelling, grammar, and punctuation count, so if time remains, give your essay a final read-through to catch and eliminate errors.

The evaluation grades your essay on a three-point scale. You receive 2, 1, or 0 points, depending on your success in meeting these criteria. You can check out a guide for teachers on the RLA Extended Response at www.gedtestingservice.com/uploads/files/ 949aa6a0418791c4f3b962a4cd0c92f4.pdf. Here, you can see a sample essay prompt and a breakdown of how it's evaluated. Be aware that evaluation of the GED test is an ongoing process. The GED Testing Service does make changes to the test timing and format at times. The website will have the latest information.

A computer performs the initial evaluation of your essay. The software, a combination of grammar- and spell-checker and evaluation algorithm, screens your essay. This mechanical process looks for very specific points. Besides evaluating the content and arguments presented, it searches for grammar errors, spelling mistakes, wordy phrases and expressions, and non-Standard English usage. After the initial evaluation, a person, often a high-school English teacher, evaluates the essay.

Read the sections on what constitutes a passing score very carefully. If you don't pass the essay, you won't accumulate a high enough score on the other sections to pass the RLA test.

Choosing a Side

The RLA Extended Response essay requires you to examine two papers, essays, articles, documents, or other passages and decide which presents and defends its position best. (Sometimes, you'll read two arguments in a single passage.) You identify the thesis and examine the evidence presented. Your essay then argues which side presents the better argument based on the evidence presented.

Choosing a side is an important first step. If you choose the wrong side, you'll have less or worse evidence from the passages to support the position you decide to argue. Although the choice is entirely up to you, we recommend that you choose the position that is better argued and more fully supported, which may not necessarily be the position you personally agree with.

The process we suggest in the following sections is time consuming. You won't have time to perform it on the test as described here. This process provides you with a way to read the two passages critically, identify strengths and weaknesses in their arguments, and gather evidence for supporting whichever side you choose. On the test, you'll do much of this work in your head, jotting down a few notes for reference. However, we recommend that you practice the full process on numerous opinion pieces so that it becomes second nature prior to test day.

Identifying the different positions

The source texts you're provided are typically written in the form of argumentation essays. An argumentation essay has a *thesis statement,* typically a single sentence that presents a point of view on a controversial topic, followed by reasoning and evidence to support that claim. The thesis statement usually appears at the beginning of a passage and is reiterated at the end. The developers of the GED test choose passages in which the positions are fairly easy to identify.

As you skim the passages, the thesis should be obvious in the first paragraph. If you're unsure, read the first and final paragraphs and skim everything between. Ask yourself, "What's the point?" or "What is the author trying to persuade me to think or do?" If you can answer either question, you've discovered the thesis statement.

Read the following passages using the method we just described and identify the thesis statement in each passage. Write your answer on the line below each passage.

Passage One

The union movement has outlived its usefulness. It is based on a model of confrontation suitable for the 19th century but no longer needed in the 21st. The movement assumes that all employers are determined and able to increase their profits at the expense of workers. Whether they are keeping wages low or stripping workers of benefits, the employers are out to get the workers.

However, today labor laws provide protection against corporate excesses. Minimum wage standards, pensions, health insurance managed by the government, and laws governing safety in the workplace are all in place to protect workers. Laws against discrimination and legal procedures for firing workers restrict an employer's ability to terminate employment unjustly. Laws are even in place to protect workers who file complaints with government agencies against employers.

With all these protections, unionization does little for workers other than add to the workers' expenses as they support a bloated union bureaucracy.

Passage One thesis: _____

Passage Two

Workers need unions today more than ever. Corporations are determined to promote profits above all else, even at the expense of their own workers. This at a time when the average CEO's hourly earnings are between 600 and 700 times that of the average worker. Workers' hours are cut or their positions are turned over to contract workers. Jobs are downsized and sent offshore, benefits cut or denied, and wages kept as low as possible. The richest corporations even lobby against improvements to the minimum wage.

According to Executive Paywatch, the CEO of Yahoo in 2013 had a total annual compensation package of nearly $25 million, while the Bureau of Labor Statistics determined the average production worker earned just over $35,000. CEO earnings in 1965 were 20 times that of their workers; today the ratio is 300 times that. While wages for workers have stagnated, executive earnings have risen some 22 percent since 2010. Workers at the lowest end of the wage scale do not earn enough to live on. Ronald Reagan once said that wealth earned by the top income earners would trickle down to all. So far, we're still waiting.

Workers' wages are low, and many workers rely on welfare and food stamps to subsidize their earnings. Many workers get too few hours to qualify for benefits. Walmart, one of America's largest employers, is once again holding food drives at several stores for its employees. This is the same company that fought against any efforts to unionize workers, going so far as to close stores where a unionization vote had succeeded.

Unions negotiate more than just wages. Typical union contracts contain provisions for health care and other benefits, pensions in addition to the basic Social Security, antidiscrimination and workplace safety clauses, even job security provisions. These provisions go well beyond legislated minimums.

Legislation has alleviated the worst abuses of industrialization, especially during the New Deal. In part, that achievement grew out of new legislation supporting unionization and workers' rights. However, corporations have found new ways around the legislated controls and worker benefits. Only a strong union organization can protect workers.

Passage Two thesis: _____

The two passages cover the same issue: the need for unions. However, the passages have diametrically opposed positions. The first passage argues that unions are no longer required, while the second passage argues that workers really need unions today. Those positions are clearly identified in the first paragraph and summarized in the final paragraph in each passage:

Passage One thesis: <u>The union movement has outlived its usefulness.</u>

Passage Two thesis: <u>Workers need unions today more than ever.</u>

If the thesis statements you wrote down differ a little from the ones given here, that's fine. Just make sure that the thesis statement you wrote down for the first passage has something about unions being unnecessary and that the second one describes the opposite viewpoint.

The testing center supplies an erasable tablet to use as a scratch pad. Pen and paper aren't allowed. Use the tablet to take notes as you prepare to compose your RLA Extended Response essay. Start by making two lists, one for each passage. Write the thesis statement from each passage, and then write additional notes for each passage as you go.

Examining the strengths and weaknesses of each argument

As you read the two passages, you must analyze the passages to decide which presents the stronger argument. To determine which argument is stronger, analyze the passages in respect to the following items:

✔ Credibility of the *premises* (stated views) and any *assumptions* (unstated views) on which the argument is based

✔ Quantity and validity of the evidence presented to support the argument

✔ Bias or emotional appeals that may diminish the writer's credibility

✔ Faulty logic that weakens or undermines the argument

The GED test doesn't allow for fact checking the information presented. You have no access to outside reference materials. You have to accept that supporting evidence presented is valid, unless you notice a glaring error in something you know as absolute fact or the presentation shows some form of bias. Your task is to determine which passage presents the most (and most convincing) supporting evidence and uses it in a valid way.

Identifying premises and assumptions

The first step in analyzing the strengths and weaknesses of an argument is to identify and write down the premises and assumptions on which each argument is based. These are the claims, stated or implied, that the writer uses as the basis of mini-arguments leading up to the overall conclusion being drawn. (For more about identifying premises and assumptions, turn to Chapter 6.) Go back through the preceding two passages, identify the premises, and note them in the spaces provided here. (Don't identify assumptions yet.)

Passage One premises

1. _____
   _____
2. _____
   _____
3. _____
   _____
4. _____
   _____
5. _____
   _____

Passage Two premises

1. _____
   _____
2. _____
   _____
3. _____
   _____
4. _____
   _____
5. _____
   _____

Leave sufficient room below each premise to jot down a list of evidence presented in support of each premise.

What you identify as the premises may not match the following responses, but they should be pretty close:

Passage One premises

1. The current union model is outmoded.
2. Modern labor laws provide sufficient worker protection.
3. Unions do little for workers other than take their money.
4. Union dues merely support a bloated union bureaucracy.

Passage Two premises

1. Corporations are profit-driven at the expense of workers.
2. CEO incomes have risen dramatically while worker wages have stagnated.
3. Workers do not earn enough to live.
4. Unions help workers obtain more than just higher wages.
5. Corporations have found ways to work around labor laws.

Underlying assumptions are more difficult to spot because they're not directly stated and have no evidence to back them up. For example, in Passage Two, the second paragraph presents information about executive salaries compared to workers' incomes. The implication is that nothing justifies such a large difference between CEO and employee compensation. Assumptions are often weak claims in an argument that are open to debate.

Don't spend a great deal of time trying to root out assumptions, but be aware of them and jot down any assumptions you happen to notice for each passage:

Passage One assumptions

1. _____

2. _____

Passage Two assumptions

1. _____

2. _____

Here are a couple of assumptions we picked out from each passage

Passage One assumptions

1. Today's employers are not out to get the workers.
2. Labor laws are effective in protecting workers.

Passage Two assumptions

1. Nothing justifies the massive difference between CEO and average worker pay.
2. Unions benefit workers more than they cost workers.

Weighing the evidence

When you've nailed down the premises and assumptions, identify the supporting evidence for each premise. Below each premise, write a brief entry describing every piece of evidence presented to support it. When the list is complete, examine each piece of supporting evidence for validity.

Evidence can be fact or opinion and can come from a variety of sources. It has been selected to support the position the author takes in the passage, but it can be skewed. The passage may give statistics in a straightforward manner, like a newspaper article, without any evidence of bias. That information is possibly valid. Statistics may be mentioned together with their sources for more validity. Evidence from a variety of sources is even better. Overall consistency of evidence is also worth considering.

You need to decide whether the evidence is factual. Does the passage contain anything that lends credibility to the evidence? Does the selected evidence in any way show bias? Does the text use loaded vocabulary? The second paragraph of Passage One presents evidence clearly, without any signs of bias, although the evidence provided isn't very specific. The style is almost like a series of bullet points. The second passage does the same, using more specific data, and it specifies sources for some of the data.

Here is a chart that can help you organize the supporting information in a passage. Complete the chart shown in Figure 8-1 or draw up your own evidence analysis chart and use it to analyze the evidence presented in the two sample passages. Create additional pages as necessary.

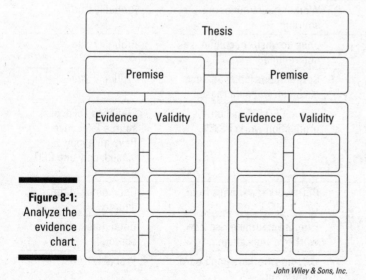

Figure 8-1:
Analyze the evidence chart.

John Wiley & Sons, Inc.

Table 8-1 shows a sample evidence analysis for the two sample passages presented in this section. Although your evidence analysis is likely to differ, it should reflect a similar unbiased analysis of the evidence.

Table 8-1   Sample Evidence Analysis for Passages One and Two

Passage	Premise	Evidence	Validity
One	Union model no longer useful	Based on model of confrontation	Probably true
		Assumes employers driven to exploit workers for their own benefit	Probably true
		Assumes employers out to get workers	Probably true
	Modern labor laws protect workers	Minimum wage, pensions, health insurance by government	Accurate
		Workplace safety laws	Accurate
		Antidiscrimination laws	Accurate
		Worker protection to file complaints	Accurate
			No discussion of how effective these laws are
	Unions do little for workers	Unions merely cost workers money	May be true
		Union dues support "bloated" bureaucracy	No support, biased
Two	Corporations profit driven at expense of workers	CEO earnings hundreds of times of average worker's	Probably true
		Worker hours cut or out-sourced	Probably true
		Jobs downsized, compensation reduced	Probably true
		Corporations lobby against minimum wage increases	Probably true
	CEO incomes rise while worker incomes sink	Yahoo CEO $25 million, production worker $35K	Statistics solid, but source Executive Paywatch may be biased; only one CEO used
		CEO: worker earnings from 20:1 to 600:1	Good detail, ditto source
		Executive earning rise 22%, worker wages stagnant	Good detail, ditto source
		Low-end workers don't earn living wage	Probably true
		Trickle down claim	Biased/emotional
		Many workers on welfare and food stamps	Probably true

Passage	Premise	Evidence	Validity
		Walmart food drive for employees	Only one example, happened at only some stores
	Unions do more than get higher wages	Health care, pensions, anti-discrimination, safety issues, job security	Probably true
		Provisions exceed legislated minimums	Probably true, good point
	Legislation not enough	Part of reason legislation has helped is that it has helped unions	Probably true, good point
		Corporations exploit loopholes in legislation	Probably true

Testing for logical errors

Logical errors are ways of thinking that lead to erroneous conclusions or fail to support those conclusions. We cover invalid reasoning in Chapter 6, but here are a few of the more common types of logical errors you need to watch out for:

✔ **Overgeneralization:** A broad conclusion drawn from a limited amount of evidence. Passage Two, for example, uses the Walmart food drive for workers to support the premise that workers are so underpaid food drives are necessary for their survival. However, you've already noted that this food drive happened in only two or three stores in the entire country. Although the point of poor wages may be true, the generalization isn't. Carefully examine any generalization. It can be a problem when based on very few facts and can easily be used to misrepresent.

✔ **Inaccurate depiction of the opposing viewpoint:** One common tactic in arguments is to mischaracterize the opposing viewpoint and then attack the fictional viewpoint. Passage One does so by comparing modern unions to those of the 19th century, during which time unions operated under the assumption that employers are "out to get the workers." However, no evidence is provided to prove that such a comparison is accurate.

✔ **Erroneous cause-effect connection:** Assuming that event A caused event B just because event A happened first is flawed reasoning. For example, the fact that childhood obesity has become more prevalent since the introduction of the chemical BPA in plastics doesn't mean that BPA caused the increase in childhood obesity. More evidence is necessary to prove the connection.

✔ **Faulty deductive reasoning:** Deductive reasoning usually involves two or more premises that lead to a conclusion. Both passages presented in this example use deductive reasoning:

- In Passage One, the reasoning goes something like this: "Labor laws accomplish what unions used to do in the past. Therefore, unions are an unnecessary expense for workers."

- In Passage Two, the reasoning goes something like this: "Corporations are profit driven and don't care about workers. Many workers don't earn enough to live. Unions help workers earn higher wages and other benefits. Corporations have found ways around labor laws; therefore, unions are still necessary."

Here's a common example of faulty deductive reasoning: "All dogs have four legs. My cat has four legs. Therefore, my cat is a dog." (See Chapter 6 for more about other logical flaws.) When evaluating arguments, carefully examine the premises and conclusion (thesis) to determine whether the conclusion follows logically from the premises.

Rooting out bias and emotional appeals

As part of your argument analysis, look for signs of bias and emotional appeals. Both of the sample passages presented contain statements that carry an emotional component instead of making a rational argument. The end of Passage One, for example, uses the phrase "bloated union bureaucracy," which is an emotionally charged value judgment with no evidence to back it up. In Passage Two, you can argue that the last sentence in the second paragraph carries emotional overtones with no evidence to support the claim against trickle-down economics. Emotional appeals can be useful in making an argument but can also mislead the reader. Consider whether these statements negate the arguments or are acceptable. You should certainly mention in your essay any incidence of bias or emotional appeal as part of the paragraph critical of what one or the other of the passages argues, so take note of them.

Picking a position you can support

You've done all the hard work of analyzing the arguments. Now you need to take a stand on the issue and pick a side. Which passage does a more effective job of presenting and supporting its point of view? More importantly, given the arguments and the evidence presented, for which side of the argument do you think the passages have best equipped you to argue? Notice that none of these questions asks you which position you agree with; that's irrelevant. When you're deciding which passage is most effective, you're not acting as a lawyer about to argue a case; instead, you're acting as a judge determining which side presented the best case. To help you decide which passage is most convincing, answer the following questions:

- ✔ Which passage presents the strongest, clearest thesis?
- ✔ In which passage do the premises lead most logically to the stated conclusion?
- ✔ Which passage provides the most and most detailed and credible evidence in support of its premises?
- ✔ Which passage is free of logical errors such as overgeneralizations?
- ✔ Which passage presents its claims in the most unbiased manner?

You have no other option. You must select one or the other passage. Although you should point out weaknesses in the passage you choose, the goal remains to show that one passage is definitely better supported than the other. You want to make sure that your position is clear.

Be aware of your own biases and preferences. If you're pro- or antiunion or are concerned about income inequality or executive wages, your own viewpoint may be biased toward one of these passages. That bias can influence your decision on which passage to argue for. Be careful to assess the material as dispassionately as possible. Keep to a strictly factual interpretation of the passage content.

Refer to the chart you used in Figure 8-1. Check off each point that has good support. Now decide which passage uses the fewest emotional appeals or least biased or loaded wording. Emotional appeals aren't in themselves wrong, but they can prejudice the way you interpret the information. Some emotion is quite normal in an essay designed to persuade; you need to decide whether a passage has too much. The same goes for loaded wording.

Writing a Clear, Direct Thesis Statement

Regardless of how you ultimately decide to introduce your Extended Response, you need to write a clear and direct *thesis statement* — a single sentence that proclaims your opinion regarding the issue discussed in the two passages. When writing your thesis statement, make sure it meets the following requirements:

- ✔ **Expresses your position on the issue discussed in the passages:** Take a stand. Pick a side.

- ✔ **Makes a statement that you're prepared to support:** Limit the scope of your thesis so it covers only the evidence presented in the passages. For example, if the passages cover why unions are or aren't beneficial for workers, and you write a thesis statement claiming that unions are good for businesses, you have no evidence from the passages to support your claim. Don't set yourself up for failure.

- ✔ **Is clear and direct:** The reader needs to know where you stand on the issue. See Chapter 7 for suggestions on how to write clearly and directly.

Here are two examples of strong thesis statements:

Based on the evidence presented in the two passages, unions are necessary to ensure fair compensation and acceptable working conditions for employees.

Although the second passage presents solid evidence in favor of unions, union dues are an added expense that modern day workers can ill afford.

Don't tell the reader what she already knows. The most common error in writing thesis statements is to write a statement of fact instead a statement of opinion. Here are a few examples of statements that fail to establish the writer's opinion on the issue:

Both passages present evidence to support their claims.

There are numerous reasons to support unions.

Some people think that unions are unnecessary.

Passage Two presents an argument in favor of unions.

Unions charge dues that some workers do not like to pay.

Take a stand on the issue and defend your position. You choose your position as though you're a judge, but when writing your thesis and essay, pretend you're a lawyer presenting your case to a judge or jurors. They need you to tell them what you're going to prove. However, keep yourself out of it. Avoid any mention of yourself with *I, me, my, myself,* or *mine:*

After reading the two passages, I have concluded that unions are good for workers.

I am of the opinion that unions should be abolished.

Evidence in the two passages leads me to believe that unions are a necessary evil.

Structuring Your Argument

You can structure your Extended Response in any number of ways. Every writer has a favorite. You've probably heard of the hamburger, pyramid, and inverted pyramid models. You can find plenty of information about those models online. We recommend what we call the *formula essay,* which is a variation of another common model, the five-paragraph essay. Here's the formula (outline), with each item in the list representing a paragraph:

1. **Introduction with thesis statement and, possibly, evidence preview:** This paragraph is where you state your position, typically identifying the passage that makes the stronger case and briefly stating why. The paragraph may also include a preview of the evidence or other introductory material to let the reader know what's coming next.

2. **Premise 1 with supporting evidence:** State your first premise and follow up with two or three sentences of supporting detail, based primarily on the evidence presented in the two passages.

3. **Premise 2 with supporting evidence:** State your second premise and follow up with two or three sentences of supporting detail, based primarily on the evidence presented in the two passages.

4. **Additional premise with supporting evidence (optional):** If you have additional evidence, state the premise drawn from that evidence along with a sentence or two of supporting detail.

5. **Acknowledgement and refutation of opposing viewpoint:** To convince a reader of a particular point of view, you must anticipate and address any *rebuttals* (counterarguments) to your argument. Because you're not in the reader's mind to respond to rebuttals, you must address them in your essay. You don't get a second chance. So just before you wrap up your essay, acknowledge at least one opposing viewpoint and refute it, preferably with evidence to show why the opposing viewpoint is wrong. Here's where your notes come in handy. If you noticed any logical errors that form the basis of the opposing viewpoint, introduce them here.

6. **Conclusion with restatement of thesis and, possibly, evidence recap:** Wrap it up. Restate your thesis in a confident tone to add closure to your essay.

Draft an outline for your formula essay starting with the thesis statement you wrote.

1. **Thesis statement:** _____
2. **Premise 1:** _____
3. **Premise 2:** _____
4. **Additional premise:** _____
5. **Opposing viewpoint:** _____
6. **Conclusion:** _____

Listen to the preacher

A visitor happened to walk into a poor backwoods church and listen to the preacher deliver a very sophisticated sermon. He asked how the preacher could make his audience understand such a complicated subject matter. The preacher replied, "Easy: First, I tells 'em what I'm gonna tell'm, then I tell'm, and then I tell'm what I tole 'em."

Follow this same approach when you're writing your Extended Response, and you can't go wrong.

Here's an example:

1. **Thesis statement:** <u>The evidence in the two passages indicates that unions are as necessary today as they were in the last century.</u>

2. **Premise 1:** <u>The argument that unions are needed to improve wages is made clearly and shown with appropriate supporting evidence.</u>

3. **Premise 2:** <u>The important role that unions play in protecting workers' benefits beyond just wages is also clearly stated and has sufficient evidence to support it.</u>

4. **Additional premise:** <u>The third key argument — the links among the need for employers to find cheaper labor to remain competitive, legislation that has encouraged many companies to outsource jobs, and the need for unions to protect domestic jobs — is also clearly presented and supported.</u>

5. **Opposing viewpoint:** <u>The counterargument that new laws preserve workers' rights is valid but ignores the fact that these laws can be and are being circumvented by employers.</u>

6. **Conclusion:** <u>The argument that unions are needed now more than ever is stronger.</u>

Putting your main points in logical order

In your opening paragraph, after your thesis statement, you presented your points in a logical order. Whether that order was in ascending or descending order of importance is a matter of personal preference, although most examiners prefer an ascending order. That builds involvement and anticipation, just like a growing crescendo in music.

If you followed our process for writing a formula essay, your main points should be in logical order, but double-check the outline you produced in the previous section to be sure. Focus especially on your premises, paragraphs 2, 3, and 4. Your thesis statement will remain at the beginning, your conclusion will stay at the end, and your second-to-last paragraph, where you address the opposing viewpoint, won't move. The only three main points you need to concern yourself with are your premises.

Building your arguments

Each paragraph in the body of your Extended Response essay deals with a single point. Structure each paragraph like a miniature essay. The first sentence in each paragraph is the *topic sentence,* a statement identifying the point to be discussed in that paragraph. The rest of the paragraph must support that main point. Supporting details may include evidence, facts from the passage, and even relevant passage quotations.

At this point in the process, imagine yourself filling out a form like the following:

Paragraph One

Thesis statement: _____

Evidence summary:

> ✔ _____
> _____
> ✔ _____
> _____
> ✔ _____
> _____

Paragraph Two

Premise 1: _____

Evidence:

✔ _____
_____
✔ _____
_____
✔ _____
_____

Paragraph Three

Premise 2: _____

Evidence:

✔ _____
_____
✔ _____
_____
✔ _____
_____

Paragraph Four (optional)

Premise 3: _____

Evidence:

✔ _____
_____
✔ _____
_____
✔ _____
_____

Paragraph Five (optional)

Opposing viewpoint: _____

Rebuttal: _____

Evidence:

✔ _____
_____
✔ _____
_____
✔ _____
_____

Paragraph Six (Final)

Thesis restatement: _____

Closure: _____

Considering Your Purpose, Audience, and Message

Whenever you write anything — your GED test Extended Response, a letter to the editor of your local paper, or a cover letter for your resume — you need to think about what you want the letter to accomplish, the person(s) you're addressing, and the message you want to convey. You don't have to write all this information down or address it any formal way in your essay, but you do need to keep purpose, audience, and message in mind as you write your Extended Response. In the following sections, we describe each of these considerations in turn.

Purpose

When writing your RLA Extended Response, the purpose is clear: You're writing to express your point of view and convince the reader that you're right. Sure, your underlying purpose is to score as high as possible on this portion of the test, but if the people scoring your Extended Response are convinced by your argument, you'll achieve that goal, too.

Purpose is important because it influences everything from organization to word choice. A letter to persuade your boss to give you a raise is quite different from instructions for connecting to a Wi-Fi hotspot.

Your purpose in an argumentative essay is to convince the reader. Don't get confused with purposes of other types of writing. Your purpose isn't to instruct, describe, or tell a story. Although you do need to inform the reader in terms of providing evidence to support your claims (thesis and premises), your primary objective isn't to inform or explain. Your objective is to *persuade*.

Audience

Like a movie, an essay is intended for a particular audience. Before you put pen to paper, you need to think about who will be reading your essay. If your essay were to be used as an industry magazine editorial, you'd know that you had an audience with a particular level of education and set of interests. Your audience may have specific political leanings, biases, and preconceptions. To persuade such an audience of your viewpoint, you need to write your essay in a way that this audience will accept your points. Whether you're writing for preteens, university professors, or your neighbors, you adjust the way you present the information to make it suitable.

Your audience for the Extended Response consists of the people who will read and score your essay. Write your essay as if to convince your high-school English teacher. The evaluators expect you to use Standard English — to demonstrate a good command of vocabulary and grammar. They want to see precision in your arguments.

Message

The message is what you want the reader to understand and accept. You want to present that message clearly and in a way that your audience will acknowledge. When you've organized the key points you want to present in your essay, you need to review how well they prove your thesis and how you present the information. You want to be convincing without being harsh. The wording needs to be strong enough to make the message clear without becoming so aggressive that the audience rejects it.

Writing and Revising Your Essay

After you've outlined your Extended Response, it should almost write itself. You've done the heavy lifting. You have a strong point of view and two or more strong premises, along with plenty of evidence to support each of them. You know which objection you're going to refute and how you're going to refute it. Now all you need to do is string together sentences to form paragraphs and paragraphs to form your Extended Response.

As you compose your Extended Response, follow the good-writing guidelines presented in Chapter 7. In the following sections, we highlight areas of writing on which to focus your efforts.

Practice writing Extended Responses on a computer so you're accustomed to typing, cutting, copying, pasting, and moving text around on-screen and, perhaps most importantly, to how to undo changes in case you delete something by mistake. The computer software used to write the RLA exam provides a very basic word processor. It allows you to cut and paste, insert and delete, and generally rewrite as you want. It doesn't contain a grammar- or spell-check function. You can outline your essay on the tablet provided. However, it will probably not allow you to do a rough draft. You'll need to write that draft on-screen and then do all your revisions there as well. Transitioning from paper to screen can be challenging. If you're not comfortable with writing and editing on-screen, the best advice is to practice, practice, and practice some more.

Choosing your words carefully

When you've completed your rough draft on-screen, reread what you've written with an eye toward word choice and efficiency. Chapter 7 explains the importance of choosing the most precise words and avoiding the pitfalls of wordiness. Specifically, look for the following signs of trouble:

- **Homonyms:** Words that sound the same but differ in meaning

- **Frequently confused words:** Words such as *accept* and *except* that people commonly misuse

- **Slang and other informal English:** Phrases such as *kind of* and *sort of* or, even worse, *kinda* and *sorta*

- **Passive voice:** Sentences that start with anything other than the person or thing performing the action

- **Negative phrases:** Phrases with "no" or "not" that can be rephrased into shorter, positive statements

- ✔ **Redundancy:** Repetition of words, statements, details, or ideas
- ✔ **Nominalizations:** Verbs used as nouns, such as *indication* (indicate) and *stabilization* (stabilize)
- ✔ **Phrasal verbs:** Two or more words used together to express action, such as *decide on* (choose) and *hold up* (delay)
- ✔ **Unnecessary use of prepositions:** Prepositional phrases that can be reduced to one or two words, such as *view of the majority* (majority's view) or *on a regular basis* (regularly)

Vocabulary in essay writing is important. When you're trying to convince an audience that your points are valid and need to be taken seriously, presentation is important. Remember that the RLA test expects you to use proper and Standard English, avoiding slang and collo-quial expressions. Review the list of homonyms and commonly mistaken words presented in Chapter 7. Be sure you're using the appropriate words in the proper manner. Check for short forms or familiar expressions, and make sure they conform to Standard English usage. You're not writing for your pals. You're writing for evaluators with very specific expecta-tions of clarity and language use.

The English language has dozens of words meaning roughly the same thing. The synonyms often have subtle differences among them. Choose the most precise word you can think of. Misusing vocabulary counts against you when your paper is marked. However, don't get so obsessed with choosing the right word that you run out of time; express yourself as clearly as possible, and then go back through if time remains and make adjustments.

Varying your sentence patterns

Nothing is more boring than sentences that are all alike. That would be like a song consist-ing of only one note or the annoying drip, drip, drip of a leaky faucet. Vary your sentence patterns by mixing simple sentences with compound, complex, and compound-complex sentences, as explained in Chapter 7.

However, complexity increases the risk of errors. The more complex your sentences become, the higher the chances that you may make grammar mistakes. Pay particular attention to subject-verb agreement and to pronouns and their antecedents. See Chapter 7 for details.

Smoothing transitions

When markers read your Extended Response, they evaluate how well you transition from one sentence to the next and from one paragraph to the next. They need to be able to follow your train of thought. If you present them with a train wreck, you'll earn a well-deserved low score. To build smooth transitions into your Extended Response, use the following three techniques:

- ✔ **Stick to your outline.** A well-organized essay doesn't have to rely so much on heavy-duty transitional words and phrases, such as "as a result," "therefore," and "due to the fact that."
- ✔ **Repeat key words and phrases.** Frequently, you can subtly transition from sentence to sentence or paragraph to paragraph by repeating one or more key words from the pre-vious sentence in the new sentence.

> ✔ **Use transitional phrases as needed.** Transitional phrases provide valuable information to readers regarding how two ideas are related, or they signal a shift or contrast between two ideas. Although you should avoid overusing them, don't avoid using them altogether.

For more about transitional words and phrases, check out Chapter 7.

Detecting and eliminating errors in spelling, grammar, usage, and punctuation

As you read and revise your Extended Response, don't overlook the little stuff. Spelling, grammar, usage, and punctuation count toward your final score, and because you're not using a full-featured word processor, you're your own editor. Be particularly mindful of the following issues:

> ✔ ***It's* versus *its*:** *It's* is the contraction of "it is." *Its* is the possessive pronoun.
>
> ✔ ***Number* versus *amount*:** Number is a count of individuals, such as rabbits. Amount is a quantity of stuff, such as mashed potatoes.
>
> ✔ **Quotation mark placement:** Periods and commas go inside quotation marks. Question marks, semicolons, and colons go inside quotation marks if they're part of the quotation and outside when they're not.
>
> ✔ **Complete sentences:** A complete sentence requires a subject and a verb, an actor and an action.
>
> ✔ **Pronoun-antecedent clarity:** Be particularly careful of demonstrative pronouns, such as *this, these,* and *those*. If the reader has to question what any of those words refers to, you need to add something from the previous sentence to clarify. For example, if you're explaining a new government policy and then write something like "*This* calls for a change in policy," you can clarify by saying something along the lines of "*This* oversight calls for. . ." or "*This* incident calls for. . . ."
>
> ✔ **Commas and conjunctions:** Place a comma before a conjunction, such as *and* and *so,* if the conjunction joins two complete sentences, each with its own subject and verb. Omit the comma if what follows the conjunction isn't a complete sentence. Be careful when the subject of a sentence performs two actions, as in "Larry mowed the lawn and planted some flowers." You don't see a comma before *and* because what follows it isn't a complete sentence.

For more about ridding your prose of common errors in grammar, usage, and punctuation, see Chapter 7.

Rereading and revising your response

The final step in preparing your essay is to reread and revise. Writing on a computer presents particular challenges. Studies show people are more likely to skim and skip over text on-screen than to read thoroughly. Now that you're aware of that, carefully reread your draft. Sometimes reading "out loud" to yourself without actually speaking is a good technique for reading more carefully. The "to yourself" part is important because actually reading out loud may get you into trouble on the actual test.

As you reread, remain especially sensitive to word choice, sentence patterns, and transitions, as explained earlier in this chapter. In addition, check the following:

- **Words or phrases that make you stumble:** If you have trouble reading something, your evaluator will have even more trouble. Rephrase to smooth out the bumps.

- **Meaningless phrases:** Sometimes a sentence or phrase seems important when you write it, but you find yourself asking, "What was I thinking?!" when you reread it. Get rid of these bits before the evaluator sees them.

- **Overly obvious phrases:** If a sentence or phrase tempts you to respond, "Yeah, duh!", it's probably too obvious to mention. Delete it.

- **Digressions:** Although the formula model is likely to keep you on track, one of the most common errors involves drifting off topic. If you start to rant, you're probably drifting off topic. Your Extended Response should follow a clear path from introduction to conclusion.

Part III
Putting Your RLA Knowledge and Skills to the Test

Five Ways to Simulate the GED RLA Test Environment

✔ Find a quiet place to work where you won't be distracted or interrupted. Put away cellphones, music players, and all other electronic devices. They won't be permitted on test day.

✔ Set a timer to count down from the total time allocated for each section of the test.

✔ *Don't* go to the next section of the test until the time allotted for the current section is up. If you finish early, check your work for that section only.

✔ Give yourself exactly one ten-minute break before writing the Extended Response essay. Don't take any other breaks.

✔ Type your Extended Response essay instead of using pen and paper. Use only a text editor, such as Windows Notepad or TextEdit on a Mac, and disable the spell-checker and grammar-checker on your word processor.

If English isn't your first language, head to www.dummies.com/extras/gedrlatest for a free article that provides information on the GED Testing Service's English as a Second Language (ESL) test.

In this part. . .

✔ See how your stamina measures up by taking a full-length practice GED RLA test, including an Extended Response prompt.

✔ Score your test quickly with the answer key.

✔ Discover how to improve your performance by reading through the answer explanations for all practice test questions and evaluating your Extended Response essay.

Chapter 9

Taking an RLA Practice Test

. . . .

*R*eady to practice your language skills? You have 95 minutes to complete the question-and-answer section, followed by a 10-minute break, and then another 45 minutes to write the Extended Response (the essay). Remember, on the actual GED test, you can't transfer unused time from one section to another.

The answers and explanations to this test's questions are in Chapter 10. Review the explanations to all the questions, not just the ones you missed. Going over the answers is a good review technique.

Practice tests work best when you take them under the same conditions as the real test. We can't provide a computer test along with this book, but you can simulate the test-taking experience in other ways. Take this test in a room with no distractions, no music, no telephone, no munchies, and no interruptions. Do the test in one sitting. You have only one ten-minute break.

Unless you require accommodations, you'll be taking the GED test on a computer. You'll see all the questions on a computer screen and use a keyboard or mouse to indicate your answers. We formatted the questions and answer choices in this book to make them visually as similar as possible to the real GED test. We had to retain some A, B, C, D choices for marking your answers, and we provide a separate answer sheet for you to do so. Also, to make it simpler for you to time yourself, we present the question-and-answer sections as one unit rather than two, followed by the Extended Response at the end.

Answer Sheet for Reasoning Through Language Arts Practice Test

1. Ⓐ Ⓑ Ⓒ Ⓓ		26. Ⓐ Ⓑ Ⓒ Ⓓ	
2. Ⓐ Ⓑ Ⓒ Ⓓ		27. Ⓐ Ⓑ Ⓒ Ⓓ	
3. Ⓐ Ⓑ Ⓒ Ⓓ		28. Ⓐ Ⓑ Ⓒ Ⓓ	
4. Ⓐ Ⓑ Ⓒ Ⓓ		29. Ⓐ Ⓑ Ⓒ Ⓓ	
5. Ⓐ Ⓑ Ⓒ Ⓓ		30. Ⓐ Ⓑ Ⓒ Ⓓ	
6. Ⓐ Ⓑ Ⓒ Ⓓ		31. [_____]	
7. [_____]		32. Ⓐ Ⓑ Ⓒ Ⓓ	
8. Ⓐ Ⓑ Ⓒ Ⓓ		33. Ⓐ Ⓑ Ⓒ Ⓓ	
9. Ⓐ Ⓑ Ⓒ Ⓓ		34. Ⓐ Ⓑ Ⓒ Ⓓ	
10. Ⓐ Ⓑ Ⓒ Ⓓ		35. Ⓐ Ⓑ Ⓒ Ⓓ	
11. Ⓐ Ⓑ Ⓒ Ⓓ		36. Ⓐ Ⓑ Ⓒ Ⓓ	
12. Ⓐ Ⓑ Ⓒ Ⓓ		37. Ⓐ Ⓑ Ⓒ Ⓓ	
13. Ⓐ Ⓑ Ⓒ Ⓓ		38. Ⓐ Ⓑ Ⓒ Ⓓ	
14. Ⓐ Ⓑ Ⓒ Ⓓ		39. Ⓐ Ⓑ Ⓒ Ⓓ	
15. Ⓐ Ⓑ Ⓒ Ⓓ		40. [_____]	
16. Ⓐ Ⓑ Ⓒ Ⓓ		41. Ⓐ Ⓑ Ⓒ Ⓓ	
17. Ⓐ Ⓑ Ⓒ Ⓓ		42. Ⓐ Ⓑ Ⓒ Ⓓ	
18. Ⓐ Ⓑ Ⓒ Ⓓ		43. Ⓐ Ⓑ Ⓒ Ⓓ	
19. Ⓐ Ⓑ Ⓒ Ⓓ		44. Ⓐ Ⓑ Ⓒ Ⓓ	
20. Ⓐ Ⓑ Ⓒ Ⓓ		45. Ⓐ Ⓑ Ⓒ Ⓓ	
21. Ⓐ Ⓑ Ⓒ Ⓓ		46. Ⓐ Ⓑ Ⓒ Ⓓ	
22. [_____]		47. Ⓐ Ⓑ Ⓒ Ⓓ	
23. Ⓐ Ⓑ Ⓒ Ⓓ		48. Ⓐ Ⓑ Ⓒ Ⓓ	
24. Ⓐ Ⓑ Ⓒ Ⓓ		49. Ⓐ Ⓑ Ⓒ Ⓓ	
25. Ⓐ Ⓑ Ⓒ Ⓓ		50. [_____]	

Reasoning Through Language Arts Test

Time: 95 minutes for 50 questions

Directions: Mark your answers on the answer sheet provided.

Questions 1–10 refer to the following article.

But not all brands of bottled water are the same, many bottlers use the same municipal water that comes from your tap. It merely has to completely remove the chlorine and do some additional filtration to enhance the taste. Bottled spring waters are different. The mineral content of waters differs from spring to spring, producing water with a unique taste. Other bottled waters are carbonated; either naturally or artificially in the bottling process; carbonation can add to the clean taste of water.

If you find mineral water whose taste you enjoy and don't mind the cost, enjoy. From a "green" perspective, the plastic litter is a huge negative. Also, the effect on the environment of moving large quantities of potable water from one area to another make this an undesirable solution.

Many people enjoy their bottled water taste. So how can you get the same clean taste without the waste? The least expensive way is to use a jug with a charcoal filter cartridge. Filling that jug with clean tap water removes the chlorine and unpleasant tastes or odors. It also removes some of the led found in the water pipes of older buildings. This is an effective and inexpensive choice. Certainly our morning coffee and tea taste better for this filtration.

A more advanced and expensive counter-top system is a distillation pot. This system boils water, collects the steam, and condensed it into absolutely pure water. But not everyone likes the taste of totally mineral-free water, and the electricity costs add up.

They're also more extensive systems available. If you get tired of changing cartridges or storing the plastic jug in your fridge, you can also have an under-the-counter system installed on your kitchen sink. In houses, you can add such a system on the main water pipe and provide the same filtration to the entire house. Some of these systems use carbon blocks and ceramic filters. The blocks are more effective than loose charcoal filters. Also removing traces of pesticides and other chemical contaminants. Ceramic filters remove cloudiness and micro-particles, spores, and other microscopic matter, but not dissolved materials. They deliver excellent drinking water. In either case, there is little waste other than the filters.

1. How would you correct the underlined portion of the following sentence?

   But not <u>all brands of bottled water are the same, many bottlers use</u> the same municipal water that comes from your tap.

   (A) all brands of bottled water are the same, many bottlers use

   (B) all brands of bottled water are the same; many bottlers use

   (C) all brands of bottled water are the same many bottlers use

   (D) all brands of bottled water are the same, but bottlers use

2. How would you correct the underlined portion of the following sentence?

   <u>It merely has to</u> completely remove the chlorine and do some additional filtration to enhance the taste.

   (A) It merely has to

   (B) They merely have to

   (C) It has to merely

   (D) They merely has to

3. How would you correct the following sentence?

   It also removes some of the led found in the water pipes of older buildings.

   (A) It also removes some of the led found in the water pipes of older buildings.

   (B) It also removes some of the led found in the water pipe of older buildings.

   (C) It also removes some of the lead found in the water pipes of older buildings.

   (D) It also removed some of the lead found in the water pipes of older buildings.

4. How would you correct the underlined portion of the following sentence?

   <u>This system boils water, collects the steam, and condensed it into absolutely pure water.</u>

   (A) This system boils water, collects the steam, and condensed it into absolutely pure water.

   (B) This system boils water, collects the steam and condensed it into absolutely pure water.

   (C) This system boils water, collects the steam, and condenses it into absolutely pure water.

   (D) This system boils water, collects the steam and condenses it into absolutely pure water.

5. How would you correct the underlined portion of the following sentence?

   Other bottled waters <u>are carbonated; either naturally or artificially in the bottling process; carbonation can add</u> to the clean taste of water.

   (A) are carbonated; either naturally or artificially in the bottling process; carbonation can add

   (B) are carbonated naturally or artificially in the bottling process, carbonation can add

   (C) are carbonated. Either naturally or artificially in the bottling process; carbonation can add

   (D) are carbonated, either naturally or artificially in the bottling process; carbonation can add

6. How would you correct the following sentence?

   They're also more extensive systems available.

   (A) They're also more extensive systems available.

   (B) There are also more extensive systems available.

   (C) Their are also more extensive systems available.

   (D) none of the above

7. What is a more effective filter than loose charcoal? ⬚.

8. What are the disadvantages of using ceramic filters?

    (A) can't remove micro-particles

    (B) don't remove dissolved chemicals

    (C) removes taste

    (D) leaves spores in water

9. How would you correct the following sentence?

    If you get tired of changing cartridges or storing the plastic jug in your fridge, you can also have an under-the-counter system installed on your kitchen sink.

    (A) change the word *fridge* to *refrigerator*

    (B) change *can also have* to *also can have*

    (C) insert a comma after *jug*

    (D) no change required

10. How would you correct the underlined portion of these sentences?

    The blocks are more <u>effective than loose charcoal filters. Also removing traces</u> of pesticides and other chemical contaminants.

    (A) affective than loose charcoal filters, also removing traces

    (B) effective than lose charcoal filters. Also removing traces

    (C) effective than loose charcoal filters; also removing traces

    (D) effective than loose charcoal filters, also removing traces

---

Questions 11–17 refer to the following business letter.

Urban Parent,
Northern Publications
447 Peer Rd.

Dear Sirs,

Please find enclosed a proposal for an article on Alternative Schools for your consideration.

(1) Your publication would be an ideal platform for an article on the alternative schools. (2) Your demographics include the very age group of parents who have concerns about the education our children are receiving. (3) However, many parents are unaware of the fascinating range of options available to them beyond the regular classroom.

(4) I and my colleague are educators, with experience at all levels. (5) We have taught elementary and secondary schools, as well as in university and adult education. (6) We both at various times Chairs of the District School Board's Alternative Schools Advisory Council. (7) We founded four different alternative schools for the school board.

(8) We hope that this proposal is of interest; and, look forward to hearing from you.

Yours truly,

Adam Jamieson

11. Sentence 1: **Please find enclosed a proposal for an article on Alternative Schools for your consideration.**

    Which revision should be made to Sentence 1?

    (A) Please find enclosed a proposal for an article on Alternative Schools for your consideration.

    (B) Please find enclosed a proposal for an article on alternative schools.

    (C) Please find enclosed a proposal for an article on Alternative Schools, for your consideration.

    (D) Enclosed is a proposal for a article on alternative schools.

12. Sentence 2: **Your publication would be an ideal platform for an article on the alternative schools.**

    Which is the best way to improve Sentence 2?

    (A) Your publication would be an ideal platform for an article on the alternative schools.

    (B) Your publication will be an ideal platform for an article on the alternative schools.

    (C) Your publication is an ideal platform for an article on the alternative schools.

    (D) Your publication might be an ideal platform for an article on the alternative schools.

13. Sentence 3: **Your demographics include the very age group of parents who have concerns about the education our children are receiving.**

    Which correction should be made to Sentence 3?

    (A) no change required

    (B) change *parents who* to *parents that*

    (C) change *our children* to *their children*

    (D) change *include* to *included*

14. Sentence 4: **I and my colleague are educators, with experience at all levels.**

    Which is the best way to correct Sentence 4?

    (A) I and my colleague are educators, with experience at all levels.

    (B) My colleague and I are educators, with experience at all levels.

    (C) I and my colleague are Educators, with experience at all levels.

    (D) My colleague and me are educators, with experience at all levels.

15. Sentence 5: **We have taught elementary and secondary schools, as well as in university and adult education.**

    Which correction should be made to Sentence 5?

    (A) We have taught elementary and secondary schools, as well as in university and adult education.

    (B) We have taught elementary and secondary, as well as university and adult education.

    (C) We have taught elementary and secondary schools; and as well, as in university and for adult education.

    (D) We teach elementary and secondary schools, as well as in university and adult education.

16. Sentence 6: **We both at various times Chairs of the District School Board's Alternative Schools Advisory Council.**

    Which correction should be made to Sentence 6?

    (A) We both at various times Chairs of the District School Board's Alternative Schools Advisory Council.

    (B) We both at various times, Chairs of the District School Board's Alternative Schools Advisory Council.

    (C) We both at various times Chairs of the District School Board's Alternative Schools Advisery Council.

    (D) We were both at various times Chairs of the District School Board's Alternative Schools Advisory Council.

17. Sentence 8: **We hope that this proposal is of interest; and, look forward to hearing from you.**

    How would you correct Sentence 7?

    (A) We hope that this proposal is of interest; and, look forward to hearing from you.

    (B) We hope that this proposal was of interest; and, look forward to hearing from you.

    (C) We hope that this proposal is of interest and look forward to hearing from you.

    (D) We hope that this proposal is of interest, and look forward to hearing from you.

Questions 18–19 refer to the following excerpt adapted from Customer Service For Dummies *by Karen Leland and Keith Bailey (Wiley).*

The Care Token Coupon

(1) A new Copie Shoppe recently opened near our office. (2) Modern and full of new, streamlined, state-of-the-art copiers; (3) the Fast Copy Company store was just what I needed. (4) The first time I went over, I waited 45 minutes before service because of a shortage of trained staff. (5) They bounced back by apologized, explained the situation, and gave me a care token coupon that was worth 100 free copies. (6) Okay, I thought, fair enough, they're new and getting their act together, no big deal. (7) A week later, I went back and waited 30 minutes for service. (8) They apologised, explained the situation, and gave me a coupon for 100 free copies. (9) This time I was a little less understanding. (10) Two weeks later, I went back and the same thing happened again. (11) I didn't want another free coupon — they had bounced back just once too often. (12) My opinion of their services were so soured that I began looking for another copy shop.

18. Sentence 1: <u>**A new Copie Shoppe recently opened**</u> near our office.

    Which correction should be made to the underlined portion of Sentence 1?

    (A) no change required

    (B) change *Copie Shoppe* to *copy shop*

    (C) change *Copie Shoppe* to *copy shoppe*

    (D) change *a* to *an*

19. Sentences 2 and 3: **Modern and full of new, streamlined, state-of-the-art copiers; (3) the Fast Copy Company store was just what I needed.**

    Which improvement should be made to Sentences 2 and 3?

    (A) no change required.

    (B) remove the hyphens from *state-of-the-art*

    (C) change the semicolon after *copiers* to a comma

    (D) change *store was* to *the copiers were*

20. **The president will visit our town today. It is a historical event.**

    What correction does this passage require?

    (A) replace *historical* with *historic*

    (B) capitalize *president*

    (C) merge the two sentences with a comma after *today*.

    (D) no correction required

21. **We were about to leave when the Bradley's arrived.**

    Which correction should be made to the following?

    (A) add a comma after *leave*

    (B) replace *were* with *are*

    (C) replace *Bradley's* with *Bradleys*

    (D) no correction required

22. What is the correct word for the following sentence, *compliment* or *complement?*

    The platoon had a full [   ] of specialists available.

23. How would you correct the following sentence?

    Considered virtually unsinkable, the captain went down with the Titanic.

    (A) delete *considered virtually unsinkable* and capitalize *the.*

    (B) Change the sentence to "The Captain went down with the Titanic that had been considered virtually unsinkable."

    (C) Change the sentence to "The captain went down with the Titanic, which had been considered virtually unsinkable."

    (D) Change the sentence to "The Captain went down with the Titanic which had been considered virtually unsinkable."

24. How would you correct the following sentence?

    The detectives could not identify the man; who had they arrested?

    (A) The detectives could not identify the man; who had they arrested?

    (B) The detectives could not identify the man; whom had they arrested?

    (C) The detectives could not identify the man who had they arrested.

    (D) The detectives could not identify the man; that they had arrested?

25. How would you correct the following sentence?

    Whenever that group of children sneeze, I get the urge to throw tissues at them.

    (A) no change required

    (B) change *get* to *got*

    (C) change *sneeze* to *sneezed*

    (D) change *sneeze* to *sneezes*

Questions 26–29 refer to the following excerpt from The Prince *by Niccolò Machiavelli* (www.gutenberg.org).

A prince ought to have no other aim or thought, nor select anything else for his study, than war and its rules and discipline; for this is the sole art that belongs to him who rules, and it is of such force that it not only upholds those who are born princes, but it often enables men to rise from a private station to that rank. And, on the contrary, it is seen that when princes have thought more of ease than of arms they have lost their states. And the first cause of your losing it is to neglect this art; and what enables you to acquire a state is to be master of the art. Francesco Sforza, through being martial, from a private person became Duke of Milan; and the sons, through avoiding the hardships and troubles of arms, from dukes became private persons. For among other evils which being unarmed brings you, it causes you to be despised, and this is one of those ignominies against which a prince ought to guard himself, as is shown later on. Because there is nothing proportionate between the armed and the unarmed; and it is not reasonable that he who is armed should yield obedience willingly to him who is unarmed, or that the unarmed man should be secure among armed servants. Because, there being in the one disdain and in the other suspicion, it is not possible for them to work well together. And therefore a prince who does not understand the art of war, over and above the other misfortunes already mentioned, cannot be respected by his soldiers, nor can he rely on them. He ought never, therefore, to have out of his thoughts this subject of war, and in peace he should addict himself more to its exercise than in war; this he can do in two ways, the one by action, the other by study.

26. Why does Machiavelli think the unarmed and armed cannot work together?

   (A) The unarmed are suspicious of the armed, and the armed disdain the unarmed.

   (B) A well-schooled prince would not allow it.

   (C) The armed are suspicious of the unarmed, and the unarmed disdain the armed

   (D) Peaceful men are respected by their soldiers.

27. What is the relationship between the armed and unarmed?

   (A) They are proportionate.

   (B) They must work together to avoid disdain and suspicion.

   (C) They are disproportionate because the armed will always defer to the unarmed.

   (D) They are disproportionate because the armed will never yield to the unarmed.

28. What is Machiavelli's underlying premise in this passage?

   (A) The art of war is the only means to power.

   (B) Unarmed men are despised.

   (C) War is the ultimate purpose of society.

   (D) None of the above.

29. What does Machiavelli mean when he states someone is a "private person"?

   (A) someone without power who is not a prince or leader

   (B) someone withdrawn from public scrutiny

   (C) reclusive aristocrat

   (D) child of aristocrats

Questions 30–34 refer to the following passage from The Adventures of Tom Sawyer *by Mark Twain (*www.gutenberg.org*).*

[Aunt Polly speaks about Tom] "Hang the boy, can't I never learn anything? Ain't he played me tricks enough like that for me to be looking out for him by this time? But old fools is the biggest fools there is. Can't learn an old dog new tricks, as the saying is. But my goodness, he never plays them alike, two days, and how is a body to know what's coming? He 'pears to know just how long he can torment me before I get my dander up, and he knows if he can make out to put me off for a minute or make me laugh, it's all down again and I can't hit him a lick. I ain't doing my duty by that boy, and that's the Lord's truth, goodness knows. Spare the rod and spile the child, as the Good Book says. I'm a laying up sin and suffering for us both, I know. He's full of the Old Scratch, but laws-a-me! he's my own dead sister's boy, poor thing, and I ain't got the heart to lash him, somehow. Every time I let him off, my conscience does hurt me so, and every time I hit him my old heart most breaks. Well-a-well, man that is born of woman is of few days and full of trouble, as the Scripture says, and I reckon it's so. He'll play hookey this evening, and I'll just be obleeged to make him work, tomorrow, to punish him. It's mighty hard to make him work Saturdays, when all the boys is having holiday, but he hates work more than he hates anything else, and I've GOT to do some of my duty by him, or I'll be the ruination of the child."

30. What does this monologue tell you about the speaker?

   (A) She hates children.

   (B) She considers herself an old fool.

   (C) She believes Tom will lead her into sin.

   (D) She is a simple country woman who wants to do the best job she can raising Tom.

31. What is the source of the phrase "spare the rod and spile [spoil] the child" that the speaker refers to? [   ]

32. Why does the speaker worry about not being strict enough?

   (A) She can't make Tom go to church.

   (B) She worries she'll lose Tom.

   (C) She fears she is not doing as the scriptures say, thus committing a sin.

   (D) She wants Tom to work on Sundays.

33. How does Tom avoid being disciplined by the speaker?

   (A) Her makes her laugh.

   (B) He stays away from home.

   (C) He pulls tricks on her.

   (D) All of the above.

34. What does "He's full of Old Scratch" mean?

   (A) He's hyperactive.

   (B) He's full of the devil.

   (C) He's injured because he was lashed.

   (D) All of the above.

Questions 35–36 refer to the following excerpt from the Central Intelligence Agency Careers & Internships web page (www.cia.gov/careers/diversity).

Instilling Inclusive Work Practices

In our organization, we are working to ensure every officer's views are heard and that their ideas and skills are given due consideration. This enables us to fully leverage our talented and dedicated workforce.

The Agency has a variety of employee resource groups comprised of employees who share a common affinity (gender, sexual orientation, disability, ethnic, and racial backgrounds) and their allies. The employee resource groups make the organization stronger by:

- increasing cultural awareness,

- providing insight, practical solutions, and best practices, and

- promoting engagement and collaboration.

In addition, mentoring, coaching, training, and recognition for collaborative and inclusive behaviors foster employee engagement, professional development, and career advancement.

35. To what does "common affinity" refer?

    (A) people sharing best practices

    (B) people sharing backgrounds

    (C) resource group allies

    (D) all of the above

36. What is the purpose of mentoring, according to the CIA?

    (A) It fosters employee engagement.

    (B) It promotes professional development.

    (C) It helps career advancement.

    (D) All of the above.

Questions 37–40 refer to the following passage from the U.S. Government Publishing Office web page (www.gpo.gov/careers/apply.htm).

What you'll need:

We need certain information to evaluate your qualifications and determine if you meet legal requirements for Federal employment. Help speed the selection process by keeping your resume or application brief and to the point and by sending only the requested material. Type or print clearly in dark ink. Be sure to include the announcement number, title and grade(s) of the job for which you are applying. You must apply for a specific announcement.

Resumes must include the following:

- Full name, mailing address (with zip code) and day and evening phone numbers with area code.

- Social security number.

- Country of citizenship (most Federal jobs require United States citizenship).

- Veteran's preference and supporting documentation (if applicable).

- Reinstatement eligibility documentation if applicable (attach SF 50 proof of your career or career-conditional status).

- Highest Federal civilian grade held (give job series and dates held).

- Name, city and state of high school and date of diploma or GED.

- Name, city and state of colleges and universities attended and list types and year of any degree received. (If no degree, show total credits earned and indicate whether semester or quarter hours.) Send a copy of your college transcript(s) only if the job vacancy announcement requests it.

Other Qualifications

Give the following information for your paid and nonpaid work experience (do not send job descriptions): Job title (include series and grade if Federal job), Duties and accomplishments, Employer's name and address, Supervisor's name and phone number, Starting and ending dates (month and year), Hours per week, and Salary

- Indicate if we may contact your current supervisor.

- Job-related training courses (title and year).

- Job-related skills, for example, other languages, computer software/hardware, tools, typing speed.

Work Experience

- Job-related certificates and licenses (current only)

- Job-related honors, awards, and special accomplishments, for example, publications, memberships in professional or honor societies, leadership activities, public speaking, and performance awards. (Give dates but do not send documents unless requested.)

- Address the knowledge, skills, and abilities listed in the vacancy announcement. Submit a separate narrative addressing each knowledge, skill and ability statement (one per page) as part of your application package.

Additional information:

Veterans Preference

Individuals who have served in the military may be entitled to additional consideration. If you are a veteran, please attach a copy of your most recent DD-214, "Certificate of Release or Discharge from Active Duty" or letter from the Veterans Administration documenting your military service.

To claim 5-point veterans' preference, attach a copy of your DD-214, Certificate of Release or Discharge from Active Duty, or other proof of eligibility.

To claim 10-point veterans' preference, attach an SF-15, Application for 10-Point Veterans' Preference, plus the proof required by that form.

For more specific information about your veteran's preference and eligibility, please visit http://www.opm.gov/veterans/.

Citizenship

You must be a United States citizen to be considered for Federal employment.

37. Why are applicants asked not to send documents regarding awards and honors with their applications?

    (A) The originals might get lost.

    (B) They won't be needed until the interview.

    (C) Documents may not be returned.

    (D) All of the above.

38. What does "veterans' preference" mean?

    (A) People who have had government jobs before are given preferential treatment.

    (B) People who join the military are given preference in hiring.

    (C) People who have served in the military are preferred.

    (D) Former military personnel may receive ten additional points toward their applications.

39. How should you present your skills, abilities, and knowledge areas on your application?

    (A) Write a separate letter for each skill, ability, and knowledge area.

    (B) Attach a detailed job description that includes your skills.

    (C) Attach letters from your employers covering your skills and abilities.

    (D) All of the above.

40. Is the GED acceptable as a high school completion certification?
    Yes or No: ☐

> *Questions 41–42 are based on the following text from the U.S. Department of Labor's Termination page (www.dol.gov/dol/topic/termination/index.htm).*

If you've lost your job, you have certain rights, such as the right to continue your health care coverage and, in some cases, the right to unemployment compensation.

Jobloss and Health Care Benefits

- Upon termination of employment, some workers and their families who might otherwise lose their health benefits have the right to choose to continue group health benefits provided by their group health plan for limited periods of time.

- Employers may be required to provide certain notices to their employees.

  - Consolidated Omnibus Budget Reconciliation Act (COBRA).

  - Health Insurance Portability and Accountability Act (HIPAA).

- For information on health insurance coverage under the Family Medical Leave Act (FMLA) upon termination, see 29 CFR 825.209(f).

Unemployment Benefits

- Workers who are unemployed through no fault of their own (as determined under state law) and meet other eligibility requirements, may be eligible to receive unemployment benefits.

- Unemployment insurance payments (benefits) are intended to provide temporary financial assistance to unemployed workers who meet the requirements of state law.

- Under the Federal-State Unemployment Insurance Program, each state administers a separate unemployment insurance program within guidelines established by federal law.

41. Does anyone unemployed qualify for the Unemployment Insurance Program?

    (A) Yes. Everyone automatically has a right to unemployment insurance.

    (B) Yes, but only if unemployed for more than 6 months.

    (C) Conditions apply. Unemployment terms are dictated by state and federal government.

    (D) Conditions apply. Unemployment terms are dictated by the state government.

42. What happens to employer health care benefits if you lose your job?

    (A) They cease immediately.

    (B) They may be continued for a limited period of time.

    (C) Unemployed workers may chose to keep them indefinitely

    (D) not stated

> *Questions 43–45 refer to the following letter.*

TO: James Tiberius

FROM: Akira Hudson

RE: Consumer Math Book Proposal

We meet mathematical problems everyday of our lives. How we handle them makes the difference between winning and losing. Many of our decisions require knowledge of "survival mathematics," the skills and concepts that help us survive in an increasingly complex world. Many students drop high-school mathematics as soon as they can. Few are willing or able to take the life skills courses in school that would help them later in life. As a result, they never learn some of the important life skills math. This book has a built-in target audience, the people who need "survival mathematics" to get ahead in this world.

The key life skills are the everyday arithmetic that helps one survive in the market place. We propose to help readers learn and practice the following skills:

- Different methods of earning a paycheck: We explain hourly wages and piecework, commission, and salary.

- Calculating deductions from pay slips: What comes off and why.

- Budgeting: Making the money last from paycheck to paycheck; creating a household budget.

- The deal: How to read ads. Just how good a deal is "the deal"?

- Credit cards: How you pay, what you pay for, and the real cost of loyalty programs.

- Compound interest: The true cost of money. Comparing interest rates on debt, ranging from bank loans to credit card debt. Working out just how expensive credit card debt is.

- Compound interest: The mortgage. Working out the true costs of "zero down" financing of a home.

- Compound interest: Earning money on money. How can one reinvest to earn more, and the magic of time in accumulating wealth.

- Keeping more of what you earn: Some simple strategies to minimize taxes, from education and retirement savings to mortgage interest deductibility.

- The car: Calculating the pros and cons: We compare used vs. new, purchase vs. lease, and examine the true cost of owning a car. Because the car is probably the second biggest purchase most people will ever make, this is an important part of consumer knowledge. This unit is specially aimed at first-time car purchasers.

The application of basic arithmetic skills will help readers become better consumers and teach them how to deal with mathematical issues in everyday life.

43. What do the authors suggest is the point of understanding "the deal?"

    (A) to avoid overspending

    (B) to ensure that buyers can determine whether "the deal" is actually a good deal

    (C) to compare prices among vendors

    (D) all of the above

44. What does "magic of time" mean?

    (A) Debts fade away as inflation whittles them down.

    (B) Interest rates may go down over time, saving money.

    (C) Security deposits earn interest over time.

    (D) Interest compounds over time, earning extra income.

45. Why are different ways of earning a living considered important enough to be given a heading of their own?

    (A) Everyone needs to earn money.

    (B) Many students don't know that different employment payment methods are available.

    (C) It looks good on the proposal.

    (D) It is a generally overlooked topic in math classes.

46. How would you correct the following sentence?

    Over there you can see <u>my mother's-in-law car</u>, parked beside the shed.

    (A) my mother's-in-law car

    (B) my mothers-in-law car

    (C) my mother-in-law's car

    (D) my mother-in-laws car

Questions 47–48 refer to this passage from The Narrative of the Life of Frederick Douglass, An American Slave, 1845 *by Frederick Douglass* (`www.gutenberg.org/files/23/23-h/23-h.htm`).

My mother was named Harriet Bailey. She was the daughter of Isaac and Betsey Bailey, both colored, and quite dark. My mother was of a darker complexion than either my grandmother or grandfather.

My father was a white man. He was admitted to be such by all I ever heard speak of my parentage. The opinion was also whispered that my master was my father; but of the correctness of this opinion, I know nothing; the means of knowing was withheld from me. My mother and I were separated when I was but an infant — before I knew her as my mother. It is a common custom, in the part of Maryland from which I ran away, to part children from their mothers at a very early age. Frequently, before the child has reached its twelfth month, its mother is taken from it, and hired out on some farm a considerable distance off, and the child is placed under the care of an old woman, too old for field labor. For what this separation is done, I do not know, unless it be to hinder the development of the child's affection toward its mother, and to blunt and destroy the natural affection of the mother for the child. This is the inevitable result.

I never saw my mother, to know her as such, more than four or five times in my life; and each of these times was very short in duration, and at night. She was hired by a Mr. Stewart, who lived about twelve miles from my home. She made her journeys to see me in the night, travelling the whole distance on foot, after the performance of her day's work. She was a field hand, and a whipping is the penalty of not being in the field at sunrise, unless a slave has special permission from his or her master to the contrary — a permission which they seldom get, and one that gives to him that gives it the proud name of being a kind master. I do not recollect of ever seeing my mother by the light of day. She was with me in the night. She would lie down with me, and get me to sleep, but long before I waked she was gone. Very little communication ever took place between us.

47. Why are children separated from their mothers when only months old?

    (A) to permit mothers to go back to work

    (B) to avoid emotional attachments between children and parents

    (C) to provide a useful purpose to slaves too old to work in fields

    (D) raising all the babies together is more efficient

48. What is the definition of a kind master in this passage?

    (A) one who allows a slave to be absent from the fields at dawn

    (B) one who allows a slave child and mother to stay together

    (C) one who fathers a child by a slave

    (D) one who does not whip slaves

Questions 49–50 refer to the following excerpt from the Environmental Protection Agency's Climate Concepts web page (`www.epa.gov/climatestudents/basics/concepts.html`).

Weather Versus Climate

- Weather is a specific event or condition that happens over a period of hours or days. For example, a thunderstorm, a snowstorm, and today's temperature all describe the weather.

- Climate refers to the average weather conditions in a place over many years (usually at least 30 years). For example, the climate in Minneapolis is cold and snowy in the winter, while Miami's climate is hot and humid. The average climate around the world is called global climate.

Weather conditions can change from one year to the next. For example, Minneapolis might have a warm winter one year and a much colder winter the next. This kind of change is normal. But when the average pattern over many years changes, it could be a sign of climate change.

49. When scientists consider weather, what length of time is involved?

    (A) hours or days

    (B) a decade

    (C) probably a few months

    (D) whatever is going on today

50. Is a report of heavy rains in a region year after year most likely a feature of weather or climate? ☐

The Extended Response

Time: 45 minutes for 1 essay

Directions: The following articles present arguments both in favor of and against a topic. In your response, analyze both positions presented in the two articles and explain which one is best supported. Use relevant and specific evidence from the articles to support your response.

Use the following sheets of lined paper for your response. You should expect to spend up to 45 minutes planning, drafting, and editing your response.

Passage One

We all want our tap water to be safe and drinkable. Unfortunately, this is not always the case. Tests of municipal water supplies across America raise concerns. They have found traces of pesticides, and residues of industrial and agricultural chemicals, as well as traces of pharmaceuticals and other contaminants. There is real concern about the effects of long-term exposure to these chemicals, even in trace amounts.

The EPA monitors and has standards for only a few chemicals. However, there are traces of more than 100,000 manmade chemicals in municipal water. Despite all the purification measures, they remain. They include antibiotics, and industrial pollutants. Tests have found traces of pesticides, including atrazine and glyphosate, linked to reproductive and neurological issues and cancer. Dissolved chemicals are not removed during filtration as long as they are below limits set by the EPA.

Municipalities filter their water, and also add treatment chemicals, including fluoride. Many people are concerned about fluoridation of water and its health effects. Water treatment plants use chlorine to sterilize and remove bacteriological contaminants. As these treatment chemicals break down, the by-products remain in the water and are potentially harmful.

Even when municipal water is perfectly clean, tap water in your home still can be contaminated. In older parts of town, lead pipes were once common. Lead pipes are still in use on many older areas, and that lead leaches into the water in the pipes. Lead ingestion can lead to developmental delays and neurological problems.

Bottled water is always an option for drinking water. However, some bottlers merely add extra filtration to the same municipal water that comes from your tap. Others don't even do that before bottling. Studies have discovered contaminants in many brands of bottled water.

The only real safe answer is some form of home filtration. The least expensive way to improve your drinking water somewhat is to use a jug with a charcoal filter cartridge. That filter removes chlorine, lead, and unpleasant tastes or odors. This is an effective and inexpensive choice. More extensive systems, ranging from distillation systems to high-quality filtration, will do much more, even removing dissolved chemicals from the water supply.

Despite municipal efforts, city water supplies still have trace contaminants. If you want the taste of truly clean water, use bottled water and supplement that with a filtration system that covers your house. These systems provide you with exceptionally clean water, free of the many chemical impurities that municipal water systems do not remove.

Passage Two

Municipal drinking water is clean and safe. It comes from two main sources: ground waters or surface water. That water is filtered, treated, and distributed in a safe manner throughout our cities. Municipalities have done this for nearly 200 years and improved the process continuously.

Municipalities started chlorinating water at the turn of the last century after several severe outbreaks of disease. Jersey City was the first, starting in 1908. In the subsequent two decades, childhood diseases from municipal water declined by 90 percent and major infectious diseases by two thirds. More recently, the water treatment process has been improved to remove dissolved chemicals, improve taste, and even reduce tooth decay. The delivery system too has been improved by removing old lead pipes, once a cause for concern.

Water flows through coarse screens to remove debris, and then filtration removes fine particles. Flocculants remove suspended solids, and chlorination removes disease-causing organisms. Some municipalities treat water with ozone or ultraviolet light rather than chlorine for extra safety. Adding activated charcoal before final filtration removes organic compounds and improves taste. The final step is aeration to reduce further dissolved chemicals that affect the taste of water.

The EPA sets standards for more than 60 contaminants, from bacteria to filtration residues and organic and inorganic chemicals. That includes microorganisms such as cryptosporidium and coliform bacteria. The standards set limits on permissible levels of the breakdown chemicals of chlorine and other treatment chemicals. Metals such as cadmium and chromium, asbestos, and arsenic are also monitored. Municipal water systems must meet all of these standards. The EPA monitors treatment plants to ensure compliance.

Municipal water can have an "off" taste. Absolutely pure water has no taste, but the water we drink is not just H_2O. Rains, snows, and runoff from various sources leach chemicals from the soil. Most of these are harmless natural salts. They add their own taste to the water. Sometimes, algae or agricultural runoff in surface water also adds an unpleasant odor and taste. None of this makes the drinking water unsafe.

Municipal water treatment guarantees clean and safe water. The water is so safe, in fact, that nearly one-third of bottled water is simply municipal water repackaged by bottlers. Why bother with bottled water or extra filtration when your municipal supply is perfectly safe?

Chapter 10

Answers and Explanations for the RLA Practice Test

• •

*Y*ou've done the test. Now you need to check your answers. If you just want a quick look at what you got right or wrong, check out the abbreviated answer key with just the answers at the end of this chapter. The better approach is to read all the answers and explanations so you find out the reasoning behind the correct answers. You can discover just as much from your errors as from understanding why the right answers are correct.

Answers and Explanations

1. **B. all brands of bottled water are the same; many bottlers use.** The sentence in question is a comma splice or run-on sentence because it links two independent clauses with a comma. To fix the error, you need to replace the comma with a semicolon, turn the clauses into two independent sentences by replacing the comma with a period, or capitalize *many*.

   Choice (A) gives no change and is therefore wrong. Choice (B) is the only correct option offered. It inserts the semicolon in place of the comma. Choice (C) only removes the comma, which leaves the same grammar issue. And Choice (D) is grammatically correct but introduces a style issue by starting both clauses with *but*.

2. **B. They merely have to.** The mistake here is the antecedent for the pronoun starting this sentence. The pronoun refers to "many bottlers," which is plural. Choice (B) is the only correct option: Change the pronoun to *they*. Choice (C) doesn't address the error, while Choice (D) corrects the pronoun but fails to correct the verb.

3. **C. It also removes some of the lead found in the water pipes of older buildings.** This is a spelling error. The word *led* is the past tense for *to lead*. The sentence requires the word *lead*, which refers to the metal. Other options introduce new errors. The error the easiest to miss is Choice (D), where the sentence changes tense to the past, when everything else in the passage is in the present.

4. **C. This system boils water, collects the steam, and condenses it into absolutely pure water.** This is a parallelism error. The three verbs, *boils, collects,* and *condenses,* must all be in the same tense. The verb to correct is *condensed* (the only one in the past tense), which you do changing it to *condenses* (the present tense). Choice (D) also corrects the tense error, but it introduces a new error by dropping the comma in front of the conjunction *and.* The other choices don't correct the error.

5. **D. are carbonated, either naturally or artificially in the bottling process; carbonation can add.** This sentence is an example of improper punctuation. It sets off an adverb clause with a semicolon when only a comma is required. Choice (B) creates a comma splice before the word *carbonation,* while Choice (C) creates a sentence fragment.

6. **B. There are also more extensive systems available.** In this case of there/their/they're confusion, the correct choice is *there*. The word *there,* when used with the verb *to be,* refers to existence. *Their* shows possession, and *they're* is the contraction of *they are*. Because the sentence is talking about the existence of more expensive systems, *there* is the correct choice.

7. **charcoal blocks.** The third paragraph states that charcoal blocks work better than loose charcoal filters to remove the taste of chlorine.

8. **B. don't remove dissolved chemicals.** The text states that ceramic filters remove all suspended particles but no dissolved chemicals. Choices (A) and (D) are wrong, since particles and spores are removed. Choice (C) is wrong because there is nothing in the passage to support that choice.

9. **A. change the word *fridge* to *refrigerator.*** When you're writing an article, you should generally use more formal language. The word *fridge* is vernacular. The preferred word here is *refrigerator.* Choice (B) is a split infinitive; avoiding split infinitives isn't a strict grammar rule, but introducing a split infinitive isn't the best correction. Choices (C) and (D) are incorrect.

10. **D. effective than loose charcoal filters, also removing traces.** The second sentence isn't a complete sentence; therefore, the only way to correct this example without a complete rewrite is to replace the period between *filters* and *also* with a comma. Adding a semicolon after the word *filters* (Choice (C)) doesn't correct the error, and Choice (A) introduces a homonym error: *effective* versus *affective.* Because the article talks about results, *effective* is the proper word here. Choice (D) is the best answer.

11. **B. Please find enclosed a proposal for an article on alternative schools.** The error is improper capitalization. "Alternative schools" isn't a title or name, so it shouldn't be capitalized. The phrase "for your consideration" is unnecessary, and removing it improves the flow of the sentence. Choice (A) suggests no change, which leaves the error, while Choice (C) introduces a new error. Choice (D) is a possibility, but it introduces an article/noun agreement error. When taking an indefinite article, nouns starting with a vowel must use *an.*

12. **C. Your publication is an ideal platform for an article on the alternative schools.** This error is stylistic. The author is trying to convince the publication's editors that this article is ideal for them. The better way to do that is to make a definite statement: "Your publication *is* an ideal platform." Choice (B) is no better than the original, and Choice (D) leaves doubt about the possibility of publication in the future.

13. **C. change *our children* to *their children.*** The sentence contains an error, so Choice (A) is wrong. Choice (B) introduces a new grammar error, changing *who* to *that.* In this case, *who* is the correct pronoun. Choice (C) corrects the pronoun error. *Parents* is in the third person and requires a third person pronoun. *Our* is in the first person and is thus wrong. Choice (D) suggests the wrong tense.

14. **B. My colleague and I are educators, with experience at all levels.** Choice (B) is the correct version: In compound subjects with *I* or *we,* the *I* or *we* always comes second. Choice (A) offers no correction for the noun order error. Choice (C) introduces a capitalization error; *Educators* isn't a title nor attached to a specific name or position, so it stays lowercase. Choice (D) corrects the word order but uses the wrong pronoun (*me*).

15. **B. We have taught elementary and secondary, as well as university and adult education.** This sentence has a parallelism error. The elementary and secondary teaching and the university and adult education must be parallel, and Choice (B) corrects that. Choice (C) creates several errors around the conjunction *and.* Choice (D) is the wrong tense because the letter introduces the authors and their experience. That experience is in the past.

16. **D. We were both at various times Chairs of the District School Board's Alternative Schools Advisory Council.** Choice (D) is the correct option. Because *chair* is often used as a verb, the authors may have overlooked the fact that this sentence actually has no verb. The correction in Choice (B), the comma after *times,* isn't required. Choice (C) misspells *advisory.*

17. **C. We hope that this proposal is of interest and look forward to hearing from you.** This example is an error of punctuation around a conjunction. *We* is the subject and performs two actions: *hope* and *look.* No punctuation is required before or after the conjunction *and,* so Choice (C) is best. If you chose Choice (D), you made a common error: thinking that *and* was serving as a coordinating conjunction joining two complete sentences. However, in this case, what comes after *and* isn't a complete sentence.

18. **B. change *Copie Shoppe* to *copy shop*.** The words *Copie Shoppe* are quaint and may have been appropriate in Williamsburg 200 years ago, but unless this is the actual name of the shop, you should use the lowercase spelling *copy shop*. The next part of the passage refers to the shop as the Fast Copy Company, so you know that Copie Shoppe isn't the business name.

19. **C. change the semicolon after *copiers* to a comma.** Joining the first clause to the second clause with a semicolon is an error because the first clause isn't a complete sentence. Choice (C) corrects the mistake by setting off the first part of the sentence with a comma as a subordinate clause. Choice (B) doesn't correct the error and introduces a new error: *State-of-the-art* is acting as a single adjective to *copiers,* and multiword adjectives are nearly always hyphenated. Choice (D) is incorrect because the first sentence is clearly describing the store, not the copiers.

20. **A. replace *historical* with *historic*.** The word *historic* conveys a sense of lasting importance. *Historical*, on the other hand, describes anything based on past events, such as a *historical* novel. Choice (B) is incorrect because you generally capitalize *president* only when it's used before the person's name, such as President Lincoln. Choice (C) is wrong because it creates a comma splice — joining two complete sentences with a comma and without a conjunction.

21. **C. replace *Bradley's* with *Bradleys*.** Using *'s* to create a plural is a common error. The comma in Choice (A) is unnecessary, and changing tenses as in Choice (B) isn't required.

22. **complement.** The proper word is *complement,* which means a complete group. A *compliment* is a kind statement.

23. **C. Change the sentence to: The captain went down with the Titanic, which had been considered virtually unsinkable.** The participial phrase "considered virtually unsinkable" needs a clear antecedent. It will attach itself to the nearest noun. In this case, it suggests that the captain was virtually unsinkable. The clause "considered virtually unsinkable" is an unrestricted clause introduced by the pronoun *which,* meaning you can omit it without changing the meaning of the sentence. The pronoun *which* must be preceded by a comma. Choices (B) and (D) also introduce a different error by capitalizing "captain". Because the captain is not mentioned by name, the word must be lower case unless at the beginning of the sentence.

24. **B. The detectives could not identify the man; whom had they arrested?** Substitute *he* or *him* in the phrase "had they arrested?" The person arrested is the direct object, so the associated pronoun must be in the objective case. The proper form is *whom*. Changing punctuation (Choice (C)) or replacing *who* with *that* (Choice (D)) creates different errors.

25. **D. change *sneeze* to *sneezes*.** The error in this sentence is one of proper verb usage with collective nouns. The noun *group* is a collective noun and is singular. It requires a singular verb. Choices (B) and (C) would work, but only if you changed both verbs to the same tense. Changing just one creates a new error.

26. **A. The unarmed are suspicious of the armed, and the armed disdain the unarmed.** The text clearly states the disdain and suspicion between the armed and unarmed. Although Choice (B) may be true, it has nothing to do with the question. Choices (C) and (D) are the opposite of what the text states.

27. **D. They are disproportionate because the armed will never yield to the unarmed.** The text contradicts Choices (A), (B), and (C), so Choice (D) is correct.

28. **A. The art of war is the only means to power.** The text states in many ways that arms and skills in war equal power. Choice (B) is only partially true. Machiavelli doesn't discuss the relationship between war and society, only princes and war.

29. **A. someone without power who is not a prince or leader.** Machiavelli refers a number of times to someone who was a private person but became a prince, or princes who paid no attention to the art of war and became private persons. The inference, then, is that private people aren't princes and not people with power. Choices (B), (C), and (D) aren't supported by the text.

30. **D. She is a simple country woman who wants to do the best job she can raising Tom.** She's a simple country woman with little education who has never had to raise a child. The pattern of speech reflects her background, and the statement about teaching an old dog new tricks refers to raising a child. Choice (A) is certainly wrong, and though she acknowledges she is an old fool (Choice (B)), that's not the main point. Choice (C) isn't supported by the text the way Choice (A) is.

31. **The Good Book (the Bible).** The speaker, Aunt Polly, refers to that line as a quote from the Good Book.

32. **C. She fears she is not doing as the scriptures say, thus committing a sin.** After the quote "spare the rod and spoil the child," the speaker goes on to say, "I'm a laying up sin." She is a good woman who wants to do the right thing. However, not being strict enough with Tom goes against Biblical rules as she understands them. Choices (A) and (B) may be partially correct but aren't the best answer. The text never gives any indication that she wants Tom to work Sundays, so Choice (D) is wrong.

33. **A. Her makes her laugh.** Early in the text, she talks about how Tom handles her. There is no evidence he stays away from home. He may pull tricks on her, but that isn't the best answer.

34. **B. He's full of the devil.** *Old Scratch* was a term country people in Twain's time used to refer to the devil. An old superstition warned against use the devil's name for fear of conjuring him up. You have to infer that meaning from the context. Tom may be hyperactive, but that's not the best choice. The text contradicts Choice (C), which also means Choice (D) must be wrong.

35. **B. people sharing backgrounds.** The text gives examples of common affinity: gender, sexual orientation, disability, and so on. They're not allies of resource groups nor do they share best practices. Choice (D) simply doesn't apply.

36. **D. All of the above.** None of the choices is a complete answer. The last paragraph states the purpose: It's all of the items listed. *Remember:* Always choose the most complete answer based on the evidence in the text.

37. **D. All of the above.** Although not stated, the comment not to send documents unless requested is repeated. You can infer that the hiring agency doesn't want to risk losing originals, won't be able to return them, and most likely won't need them until an interview. Choices (A), (B), and (C) are all correct inferences, so Choice (D) is your best choice.

38. **D. Former military personnel may receive ten additional points toward their applications.** The text states that veterans may claim a ten-point preference if they submit the appropriate forms. Choice (A) is wrong because having had a government job doesn't necessarily make you a veteran. Choice (B) may be correct, but it's not true until the person leaves the military. Choice (C) is correct but incomplete. That leaves Choice (D) as the best option.

39. **A. Write a separate letter for each skill, ability, and knowledge area.** The instructions state that you shouldn't send job descriptions, so Choice (B) is wrong. That means Choice (D) is also wrong. Nowhere does the information ask for letters from former employers, so Choice (C) is also wrong. Choice (A) is the best answer.

40. **Yes.** The text lists the GED along with high school diplomas.

41. **C. Conditions apply. Unemployment terms are dictated by the state and federal governments.** The passage states that unemployed people must meet certain requirements. This text comes from is a federal government organization, so the rules are federal. It also asserts that state governments determine what constitutes "through no fault of their own."

42. **B. They may be continued for a limited period of time.** The text states that unemployed workers have "the right to choose to continue group health benefits provided by their group health plan for limited periods of time." Choices (A) and (C) contradict this statement and are wrong. Because the answer does appear in the text, Choice (D) is also incorrect.

43. **B. to ensure that buyers can determine whether "the deal" is actually a good deal.** Although a few choices are partially correct, you must select the most correct answer. The item about "the deal" implies learning how to assess deals to ensure you're really getting a valuable offer. Choice (B) is the most correct answer.

44. **D. Interest compounds over time, earning extra income.** The "magic of time" refers to compound interest and the effect it has on both savings and debt. Compounding significantly increases long term earnings. The other choices may be partially correct but aren't the best answer.

45. **B. Many students don't know that different employment payment methods are available.** Choice (D) is partially correct, while Choice (A) is true but doesn't answer the question. Choice (C) may also be true but doesn't explain why these different ways of earning a living are important enough to have individual headings. Choice (B) is the best, most complete, answer.

46. **C. my mother-in-law's car.** When creating the possessive form of compound nouns, you apply the apostrophe and *s* to the last word, so the correct answer here is "mother-in-law's."

47. **B. to avoid emotional attachments between children and parents.** Douglass states that the only purpose he can see is "to blunt and destroy the natural affection" between mother and child. Choices (A) and (C) are partially correct but not the best answers. Choice (D) is wrong because there is nothing in the text to support that idea.

48. **A. one who allows a slave to be absent from the fields at dawn.** The text specifically refers to owners who do not whip slaves who aren't in the fields at dawn (when Douglass talks about his mother visiting him at night). The other choices may be partially correct, but nothing in the text supports these choices.

49. **A. hours or days.** The text states that *weather* refers to the events that last for only hours or days, as opposed to *climate,* which is the average weather conditions over many years.

50. **climate.** Climate is the average of weather conditions over many years, while weather varies from day to day.

Sample Extended Response

Here's an example of an essay in response to the articles about higher education. Your essay will look different, but this example can help you compare your response to a well-structured essay. Your essay may raise many of the same points that this essay does and perhaps be organized differently, but above all, it should be well organized with a clear introduction, conclusion, and supporting evidence.

Compare the following sample to the response you wrote, and check out Chapter 8 for the scoring criteria and what evaluators look for in a response.

The two passages present different views. One argues that municipal water is safe, the other that municipal water can't be trusted. Both passages present some facts to back their positions, but passage two presents the stronger case.

Both passages present some data to support their arguments. Passage one argues that municipal water supplies cannot be trusted. It states that trace chemicals remain despite all filtration. It further argues that the EPA monitors only a few chemicals in the water supply. It states that many trace elements remain in the water, including medication, pesticides and industrial pollution.

However, passage two contradicts part of this. It states that the EPA has standards for over 60 chemicals. It discusses some specific examples of chemicals and bacteria in the water, and it states that the EPA monitors to ensure the water supply reduces these to safe levels. It also mentions the use of charcoal to remove chemicals and the replacement of chlorine with ozone or ultraviolet light. All these steps remove trace pollutants. These statements are specific and strongly contradict passage one, making a stronger case.

The safety of the water supply is reinforced by the second passage's argument that water filtration has eliminated outbreaks of diseases spread by municipal water. The data for that is old, but still valid. The second passage also uses the fact that water bottlers use city water to makes a strong case for its safety.

Both passages even address the issue of foul-smelling and bad-tasting water. People are naturally concerned when city water smells or tastes bad. The first passage suggests filtration to remove odors and lead. The second passage explains that taste and odor are not a safety issue. It identifies the source of the odor and taste, which is reassuring and reinforces the case that municipal water is safe.

The first passage discusses the use of additional filters in the home. It argues that extra filters are the only way to ensure that trace contaminants are removed. The second passage does not deal specifically with the issue of pesticide or medication residues. However, the first passage does not explain at what levels these contaminants are found, only that there are traces. By definition, trace contaminants are just that, traces. Nothing in the first passage explains why people need to be worried about traces of chemicals. Only one statement suggests that these trace amounts might be harmful, and even that offers no supporting evidence.

The second passage makes a more convincing case because it presents more evidence. It has clear examples of EPA standards and of efforts to deal with lead in pipes. It also successfully addresses taste and odor problems. The other passage never expands on the one area of concern it does present, the presence of trace contaminants. The second passage makes the better case.

Answer Key

1. B

2. B

3. C

4. C

5. D

6. B

7. charcoal blocks

8. B

9. A

10. D

11. B

12. C

13. C

14. B

15. B

16. D

17. C

18. B

19. C

20. A

21. C

22. complement

23. C

24. B

25. D

26. A

27. D

28. A

29. A

30. D

31. The Good Book (the Bible)

32. C

33. A

34. B

35. B

36. D

37. D

38. D

39. A

40. Yes

41. C

42. B

43. B

44. D

45. B

46. A

47. B

48. A

49. A

50. climate

Part IV

The Part of Tens

For a list of ten spelling rules to help keep you out of trouble, check out www.dummies.com/extras/gedrlatest.

In this part. . .

- ✔ Discover how to guess a word's meaning from its context, use common organizational structures to unlock the meaning of a passage, and detect bias and the signs of faulty logic, along with other ways to read faster and understand and retain more of what you read.

- ✔ Catch and eliminate common errors from your writing, including misused words and punctuation, verb and word choice issues, choppy transitions, and proofreading errors.

Chapter 11

Ten Tips for Faster Reading and Improved Comprehension

In This Chapter

▶ Working on reading skills and approaches

▶ Evaluating content as you read

▶ Rehearsing the test-taking experience

To excel in school and in the workplace, you need to be able to read and comprehend written communication — letters and memos, policy and procedural manuals, work orders, reports, safety instructions, and so on. If you plan to study in college or pursue a career in journalism or publishing, the ability to read and decipher complex documents becomes even more important and valuable. In fact, a person's reading level is one of the best predictors of academic and employment advancement. The GED test developers recognize the importance of reading skills. As a result, every section of the test, especially the RLA section, is designed to assess your ability to read and comprehend the written word.

In this chapter, we focus on helping you hone and tone your reading and comprehension skills.

Understanding Words from Context

You don't need to memorize the dictionary to understand vocabulary. Good thing, too, because the English language contains over one million words. If you have an average *working vocabulary* (the number of words you use daily), you know the meaning of about 15,000 to 20,000 words. However, your *reading vocabulary* is probably much higher. In other words (no pun intended), you probably understand many more words when reading than the limited number you use daily.

Part of the reason you understand more words than you use is that you have the ability to *infer* the meanings of words from context — from how the word is used in a sentence. The surrounding text contains clues to the meaning of unknown words. Here's an example:

> The teacher's <u>brusque</u> manner that evening irritated most parents, who were used to longer discussions about their children.

From the context of the sentence, you know that *brusque* refers to the teacher's behavior toward the parents. If they expected more, then *brusque* must mean *harsh* or *rude* in some way. In this case, it means *abrupt* or *dismissive.* You can work out other vocabulary the same way. Though this technique may not give you the precise meaning of a word, the meaning you infer is usually close enough to work with the passages you're reading.

Try these example questions. If you don't know the meaning of the underlined word, try to infer the meaning from its context:

1. They found the <u>desiccated</u> remains near a cactus only a few miles from an oasis.

   (A) shredded or torn up

   (B) dried out

   (C) abandoned

   (D) painted, decorated

2. The home showed not even a <u>modicum</u> of taste, what with plaid purple upholstery and yellow wallpaper offset by a collection of dusty debris in every nook and cranny.

   (A) tiny trace

   (B) sign

   (C) hope

   (D) growing

3. The war quickly became <u>ubiquitous.</u> After Germany declared war on Russia and France, Britain and the British Empire declared war on Germany. The other European nations followed. Then Japan declared war on Germany, followed by countries from around the world.

   (A) fierce

   (B) unwinnable

   (C) bogged down

   (D) widespread

These three examples are enough to show you how well logical deduction can help you decipher words when you're uncertain of their meanings.

Check your answers to see how well you did:

1. The reference to an oasis and a cactus indicates that *desiccated* describes remains found in a desert. Remains found in a desert have most likely dried out, and this word means just that: "dried out" or "mummified."

2. *Modicum* modifies taste. Based on the description of the apartment, the owner shows very little taste. Choices (A), (B), and (C) are all somewhat similar, which should give you a sense of what the sentence means. Choices (B) and (C) are partly correct, but the best interpretation is Choice (A), not even a tiny trace. Choice (D) is completely wrong.

3. *Ubiquitous* means "widespread." You can deduce that from the way other countries joined in, first in Europe, then from the British Empire, and finally even from other continents.

If this practice leaves you uncomfortable, lots of websites offer lists of the most important words to know. One example is the top 1,000 list at www.vocabulary.com, but entering "most important words to know" in your favorite search engine will take you to others.

Balancing Speed and Comprehension

Reading quickly and comprehending what you read aren't mutually exclusive; however, you need to find your comfort level. Practice reading newspapers to see how much you retain from a very quick skim of an article. Skim an article and write down all the key points you remember. Then reread the article carefully to see what you missed. Skim a different article and try again. Slow your pace to a point where you pick out most key points without reading every single word. When you reach a comfortable speed and comprehension level, increase your speed again. With practice, you can improve both speed and comprehension.

The RLA test contains reading passages for both the short answer items and the Extended Response. Take a different approach depending on the test section. Short answer items consist of a stimulus text (the passage on which the question is based) and answer options. You're looking for a specific answer in the brief passage. Consider this approach:

1. **Read the question and answer options very carefully.**

2. **Skim the stimulus passage.**

3. **Isolate the key terms.**

4. **Reread those sections carefully for answer matches.**

This method works for this type of question because you're looking for something specific. Reading the question and answer choices identifies what you're looking for. Skimming helps you find it in the passage.

For the RLA Extended Response, you're reading a longer passage that you must analyze. Reading the passages for the Extended Response requires a different approach:

1. **Read the first and last paragraph carefully to identify the thesis statement.**

2. **Skim the remaining paragraphs to identify key points or premises.**

3. **Read the remaining paragraphs more closely to note the evidence presented to support each premise.**

You can always go back and reread more slowly if you're worried you missed something.

Skimming on a Computer Screen

Skimming on a computer screen is more difficult, in part because the screen is vertical. You can't use fingers to trace the lines. The screen also presents much more of the image at once, and your eyes may wander. Further, with printed text, you can highlight key words as you skim, which isn't an option on a computer screen.

Try the following techniques to improve your reading comprehension on a computer screen:

- **Let your eyes wander.** Select key words you need to find, and then scan the screen for them. Then carefully read the adjacent text.

- **Cover the screen with a sheet of paper, moving it down to reveal one line at a time.** That forces your eyes to focus on the text. Then you can move down as quickly as is comfortable.

- **Lean back from the screen.** This approach makes the text a smaller part of your field of vision and allows you to concentrate better. Studies have shown that a narrower *field,* the width of text you see at any one time, actually improves reading speed on the computer screen.

- **Increase the font size, if possible, which creates a narrower field.** That allows you to focus better. However, be aware that some programs don't reformat the content to fit a narrower image but rather cut off the sides. That forces you to scroll sideways as well as up and down, removing any benefit.

Which of these strategies works best for you is a matter of individual preference.

Remembering the Essay Models

Essays, whether they're the formula essay (see Chapter 8) or some other format, all follow a three-part structure: the opening with the thesis, the middle with the evidence and arguments, and the end with the conclusion. Use the structure of the passage as a key to unlocking its content. Read the first and last paragraphs carefully to identify the main point and the author's point of view. Then skim through the middle, looking for evidence to support the claim. If the essay is well written, the first and last sentence in each paragraph reveal the paragraph's meaning.

If the Extended Response text is a newspaper article, expect a different format. Newspaper articles put all the key information in the first sentence. The headline and the first sentence summarize the story; all the rest of the article is details.

Detecting Bias and Faulty Logic

All writing contains some degree of bias, intentional or not. On the RLA test, you can't check the validity of any evidence presented, but you can look for bias and flaws in the reasoning. Here's a quick checklist:

- **Analyze the scope of the essay.** In an attempt to persuade readers, writers often limit the scope of an essay to such a degree that no room is left for valid objections. Ask yourself how complete the argument and evidence are and what the passage omits.

- **Look for signs of bias.** Consider the evidence and the words used to present it. Does the writer present facts objectively or merely express opinions? Do certain claims appear to be exaggerated? Is the evidence precise, or does the author overgeneralize? The more specific and factual the evidence, the more likely it is to be free of bias.

- **Check the logic.** Write down the thesis statement, followed by the premises and any unstated assumptions on which the argument is based. Does the thesis follow logically from the premises and assumptions? If the argument is based on any assumptions, are the assumptions reasonable? An argument based on false assumptions has no merit.

- **Tune in to the tone.** Impassioned speeches can whip a crowd into a frenzy even when the logic is flawed. Emotionally charged language, exaggerations, and unfair or disparaging treatment of opposing views are all signs of bias. Rhetorical questions can also be used to mislead the reader.

- **Consider the source.** Are the authors associated with any special interest groups? Do they have any political or ulterior motives for writing the passage? The writers may have personal agendas. Articles from a pro- or anti-anything group are suspect, and you should weigh the evidence presented very carefully for validity, exaggeration, and bias.

Reading for Details (Picking Out Key Words)

Reading for detail is the intense version of reading. You read every word and keep asking yourself how what you read relates to the task required of you. If you're looking at a grammar question, try to remember which grammar rule applies as you read. If the question is about mood or style of a passage, keep the appropriate tools and approaches in the back of your mind. Considering the limited time on the test, you should practice careful reading to build up both your confidence and your speed before attempting the test.

Approach the two sections of the RLA test differently:

✔ As you look for specific information and detail on the Extended Response and in longer passages, start by skimming. Connect the point of the passage to the supporting detail. Then list those details in your own words. This approach helps you absorb the material because you're interpreting it as you gather content. Finally, scan for specific terms and read those sections carefully to pick out all the detail you need.

✔ For the short answer items, read the answer choices carefully and then scan the question for key terms related to the answers. When you find them, read that section carefully to extract the details needed to select the correct answer.

Tracking Tone in Longer Passages

An author creates the tone of a passage through the choice of words, the point of view, and the details presented. In fiction, the imagery and attitude of the writer to the subjects is also important. When you're assessing the essays in the Extended Response, tone provides insight into the author's motivations and point of view and may raise concerns about bias. To evaluate tone, ask the following questions:

✔ **Is the language impartial, or does it contain *loaded* — exaggerated or emotional — words?** For example, describing someone as *twisted* rather than *confused* suggests that the person has a sick mind. Likewise, describing an opposing view as *ludicrous* rather than *ill-informed* conveys a value judgment.

✔ **Is the material presented impartially, or does it appear slanted?** You've probably heard of politicians *spinning* a story or a report to make themselves or a certain situation appear better or worse than it really is. You may find the same sort of spin in a written passage on the test. Ask yourself whether the writer is being objective or trying to twist the truth.

✔ **Did the writer cherry-pick the data?** *Cherry-pick* is an idiomatic expression that means to selectively present only those facts that support your point of view and exclude all others. A passage that addresses evidence that challenges the position stated in a passage indicates that the author at least acknowledges the presence of such evidence.

✔ **Is the writing humorous or sarcastic, factual or passionate?** Try to plug into the writer's feelings as she wrote the piece. Is she angry, happy, sarcastic, sad, bitter? An author's feelings are commonly conveyed through the tone of a passage, and they help you identify the author's purpose in writing the piece.

Paraphrasing

Paraphrasing (putting information into your own words) is a useful tool for expanding your understanding of what you're reading. It forces you to process and internalize the information, and the physical act of jotting notes as you read reinforces your comprehension of the material.

Paraphrasing works especially well when trying to reduce a longer passage to a few short points. Take the following steps when reading a long passage:

1. **Read.**

   Isolate the key points.

2. **Interpret.**

   Ask yourself what the meaning and intended purpose of the key points are in the passage.

3. **Restate.**

   Write down the points from the passage. Then, using only your own notes, write them down in your own words.

By reading, interpreting, and restating, you've manipulated the data in your mind, which enhances your learning and the clarity of your thinking.

Paraphrasing is a skill that takes time to develop. Practice isolating key points from newspaper stories and then take the next step: Rewrite the story in your own words, using only the key points you wrote down. At the end, compare the original with your own story to see how accurately you were able to paraphrase.

Practicing Under Pressure

Studies show that people often choke under pressure. However, you can reduce the risk. You're already taking the most important step to deal with test anxiety and the pressure of actually taking the test on test day — you're preparing for the test. Reading speed makes a difference. Apply the tips you have learned here about reading quickly and finding key facts in the text. Find a longer passage online or a document you can read on your computer screen. Count the number of words and then time yourself to see how quickly you can read it. We suggest reading on screen because that is how you will do the test. Then, without rereading the story, write down the five most important points and five pieces of supporting evidence in that story.

The average reader achieves 200 words per minute, with about 60 percent comprehension. If your reading speed is less than that, you need more practice. If you cannot remember at least five or six points, you need more practice.

The next step is to take practice tests under conditions similar to those on test day.

 Simulate the test-taking experience. Astronauts and pilots do it, and so should you. We're not suggesting that you build your own testing center, but you can certainly find a quiet place with fluorescent lights, a desk, an uncomfortable chair, and perhaps even a computer. Your local library may be the perfect place. If not, find a quiet room in your home and take the practice test in Chapter 9. To make the simulation even more realistic, do the following:

- ✓ **Turn off the music, TV, smartphone, and any other digital distractions.**

- ✓ **Lose the drinks and snacks.** They're allowed in the testing room only as accommodations for special needs.

- ✓ **Set a timer.** The biggest source of pressure for most test-takers is the limited amount of time they have to complete the test.

- ✓ **Don't take bathroom breaks.** They may not be allowed during the test.

Maintaining Focus

When you take the actual GED tests, you're under time pressure as well as the pressure you put on yourself to succeed. Clearing your mind of everything other than the test is easier said than done. After all, you have a life with responsibilities and worries.

As you're sitting in front of that test, whether it's the real GED test or the practice test in this book, take a few deep breaths. Breathe in, hold, and breathe out. Repeat three or four times. Deep breathing keeps you from hyperventilating and getting flustered. As you breathe, think of a time when you were successful and happy in your achievement. Think of how completing the GED test successfully will improve your life. Tell yourself, "I can do this. I am prepared."

Center yourself with deep breathing and positive affirmations before the test, as you get started, and during the test. If you feel distracted or your attention wavers, repeat the breathing exercises. They really do help you focus and keep your reading speed and comprehension on track.

For steps to take in the days and weeks before the test, refer to Chapter 4.

Chapter 12

Avoiding Ten Tricky Writing Errors

In This Chapter

▶ Rooting out misused words, mixed tenses, and misplaced commas

▶ Sticking to appropriate writing techniques

▶ Finding the errors after writing your essay

*E*ven the most talented writers make errors without realizing they're breaking the rules. In this chapter, we call your attention to ten common writing errors that test-takers make when writing the Extended Response so you know what the rules are and how to steer clear of these common pitfalls. If you notice that you're prone to making any of the errors described in this chapter, we encourage you to revisit Chapter 7, where many of these topics are covered in more detail.

Misusing Words

Vocabulary errors instantly undermine your sophisticated writing. Confusing homonyms such as *its* and *it's* and *principle* and *principal* create an unflattering image. Good writing requires that you take risks, so you don't want to be so afraid to use higher level vocabulary to the point at which you don't use it at all. However, you can avoid misusing words by doing the following:

✔ **Review the list of commonly misused words and phrases in Chapter 7.**

✔ **Use precise words where you're sure of the meaning.**

✔ **Build your vocabulary.** The more words you know, the more choices you have when writing. You can grow your vocabulary in several ways. Read more, looking up the definitions of unfamiliar words. Work crossword puzzles and play word games such as Scrabble. Find and study word lists online. Visit "word of the day" websites or get a similar app for your smartphone. Use the new words you discover in your daily communications to make them part of your working vocabulary.

✔ **Tune in to subtle variations in the meanings of words.** Words have shades of meaning. *Anger, fury, ire,* and *wrath* are all related but convey slightly different meanings. *Ire* is mild anger, while *fury* and *wrath* are extreme anger. A great way to become more sensitive to variations in meaning is to use a thesaurus and dictionary together when you write or read. Look up a word in the thesaurus to find words with similar meanings, and then look up several of those words in the dictionary to see how they differ in meaning.

Guessing the meaning of a word from context is fine when you're reading but not when you're writing. When writing the RLA essay, stick to vocabulary you know. You don't want your vocabulary to be simplistic, but you do want to avoid errors. You want to use the right words.

Overlooking Subject-Verb Disagreement

This writing error is among the most common. Collective nouns, nouns joined by conjunctions, and relative pronouns (*who, which,* and *that*) often trigger disagreement. Here are some rules to write by regarding subject-verb agreement:

✔ When using *anyone, everyone, someone, no one, nobody, none,* or *each of,* use a singular verb.

✔ Use a singular verb with *either* and *neither,* but when using *neither/nor* or *either/or,* choose the verb form based on the subject that's closer to *nor* or *or.* For example, "Neither the cats nor the mouse was hungry," but "Neither the mouse nor the cats were hungry."

✔ When using *all, or some,* look to the "of" phrase that follows the word to determine whether to use the singular or plural verb form. For example, "Some of my friends are going to the movie," but "None of the food was eaten." The same is true of words and phrases that describe a portion, such as *percentage of* or *fraction of.*

✔ When using *along with, as well as,* or *together with,* choose the verb form that agrees with the subject of the sentence (ignoring any nouns in the "along with"-type phrase). For example, "Jerry, along with his brother, loves to camp out."

✔ Although we discourage the practice of starting a sentence with "There is," "There are," "Here is," and "Here are," if you do so, keep in mind that *there* and *here* never serve as the subject of the sentence. Another noun or other nouns in the sentence do. For example, "Here are the paper and ink you ordered," not "Here's the paper and ink you ordered."

✔ When using a collective noun, such as *team, swarm,* or *litter,* use a singular verb, regardless of how many individuals are on the team or in the swarm or litter.

✔ If a sentence excludes part of the subject, choose the verb form that agrees with the positive subject; for example, "The resulting tornadoes, not the hurricane itself, cause the most damage."

Mixing Verb Tenses

Slipping from one tense to another, especially from the present tense to the past and back, is a mistake most people make in spoken communication. Telling a story, you may say something like, "Yesterday, I went to the convenience store to buy a slush, and the guy behind the counter tells me they're really not good for you." Unfortunately, mixing tenses is a bad habit that follows you when you write and is difficult to break.

Pick a tense and stick with it unless you have a very good reason to change tense. We recommend writing in the present tense because as you're writing, you're doing so in the present. However, if you need to describe an event that occurred in the past, such as the signing of the Declaration of Independence, you have no choice but to shift to the past tense.

Whatever a document claims, it does so in the present. For example, even though the U.S. Constitution was written hundreds of years ago, it exists right now, and whatever statement you quote from it has a bearing on the present.

Using the First or Second Person in Analysis

There's no *I* in analysis, or at least there shouldn't be. We're not talking about the spelling. In this case, we mean referring to yourself in an analytical formal essay. A formal essay is supposed to be a factual analysis, not a subjective opinion piece. Using the first person singular *I* suggests personal opinion, which undermines the factual nature of your argument. State your argument without using the first person. It makes your writing more assertive and more factual. The reader already knows that you're stating your arguments. Instead of writing "It seems to me that the first passage is. . .", write "The first passage is. . ." You don't need to insert your opinion with a first person statement, nor do you need to address the reader by using phrases such as "as you can see." By referencing the reader, you take the focus off the ideas and facts and create a distraction that focuses on the writing and reading process. In addition, you risk coming across as condescending or pandering to the reader.

Missing and Misplacing Commas

Commas group thoughts, introduce pauses in reading, separate two or more adjectives or adverbs used in succession and items presented as a list, and precede conjunctions. The previous sentence is a good example.

Commas can change the meaning of sentences. The sentences "Tomorrow we hunt Bill" and "Tomorrow we hunt, Bill" have very different meanings (we think Bill would prefer the latter). The comma groups the words "Tomorrow we hunt" and separates it from what would otherwise be the direct object, "Bill."

Very few people really know when to use a comma and when not to in all situations, but here are a few rules to steer you clear of the worst offenses:

- Use a comma before the conjunctions *and, but, or, for, nor,* and *yet* when the conjunction joins two complete sentences.

- Don't use a comma to separate verbs that form a *compound predicate* (a situation in which one actor performs two or more actions): "Sally hit a line drive between second and third base and made it to first base without breaking a sweat."

- Don't use only a comma to join two complete sentences. This error is commonly referred to as a *comma splice.* Here's an example: "Jerry used to be a Freemason, now he's a member of Kiwanis." You can add a conjunction after the comma, separate the two sentences with periods, or choose another option like a semicolon to fix the problem.

- Use a comma following an introductory phrase, such as "When television broadcasts travelled through airwaves, many homes had large TV antennas."

- Use two commas to set off nonessential clauses: "The science professor, who happened to be fluent in Spanish, visited us over the summer." However, if the phrase is essential in identifying a specific individual, drop the commas; for example, "The child who had developed a severe infection was separated from the other children."

- Use commas to separate coordinate adjectives or adverbs but not to separate cumulative adjectives or adverbs. For example, you'd use commas in "That tall, handsome man is my father," but not in "He had a close personal relationship." To determine whether adjectives or adverbs are coordinate or cumulative, rearrange them and separate them with the word *and.* You may hear someone say, "that handsome and tall man," but nobody would ever say, "he had a personal and close relationship."

✔ Use commas to introduce or set off a quotation: "The lack of money is the root of all evil," said Mark Twain.

✔ Use a comma if not doing so is likely to confuse the reader: "Instead of reviewing, the teacher started the test."

Use commas only when necessary. Most people overuse rather than underuse commas.

Being Inconsistent

You may have heard that "foolish consistency is the hobgoblin of little minds," but consistency on the GED Extended Response is essential, and it applies to two areas of your writing:

✔ **Content:** Rely on your thesis statement to ensure consistency. All premises should lead up to the conclusion you present in the thesis statement. Every paragraph must state a premise, and the evidence in each paragraph must support the premise stated in its paragraph. You present the point, explain it, and show how it links to your thesis. Inconsistencies undermine your efforts to persuade the reader and often lead you off point.

✔ **Style:** Adopting a formal writing style is one of the best ways to ensure consistency in style. State your thesis clearly and as briefly as possible and stick to the facts. Don't try to introduce humor or sarcasm or use conversational language in an attempt to endear yourself to the reader. Take the essay seriously.

Writing in Non-Standard English

Standard English is a form of the language that any English speaker anywhere would understand. Non-Standard English is somewhat subjective, but it applies to only some people in some part of the country or an individual group of people. Regional or ethnic differences in language play an important role in speech patterns. Phrases such as "we seen that," "all y'all," or "wazzup" may be commonly used, but they're neither grammatically correct nor acceptable in essay writing. Don't use any text or email short forms, street language, or ethnic terms. Avoid double negatives such as "We don't need no help" and everyday expressions such as "no way" or "really bad." Model your writing after the language used in textbooks. If in doubt, rephrase it.

Creating a Choppy Progression

To earn a high score on the Extended Response, your essay must flow smoothly from beginning to end. To ensure a smooth, logical flow, use the following three techniques:

✔ **Get organized.** A well-organized essay requires fewer heavy-handed transition words because the reader knows what to expect, and the essay presents the ideas and information that fulfill those expectations.

✔ **Repeat key phrases.** For example, the two sentences in the first paragraph of this section both contain the words *flow* and *smooth*. These words link the sentences thematically and don't require the use of a transition word.

✔ **Use transition words when necessary.** Transition words and phrases, such as *therefore, however, for instance,* and *likewise* refer back and look forward to clearly connect one statement with the statement that preceded it while preparing the reader for what's about to be stated. Transition words can introduce contrast and emphasis, conclusions and contradictions.

For a longer list of transition words and phrases, see Chapter 7.

Building Your Essay on Sloppy Thinking

Sloppy thinking comes in four forms:

✔ **Regurgitation:** The essay merely presents a laundry list of evidence from the two sources without drawing any conclusions from the evidence.

✔ **Gibberish:** The essay drones on making one point after another, none of which connects to a single, unified idea.

✔ **Unsupported claims:** The essay makes claims but doesn't support them with enough evidence.

✔ **Faulty reasoning:** Overgeneralization, mistaking correlation for causation, and drawing conclusions based on erroneous logic are all forms of faulty reasoning.

See Chapter 6 for additional insight into sloppy thinking that chips away at the effectiveness of an argument.

To test your writing for signs of sloppy thinking, write down your thesis statement followed by the premise or main idea expressed in each paragraph that follows it. If you can't draw a line from a premise to the premise above it or directly to the thesis statement, your essay probably suffers from sloppy thinking. See Chapter 8 for suggestions on how to write a coherent essay.

Ignoring Proofreading Errors

The problems with errors in grammar, punctuation, and spelling aren't the errors themselves but rather the fact that they distract and confuse the reader. If you write a well-structured, insightful, persuasive essay, several spelling and punctuation errors won't hurt your score. On the other hand, if the errors are serious enough to distract or confuse the reader, you're score will suffer. If you have time after writing the essay, read it carefully and correct all errors you notice. Catching errors in your own essay so soon after having written it, especially on a computer screen, is very difficult, but you should still try your best to eliminate any errors in the time remaining. Here are a few techniques that may help:

✔ **Read your essay word for word.** Don't skim when you're proofreading. If you rush through the process, you'll read what you think is there and not what you actually wrote.

✔ **Read out loud to yourself; sub-vocalize.** Errors become more obvious when you "sound out" the words in your head. You stumble over punctuation errors. You see misspelled words. You hear faulty parallelism in sentence structures.

✔ **Concentrate on errors you commonly make.** If you're prone to overusing passive voice, look more closely for those constructions. If you struggle with word choice, look at key words in the essay to see whether you can think of a more precise replacement.

Index

• A •

accept/except, 129
active voice, 89, 138–139
ad/add, 127
addition, transition words indicating, 143
additional premise, in formula essay, 162, 163
adjectives
  commas to separate, 213
  misplaced, 134
adverbs
  commas to separate, 213
  misplaced, 134
advice/advise, 129
affect/effect, 129
agreement
  pronoun-antecedent, 122–126
  subject-verb, 119–122
alliteration, 81
amount, 168
analysis, first or second person in, 213
analysis questions, overview, 56–57
analysis skills, overview, 18
answer sheet, for diagnostic test, 28
answers, eliminating some, 58
antecedents, 123
AP English Literature & Composition For Dummies (Woods), 57
application questions, 57
application skills, overview, 18
applying information to other situations, 116–117
arguments. *See also* position(s)
  building your, 163–164
  comparing two, 112–117
  definition and overview of, 93
  examining the strengths and weaknesses of, 155–160
  finding the premise of, 110–111
  structuring, 161–163
  synthesizing two, 115
assumptions
  credibility of, 155
  defined, 110
  identifying, 111–112, 155–157
  rooting out premises and, 110–112
  unstated, 56

assure/insure/ensure, 129
audience, 165
  analyzing passages for, 91
awkward sentences, 141–142

• B •

bare/bear, 127
be verbs, overuse of, 139
beginning, starting at the, 51
besides the point, 130
bias
  detecting, 206
  personal, 102
  rooting out, 160
Bill of Rights, 9
borrow/lend/loan, 129
breakfast, on day of test, 51
brushing up on test-taking strategies, 54
bullet points, 69

• C •

calm, staying, 60
can't hardly, 130
capital/capitol, 127
capitalization
  overview, 16, 146–147
  practicing with, 148–149
categorical structure, 88
causal structure, 88
cause and effect
  erroneous, 159
  identifying, 56
  overview, 70
cereal/serial, 127
characters, 66–68
cherry-picking data, 207
chronological structure, 88
cite/sight/site, 127
claims, distinguishing between supported and unsupported, 100–102
clarity and command of standard English conventions, 21
clauses
  dependent, 134
  independent, 134

clothes, comfortable, 53
cognitive skills, definition and
        importance of, 58
collective nouns, 120–121, 212
collective pronouns, 125
colon, 148
comma, 147–148
comma splice, 213
commas
    detecting and eliminating errors with, 168
    missing and misplacing, 213–214
Common Core standards, 7
comparative structure, 88
comparing
    defined, 57
    transition words indicating comparison, 143
    two passages, 85–92
        impact, 88–89
        perspective, 86–87
        purpose, 87–88
        structure, 88
        style, 87
        tone, 87
complement/compliment, 127
complete sentences, 168
complex sentences, 134
compound predicate, 213
compound sentences, 134
compound-complex sentences, 134
comprehension. See also reading
        comprehension
    balancing speed and, 204–205
    overview, 18, 57
computer, GED test administered by, 7–8
computer screen
    keeping your eyes on your, 60
    skimming on a, 205
computers, becoming comfortable with, 8
conclusion
    in formula essay, 162, 163
    illogical, 102
    overview, 70–71
conclusions, drawing new, 115–116
conjunctions
    commas before, 213
    coordinating, 136, 144, 147, 148
    correlative, 136
    defined, 120
    detecting and eliminating errors with, 168
connection, of ideas or events, 69–70
consequence, transition words indicating, 143

Constitution, 9
construction shift, 9
context
    deriving meaning from, 71–72
    understanding words from, 203–204
contractions, 147
    overview, 16
    practicing with, 148–149
contrasting, 57
coordinating conjunctions, 136, 144, 147, 148
coordination, 135–137
corporate statements, 20
corrections, in general, 9
correlative conjunctions, 136
could care less, 130
could/should/would of, 130
council/counsel, 129
creation of argument and use of evidence, 21
critical reviews of visual and
        performing arts, 19

• D •

dangling modifiers, 135
data, used as evidence, analyzing, 107–110
deductions, defined, 107
deductive argument, 103
deductive reasoning, faulty, 159–160
deep breathing, 51
dependent clauses, 134
desert/dessert, 129
details
    function of, 72–74
    inferring the main idea from, 96
    reading for, 206–207
    summarizing, 99
development and organizational structure, 21
diagnostic GED RLA tests, importance of
        taking, 52
diagnostic test, 27–50
    answer sheet for, 28
    Extended Response
        arguments both for and against making
            cyberbullying a criminal offense, 40–41
        sample, 49
        scoring your essay, 50
    overview, 27
    reviewing answers and explanations, 44–48
    source texts for, 29
        business letter (CanLearn Study Tours),
            31–33

business letter (GED Enterprises LLC), 36–37

Customer Service For Dummies (Leland and Bailey), 35–36

"How Must Employees Behave?", 30–31

Photography For Dummies (Hart), 39

"Rip Van Winkle" (excerpt), 33–34

"Something to Remember Me By" (Saul Bellow), 38–39

"The Man Who Was Almost a Man" (Richard Wright), 34–35

"What Is the History of the Social Enterprise Movement?", 29–30

dictionary, using a, 25

did good, 130

digressions, 169

diploma, available online, 8

disabilities

  accommodations for, 12

  special accommodations for people with, 11

drama passages, 19

"due to," 70

• E •

editing, practicing skill of, 22

either/or, 120

eligibility requirements for taking the GED test, 10

  website, 13

ELPT (English Language Proficiency Test), 13

emigrate/immigrate, 129

emotional appeals, rooting out, 160

emphasis

  analyzing passages for, 91

  transition words indicating, 143

English, taking the GED test if it isn't your first language, 12–13

English Language Proficiency Test (ELPT), 13

errors in writing, avoiding

  being inconsistent, 214

  choppy progression, 214–215

  first or second person in analysis, 213

  missing and misplacing commas, 213–214

  misusing words, 211

  non-standard English, 214

  proofreading errors, 215

  sloppy thinking, 215

  subject-verb disagreement, 212

the essay. *See* Extended Response

essays. *See also* Extended Response

  structure of, 206

Euler diagram, 103

evaluation, importance of, 57

evaluative structure, 88

evidence

  analyzing, 104–110, 157–159

  analyzing data, graphs, and pictures used as, 107–110

  analyzing differences in interpretation and use of, 113–115

  in formula essay, 162

  ignored, 106

  in introduction paragraph, 162

  relevant, 104–105

  sufficient, 106

  supporting your position with, 152

ewe, you, 127

Example icon, 2

examples

  thinking about and using appropriate, 23

  transition words indicating, 143

exception, transition words indicating, 143

expletives, 139

Extended Response (essay), 20–23. *See also* formula essay

  audience for, 165

  choosing a side for, 153

  criteria or skills covered in, 21

  evaluation of, 22, 152

  format of, 21–22

  guidelines, 151–152

  message of, 166

  planning skills to succeed on, 22–23

  preacher's approach, 162

  purpose of, 165

  structuring, 161–163

  thesis statement

    in formula essay, 162, 163

    identifying, 153, 154

    writing a clear and direct, 161

  time allowed for, 8

  writing and revising, 166–169

• F •

faulty logic, detecting, 206

faulty reasoning

  examples of, 215

  identifying, 102–103

fees you owe, bringing, 53

fiction, 19

figurative language, 78

  interpreting, 80–81

fill-in-the-blank questions, 9

first or second person in analysis, 213

five-paragraph essay, 162. *See also* formula
    essay

flee/flea, 127

flew/flu/flue, 127

flow, extracting meaning from, 81–83

focus, maintaining, 209

font size, 205

foreign languages, taking the GED test in, 12–13

formula essay, 162–163
  outline for, 162–163

founding documents, 20

French, taking the test in, 12

frequently confused words, 166

fused sentences, 143–146

• G •

GED RLA (Reasoning Through Language Arts)
    test, 7
  eligibility to apply to take, 10
  evaluating the different questions, 56–58
  in general, 7
  getting comfortable before, 54
  importance of taking, 52
  literacy component, 8
  packing for day of, 53–54
  preparing for, 23–26
  scheduling, 9–10
  sections available in booklet format, 8
  sharpening your mental focus, 59–60
  time allowed for, 8
  what to bring to, 53
  when you can take, 10–11

GED Test For Dummies (Shukyn, Shuttleworth,
    and Krull), 52

GED Testing Service, 10, 11

generalization, 96–97
  transition words indicating, 143

gibberish, 215

glasses, reading, 53

grammar
  detecting and eliminating errors in, 168
  in everyday speaking, practicing, 24
  mastering the rules of basic, 24

grammar and writing component of the RLA test
  format of, 17
  overview, 15
  skills covered in, 16–17

graphs used as evidence, analyzing, 107–110

guerilla/gorilla, 129

guessing, intelligent, 58–59

• H •

hare/hair, 127

here/hear, 127

heroin/heroine, 129

high-school equivalency diploma, 7

high-school graduates, upgrading or updating
    skills, 10

historic documents, 20

homonyms, 126–128, 166

hyperbole, 80

hypotheses, 96–97

• I •

icons, explained, 2

ideas
  analyzing passages that present related,
      89–92
  analyzing relationships among, 69
  overview, 68–69

identification (ID), to bring
    to test, 53

idiomatic expressions, 81

illogical conclusion, 102

immigrate/emigrate, 129

impact
  analyzing differences in, 88–89
  analyzing passages for, 92

impartial language, 207

indefinite pronouns, 119

independent clauses, 134

inference, defined, 107

inferring, 65
  the main idea from details, 96

informal language, 131–133

information, applying to other situations,
    116–117

informational texts, 9, 17, 19, 107

instincts, trusting your, 59

intelligent guessing, 58–59

interpretation, analyzing differences in,
    113–115

introduction paragraph, 162

introductory phrases, commas
    following, 213

invalid reasoning, identifying valid and,
    102–104

irregardless/regardless/irrespective, 130

"it is" constructions, 89

its/it's, 127, 168

• J •

journals and blogs, keeping, 24

• K •

key phrases, repetition of, 83, 214

• L •

lay/lie, 130
lead/led, 127
learning disabilities, 11
legal documents, 20
letters (written communication), 20
like/such as, 130
literacy components of the GED test, 8
literally, 130
literary passages, 19
literature sources, 9
logical errors, testing for, 159–160
logical order, putting your main points in, 163
loose/lose, 130

• M •

main idea, identifying and summarizing, 93–95
main points, putting in logical order, 163
male/mail, 127
manuals, 20
marry/merry, 127
meaning
  big picture look at flow and, 82–83
  from context, 71–72
  from flow, 81–83
  variations in, 78–80
meaningless phrases, 169
mechanics, overview, 16
medical disabilities, 11
message, 166
metaphor, 80
misplaced modifiers, 134–135
modifiers
  dangling, 135
  misplaced, 134–135
mood, 79
multiple-choice questions
  in general, 9
  in grammar and writing component
    of the RLA test, 17
  intelligent guessing and, 58–59
  practicing, 25

• N •

negative phrases, 166
negative statements, 140
neither/nor, 120
nervousness, 60
nominalizations, 140, 167
nonessential clauses, commas to set off, 213
nonfiction, practicing reading, 23–24
nonfiction passages, 19–20
nonfiction prose, 20
not/knot/naught, 127
nouns, collective, 120–121, 212
number, 168

• O •

obvious phrases, 169
onomatopoeia, 81
opinions, separating facts from, 56
opposing viewpoint, in formula essay, 162, 163
order of events, recognizing, 63
organization
  flow and, 83
  of passages, 16–17
outline for formula essay, 162–163
overgeneralization, 72, 102, 159
overthinking, 58

• P •

paper version of the GED test, 8, 11
paragraphs, organization of, 16–17
parallelism, 135–138
paraphrasing, 207–208
parts of the whole, recognizing, 83
passages (source texts)
  comparing two, 85–92
  for diagnostic test. *See* diagnostic test, source
    texts for
  format of, 18–19
  in general, 9
  identifying the types of, 19
  reading tactics, 25–26
  tone in longer, 207
passive voice, 138–139, 166
peace/piece, 127
peak/peek, 127
period, 147
personal bias, 102
personification, 81
perspective, analyzing differences in, 86–87

phrasal verbs, 140, 167
pictures, used as evidence, analyzing, 107–110
planning an essay, 22
plot, 63, 65–66
points of view (viewpoints)
  analyzing the author's response to
    opposing, 76–77
  comparing, 74
  determining the author's, 75–76
  inaccurate depiction of the opposing
    viewpoint, 159
position(s)
  identifying different, 153–154
  picking a position you can support, 160
positive statements, 140
possessives
  difference between contractions and, 147
  overview, 16
  practicing with, 148–149
practice essays. *See also* diagnostic test
  writing, 23
practice GED RLA tests, importance
    of taking, 52
practice test
  answers and explanations for, 193–199
  taking, 25, 26, 171–190
practicing under pressure, 208
preacher's approach, 162
precise words, 138, 152
predicate, 134
  compound, 213
Premise 1 with supporting evidence,
    in formula essay, 162, 163
Premise 2 with supporting evidence,
    in formula essay, 162, 163
premises
  credibility of, 155
  defined, 110
  identifying, 155–156
  overview, 110–111
prepositions
  unnecessary use of, 167
  wordiness and, 140
prey/pray, 127
principal/principle, 127
pronoun-antecedent agreement, 122–126, 168
pronouns
  choosing the right verb when you have
    multiple, 123–124
  collective, 125
  definition of, 122
  indefinite, 119

overview, 122–123
  proper, 125
  reflexive, 124
  relative, 124
proofreading errors, 215
proper pronouns, 125
prose, nonfiction, 20
prose fiction, 19
psychological disabilities, 11
punctuation, 147–148
  detecting and eliminating errors in, 168
  overview, 16
  practicing with, 148–149
  understanding, 24
purpose, 165
  analyzing passages for, 87–88, 90

• Q •

question-and-answer part of the GED test, 8, 9
questions
  addressing and answering, 58
  asking yourself, 25
  evaluating types of, 56–58
  leaving time for review of, 59
quotation marks, placement of, 168
quotations, commas to introduce or set off, 214

• R •

rain/reign/rein, 127
reading
  carefully, 25
  practicing skill of, 22
  sharpening your skills, 23–24
  tips for faster, 203–209
    balancing speed and comprehension,
      204–205
    detecting bias and faulty logic, 206
    maintaining focus, 209
    paraphrasing, 207–208
    practicing under pressure, 208
    reading for details, 206–207
    skimming on a computer screen, 205
    structure of passage as key
      to its content, 206
    tracking tone in longer passages, 207
    understanding words from context, 203–204
reading comprehension, 17–20
  analysis skills, 18
  application skills, 18
  comprehension skills, 18

on a computer screen, 205
format of, 18–19
in general, 17
skills required for, 18
synthesis skills, 18
reading glasses, 53
reading speed, 24
reading vocabulary, 203
Reasoning Through Language Arts (RLA) test,
    overview, 8
rebuttals (counterarguments), in formula
    essay, 162
redundancy, 139, 167
reflexive pronouns, 124
registration confirmation, bringing, 53
registration receipt, bringing, 53
regurgitation, 215
relative pronouns, 124
relax, taking time to, 59
relevant evidence, 104–105
Remember icon, 2
repetition, of key phrases, 83
rereading your final essay, 59, 168–169
residency requirements, 10
rest, taking time to, 59
restatement, transition words indicating, 143
retaking the GED test
    in general, 11
    if you score poorly, 14
reviewing
    your answers, 59
    your final essay, 59
reviews of visual and performing arts, 19
revising, 9, 59, 168–169
rules of the room, 60
run-on sentences, 143–146

• S •

scheduling the GED test, 9–10
scope, analyzing passages for, 90
scope of the essay, 206
scores
    how scores are determined, 14
    overview, 13
    what to do if you score poorly, 14
second-guessing yourself, 59
sections of the GED test
    in booklet format, 8
    taking, 7, 10–11
selection bias, 102
semicolon, 148

sentence fragments, 143–145
sentence structure
    overview, 17
    varying, 89, 152, 167
sentences
    awkward, 141–142
    commas to join, 213
    complete, 168
    complex, 134
    compound, 134
    compound-complex, 134
    with misplaced modifiers, 134–135
    parallelism, coordination, and subordination
        in, 135–138
    run-on or fused, 143–146
    topic, 163
    transitional words and phrases in, 142–143
    wordy, 138–141
sequence of ideas or events
    analyzing, 69
    recognizing and ordering, 63–64
    transition words indicating, 143
sequential structure, 88
serial/cereal, 127
setting, 66
shoes, comfortable, 53
sight/site/cite, 127
signing up for the test, 12
simile, 80
skimming
    on a computer screen, 205
    questions, 56
slang and other informal English, 166
sleeping before test, 51
sloppy thinking, 215
source texts (text passages)
    comparing two, 85–92
    for diagnostic test. *See* diagnostic test,
        source texts for
    format of, 18–19
    in general, 9
    identifying the types of, 19
    reading tactics, 25–26
    tone in longer, 207
Spanish, taking the test in, 12
special circumstances, working with, 12
Speed Reading For Dummies (Sutz and
    Weverka), 24
spelling
    detecting and eliminating errors in, 168
    improving your, 24
    overview, 16

stage directions, in drama passages, 19
starting at the beginning, 51
stationary/stationery, 127
stress, 52
structure, analyzing differences in, 88
style, analyzing differences in, 87
subject-verb agreement, 119–122, 212
subordination, 135, 137
such as/like, 130
sufficient evidence, 106
summarizing, details, 99
summary, transition words indicating, 143
supported claims, distinguishing between
     unsupported and, 100–102
synthesis questions, 57
synthesis skills, overview, 18
synthesizing two arguments, 115

• T •

tenses, mixing, 212
Test of English as a Foreign Language
     (TOEFL), 13
testing centers, 9, 10
text analysis, 9
their/there/they're, 127
"there are" constructions, 89
thesis statement
  in formula essay, 162, 163
  identifying, 153, 154
  writing a clear and direct, 161
time
  available per item, 59
  to rest and relax, 59
  of test
    gearing up for, 51–52
    packing for, 53–54
    using your time wisely, 55–56
Tip icon, 2
to be, overuse of, 139
TOEFL (Test of English as a Foreign
     Language), 13
tone
  analyzing differences in, 87
  faulty logic and, 206
  tracking, in longer passages, 207
  variations in meaning and, 78–80
topic, practicing writing on a, 22–23
topic sentence, 163
to/too/two, 127
train of thought, following the, 99–100
transcript of your scores, 8

transitional words and phrases
  analyzing, 83–85
  effective use of, 142–143
  in Extended Response (essay), 152
  smoothing, 167–168
  using, when necessary, 215

• U •

unsupported claims, 215
  distinguishing between supported and,
     100–102
unusual circumstances, working with, 12
usage
  detecting and eliminating errors in, 168
  in grammar and writing component of the
     RLA test, 17

• V •

vague language, 131, 138
valid reasoning, identifying invalid and,
     102–104
verbs
  mixing tenses, 212
  phrasal, 140, 167
vice/vise, 127
viewpoints
  analyzing the author's response to
     opposing, 76–77
  comparing, 74
  determining the author's, 75–76
  inaccurate depiction of the opposing
     viewpoint, 159
vocabulary. *See also* word choice
  building your, 211
  reading, 203
  working, 203

• W •

Warning icon, 2
weather/whether, 127
websites, helpful, 13
word choice. *See also* vocabulary
  frequently confused words,
     129–130
  homonyms, 126–128
  importance of, 78–81
  for overall effect, 78–79
  overview, 126
  revising your essay and, 166–167

words
  key, 206–207
  misusing, 211
  precise, 138
  subtle variations in the meanings of, 211
  using new, 25
wordy sentences, 138–141
working vocabulary, 203
workplace and community documents, 20
workplace materials, 9
writing
  avoiding errors
    being inconsistent, 214
    choppy progression, 214–215

first or second person in analysis, 213
    missing and misplacing commas,
      213–214
    misusing words, 211
    non-standard English, 214
    proofreading errors, 215
    sloppy thinking, 215
    subject-verb disagreement, 212
  practicing, 22–24

your/you're, 127

About the Authors

Murray Shukyn, BA, is a graduate of the University of Toronto with professional qualifications as a teacher at the elementary and secondary levels, including special education. He has taught at the elementary, secondary, and university levels and developed training programs for adult learners in the coffee and foodservice industries. During his extensive career spanning more than 50 years, Murray has taught professional development programs for educators and is acknowledged as a Canadian leader in the field of alternative education. He was instrumental in the creation of such innovative programs for the Toronto Board of Education as SEED, Learnxs, Subway Academy, SOLE, and ACE. In 1995, Murray became associate director of the Training Renewal Foundation, which introduced the GED in the province of Ontario. As a consultant to government, media, and public relations companies, he has coauthored numerous textbooks and magazine and periodical articles with Achim Krull and coauthored several books to prepare adults to take the GED test with both Achim Krull and Dale Shuttleworth.

Achim K. Krull, BA, MAT, is a graduate of the University of Toronto with specialist qualifications in history and geography. He has taught at both the high-school and adult education levels. Achim worked for many years in the academic alternative schools of the Toronto District School Board as administrator/curriculum leader of Subway Academy One and cofounder of SOLE. He has written textbooks, teachers' guides, and a large variety of other learning materials with Murray Shukyn, including scripts for educational videos, as well as newspaper and magazine articles. Achim designed and currently teaches an academic upgrading program for young adults preparing to enter apprenticeships.

Dedication

From Murray: To Bev, Deb, and Ron, who have always provided ongoing support and encouragement for all the projects I find myself involved in.

Authors' Acknowledgements

We wish to say a special word of thanks to Grace Freedson of Grace Freedson's Publishing Network for all her efforts in negotiating for these books and guiding us through the often murky waters of negotiations.

Thanks to John Wiley & Sons acquisitions editor Lindsay Lefevere for choosing us to write this book and for pulling together a talented team of professionals to help us produce a top-quality product. Thanks to wordsmith Joe Kraynak at joekraynak.com for teaming up with us during the early stages of the project to produce a quality manuscript and deliver it in a timely manner.

We thank Chrissy Guthrie of Guthrie Writing & Editorial, LLC, for shepherding our manuscript through the editorial process and to production and providing the guidance we needed to make a good manuscript great. Thanks also to our copy editor, Megan Knoll, for weeding out any errors in spelling, grammar, and punctuation and, more importantly, ensuring the clarity of our prose.

Special thanks to our technical editor, Sonia Chaumette, for detecting and eliminating any substantive errors and omissions that would otherwise undermine the accuracy and utility of this workbook.

Publisher's Acknowledgments

Executive Editor: Lindsay Lefevere

Editorial Project Manager and Development Editor: Christina Guthrie

Copy Editor: Megan Knoll

Technical Editor: Sonia Chaumette

Art Coordinator: Alicia B. South

Production Editor: Vinitha Vikraman

Cover Image: © Getty Images/blackred

Apple & Mac

iPad For Dummies, 6th Edition
978-1-118-72306-7

iPhone For Dummies, 7th Edition
978-1-118-69083-3

Macs All-in-One For Dummies,
4th Edition
978-1-118-82210-4

OS X Mavericks For Dummies
978-1-118-69188-5

Blogging & Social Media

Facebook For Dummies, 5th Edition
978-1-118-63312-0

Social Media Engagement For Dummies
978-1-118-53019-1

WordPress For Dummies, 6th Edition
978-1-118-79161-5

Business

Stock Investing For Dummies,
4th Edition
978-1-118-37678-2

Investing For Dummies, 6th Edition
978-0-470-90545-6

Personal Finance For Dummies,
7th Edition
978-1-118-11785-9

QuickBooks 2014 For Dummies
978-1-118-72005-9

Small Business Marketing Kit
For Dummies, 3rd Edition
978-1-118-31183-7

Careers

Job Interviews For Dummies, 4th Edition
978-1-118-11290-8

Job Searching with Social Media
For Dummies, 2nd Edition
978-1-118-67856-5

Personal Branding For Dummies
978-1-118-11792-7

Resumes For Dummies, 6th Edition
978-0-470-87361-8

Starting an Etsy Business For Dummies,
2nd Edition
978-1-118-59024-9

Diet & Nutrition

Belly Fat Diet For Dummies
978-1-118-34585-6

Mediterranean Diet For Dummies
978-1-118-71525-3

Nutrition For Dummies, 5th Edition
978-0-470-93231-5

Digital Photography

Digital SLR Photography All-in-One
For Dummies, 2nd Edition
978-1-118-59082-9

Digital SLR Video & Filmmaking
For Dummies
978-1-118-36598-4

Photoshop Elements 12 For Dummies
978-1-118-72714-0

Gardening

Herb Gardening For Dummies,
2nd Edition
978-0-470-61778-6

Gardening with Free-Range Chickens
For Dummies
978-1-118-54754-0

Health

Boosting Your Immunity For Dummies
978-1-118-40200-9

Diabetes For Dummies, 4th Edition
978-1-118-29447-5

Living Paleo For Dummies
978-1-118-29405-5

Big Data

Big Data For Dummies
978-1-118-50422-2

Data Visualization For Dummies
978-1-118-50289-1

Hadoop For Dummies
978-1-118-60755-8

Language & Foreign Language

500 Spanish Verbs For Dummies
978-1-118-02382-2

English Grammar For Dummies,
2nd Edition
978-0-470-54664-2

French All-in-One For Dummies
978-1-118-22815-9

German Essentials For Dummies
978-1-118-18422-6

Italian For Dummies, 2nd Edition
978-1-118-00465-4

Math & Science

Algebra I For Dummies, 2nd Edition
978-0-470-55964-2

Available in print and e-book formats.

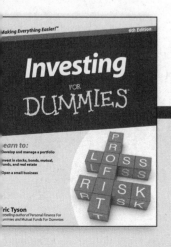

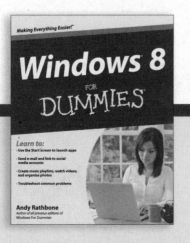

Available wherever books are sold. **For more information or to order direct visit www.dummies.com**

Anatomy and Physiology For Dummies, 2nd Edition
978-0-470-92326-9

Astronomy For Dummies, 3rd Edition
978-1-118-37697-3

Biology For Dummies, 2nd Edition
978-0-470-59875-7

Chemistry For Dummies, 2nd Edition
978-1-118-00730-3

1001 Algebra II Practice Problems
For Dummies
978-1-118-44662-1

Microsoft Office

Excel 2013 For Dummies
978-1-118-51012-4

Office 2013 All-in-One For Dummies
978-1-118-51636-2

PowerPoint 2013 For Dummies
978-1-118-50253-2

Word 2013 For Dummies
978-1-118-49123-2

Music

Blues Harmonica For Dummies
978-1-118-25269-7

Guitar For Dummies, 3rd Edition
978-1-118-11554-1

iPod & iTunes For Dummies, 10th Edition
978-1-118-50864-0

Programming

Beginning Programming with C
For Dummies
978-1-118-73763-7

Excel VBA Programming For Dummies,
3rd Edition
978-1-118-49037-2

Java For Dummies, 6th Edition
978-1-118-40780-6

Religion & Inspiration

The Bible For Dummies
978-0-7645-5296-0

Buddhism For Dummies, 2nd Edition
978-1-118-02379-2

Catholicism For Dummies, 2nd Edition
978-1-118-07778-8

Self-Help & Relationships

Beating Sugar Addiction For Dummies
978-1-118-54645-1

Meditation For Dummies, 3rd Edition
978-1-118-29144-3

Seniors

Laptops For Seniors For Dummies,
3rd Edition
978-1-118-71105-7

Computers For Seniors For Dummies,
3rd Edition
978-1-118-11553-4

iPad For Seniors For Dummies,
6th Edition
978-1-118-72826-0

Social Security For Dummies
978-1-118-20573-0

Smartphones & Tablets

Android Phones For Dummies,
2nd Edition
978-1-118-72030-1

Nexus Tablets For Dummies
978-1-118-77243-0

Samsung Galaxy S 4 For Dummies
978-1-118-64222-1

Samsung Galaxy Tabs For Dummies
978-1-118-77294-2

Test Prep

ACT For Dummies, 5th Edition
978-1-118-01259-8

ASVAB For Dummies, 3rd Edition
978-0-470-63760-9

GRE For Dummies, 7th Edition
978-0-470-88921-3

Officer Candidate Tests For Dummies
978-0-470-59876-4

Physician's Assistant Exam For Dummies
978-1-118-11556-5

Series 7 Exam For Dummies
978-0-470-09932-2

Windows 8

Windows 8.1 All-in-One For Dummies
978-1-118-82087-2

Windows 8.1 For Dummies
978-1-118-82121-3

Windows 8.1 For Dummies, Book + DVD
Bundle
978-1-118-82107-7

Available in print and e-book formats.

Available wherever books are sold. **For more information or to order direct visit www.dummies.com**